THE ADMISSIBLE CONTENTS OF EXPERIENCE

THE ADMISSIBLE CONTENTS OF EXPERIENCE

Edited by

KATHERINE HAWLEY

and

FIONA MACPHERSON

A John Wiley & Sons, Ltd., Publication

This edition first published 2011

Originally published as Volume 59, Issue 236 of *The Philosophical Quarterly*

Chapters © 2011 The Authors

Book compilation © 2011 The Editors of *The Philosophical Quarterly*

Blackwell Publishing was acquired by John Wiley & Sons in February 2007. Blackwell's publishing programme has been merged with Wiley's global scientific, technical and medical business to form Wiley-Blackwell.

Registered Office
John Wiley & Sons Ltd, The Atrium, Southern Gate, Chichester, West Sussex, PO19 8SQ, UK.

Editorial Offices
350 Main Street, Malden, MA 02148-5020, USA
9600 Garsington Road, Oxford, OX4 2DQ, UK
The Atrium, Southern Gate, Chichester, West Sussex, PO19 8SQ, UK.

For details of our global editorial offices, for customer services, and for information about how to apply for permission to reuse the copyright material in this book, please see our website at www.wiley.com/wiley-blackwell.

The right of Katherine Hawley and Fiona Macpherson to be identified as the authors of the editorial material in this work has been asserted in accordance with the UK Copyright, Designs and Patents Act 1988.

Library of Congress Cataloging-in-Publication Data

The admissible contents of experience
edited by Katherine Hawley, Fiona Macpherson
pp.   cm.
Includes bibliographical references and index
ISBN 978-1-4443-3335-0 (pbk.)

1. Experience. 2. Perception. 3. Evidence. 4. Belief and doubt.
I. Hawley, Katherine, Dr. II. Macpherson, Fiona
B105.E9A35.2011
128'.4–dc22
2011001480

A catalogue record for this book is available from the British Library.

Set in 10.5 pt Baskerville by Christopher Bryant
Printed in Malaysia by Ho Printing (M) Sdn Bhd

CONTENTS

Preface and Acknowledgements   vi

1 Introduction:
   The Admissible Contents of Experience   *Fiona Macpherson*   1

2 Perception and the Reach of Phenomenal Content *Tim Bayne*   16

3 Seeing Causings and Hearing Gestures   *S. Butterfill*   36

4 Experience and Content   *Alex Byrne*   60

5 Is Perception a Propositional Attitude?   *Tim Crane*   83

6 Conscious Reference   *Alva Noë*   101

7 What are the Contents of Experiences?   *Adam Pautz*   114

8 Aspect-Switching and
   Visual Phenomenal Character   *Richard Price*   139

9 The Visual Experience of Causation   *Susanna Siegel*   150

10 The Admissible Contents of
   Visual Experience   *Michael Tye*   172

   Index   194

PREFACE AND ACKNOWLEDGEMENTS

This volume collects together chapters that were originally delivered at a conference on the Admissible Contents of Experience that took place at the University of Glasgow in March 2006. The original papers were first published in a special edition of *The Philosophy Quarterly* (July 2009), and the journal, together with The British Academy, The Mind Association, The Analysis Trust, and The Faculty of Arts Strategic Research Fund at Glasgow University, provided grants that funded the conference.

The conference was held under the auspices of the Centre for the Study of Perceptual Experience (CSPE), which is based in the Department of Philosophy at the University of Glasgow. The primary aim of the Centre is to conduct and facilitate analytical philosophical research into the nature of perceptual experience. A secondary aim is to facilitate communication and collaboration between researchers in philosophy and other disciplines whose research remit includes perceptual experience. At the time of writing, in its five-year history, the Centre has hosted, or co-hosted, eight international conferences: *The Individuation of the Senses*; *Disjunctivism: Perception, Action, Knowledge*; *Graduate Interdisciplinary Conference on Perception*; *The Admissible Contents of Experience*; *Hallucination on Crete*; *Varieties of Experience Graduate Conference*; *Phenomenal Presence*; *Graduate Conference on Mind, Science and Everything!*. This is in addition to numerous smaller workshops and events. Further information about these events and the CSPE is available on the web: www.gla.ac.uk/philosophy/cspe.

I would like to thank all of the contributors to this volume for their contributions. I am very grateful to them for producing these excellent, thought-provoking chapters.

Finally, I would like to thank Moira Gilruth, the administrator at *The Philosophical Quarterly*, for helping to prepare the volume, Katherine Hawley, the editor of *The Philosophy Quarterly*, for making this publication possible, and Michael Brady and Stuart Crutchfield for their comments and advice on this volume and for helping with the conference. And, of course, I owe much to the staff at Wiley-Blackwell, for publishing the book and bringing it to press.

Fiona Macpherson
Glasgow, September 2010

I

INTRODUCTION: THE ADMISSIBLE CONTENTS OF EXPERIENCE

By Fiona Macpherson

This introduction provides an overview of the debate concerning the admissible contents of experience, together with an introduction to the chapters in this volume. The debate is one that takes place among advocates of a certain way of thinking of perceptual experiences: that they are states which represent the world. For to say that a state has content is to say that it represents; and its content is usually taken to be that which is represented. One should not be tempted to think that the debate is therefore marginal or esoteric, for this view of perceptual experience has been by far the dominant view of perceptual experience in recent years in philosophy (and in psychology and neuroscience). The debate is about what answer to give to a fundamental question about the nature of perceptual experience, namely, what objects and properties can it represent?

One can ask this question about the admissible contents of perceptual experience about perceptual experience *in toto*, but one can also ask it about the perceptual experiences associated with each sensory modality. Thus one can ask what objects and properties visual or auditory or tactile experiences can represent, and so on. One can also ask the same question of experiences which are not in any one modality (if indeed there are any such experiences, for it is controversial whether there are). Such experiences are sometimes called 'cross-modal' experiences or 'amodal' experiences.[1] A good example of such an alleged experience would be a perceptual experience which represented that the flash of light that one saw was the cause of

---

[1] The term 'cross-modal' experience is in fact used to refer to many different sorts of experience, but the usage in the main text is one standard type.

the sound that one heard. In fact, the question about what the admissible contents of experience are is most frequently asked about the experiences in one modality at a time. Somewhat predictably among these, it is vision that has received the most attention. In this introduction, I shall focus on outlining the debate concerning visual experience, and one can extrapolate to how the debate would go in other cases.

I. PERCEPTUAL EXPERIENCE AS A REPRESENTATIONAL STATE

As was mentioned above, many people hold that perceptual experiences are representational states. What does this mean, and why do people hold it to be true? To say that one state represents another is to say, at least in part, that one state is about another. Consider examples of things other than experience which are said to represent. Some are man-made. For example, photographs typically represent that which was in front of the lens when they were taken. A photograph of a tree, we might say, represents a tree. A painting of a flower represents a flower. Certain natural, non-man-made states of the world are sometimes said to represent too. The angle of a column of smoke represents the speed of the wind. The number of rings in the trunk of a tree represents its age. Another case, quite different from the other two, is language. Sentences represent or are about things. The sentence 'The wind blew through the branches of the tree' represents that the wind blew through the branches of the tree. The paradigm case of mental states that represent are the propositional attitudes, such as belief and desire. Propositional attitudes are so-called because one takes an attitude (holding true, in the case of belief; wanting to be true, in the case of desire) towards a proposition. For example, if I believe that basking sharks swim in the Firth of Clyde, then I take the attitude of holding it to be true towards the proposition that basking sharks swim in the Firth of Clyde. If I desire it, then I want it to be true that basking sharks swim in the Firth of Clyde. If I believe or desire that basking sharks swim in the Firth of Clyde, then my mental state is about or represents that basking sharks swim in the Firth of Clyde.

Why do people think that beliefs are representational states? One reason is that beliefs have accuracy- or correctness-conditions. That is to say that there is a way the world could be which would make the belief true and a way the world could be which would make the belief false. In the case of my belief that basking sharks swim in the Firth of Clyde, the way the world would have to be in order to make the belief true is if basking sharks swim in the Firth of Clyde, and the belief would be false otherwise.

This feature of beliefs, which at least in part makes them representational states, explains why some people think that in order for a state to be a representational state it has to have the possibility of misrepresenting the world. However, this claim is not obviously true. The reason is that beliefs about necessary states of affairs, particularly logically or conceptually necessary states of affairs, do not, at least in one sense, have the possibility of misrepresenting. For example, my beliefs that two plus two equals four, that vixens are female foxes and that David Hume is David Hume could not misrepresent the way the world is, since these states of affairs necessarily obtain.

Do declarative sentences also have accuracy-conditions? Consider the sentence 'There are basking sharks in the Firth of Clyde'. Just as the belief which I would express by uttering this sentence has accuracy-conditions, so too, it might seem, does the sentence. One complication here, however, is that some philosophers think that some or all sentences are context-sensitive. That is to say that what sentences mean changes according to their context. For example, the sentence I asked you to consider might mean (and probably typically means) that there are *Cetorhinus maximus* in the Firth of Clyde. But in a context where I was telling you about Glasgow gangsters and their penchant for sunbathing on the *Waverley*, a ship that frequently sails down the Firth of Clyde, then the sentence might mean that there are loan sharks on sun loungers in the Firth of Clyde. If some sentences are context-sensitive, then it would be accurate not to say that sentences have correctness-conditions, full stop, but that sentences in a particular context have correctness-conditions.

What of natural, non-man-made states of the world, such as the angle of the column of smoke or the rings in the trunk in the tree? There is a tradition in philosophy which holds that these natural indicators cannot misrepresent, for they are conceived of as states that co-vary without exception with that which they represent. This is because it is claimed that it is in virtue of their strictly co-varying that they are representational states. In other words, if an exception to strict co-variance was found, then the alleged natural indicator would not be held to represent that which it failed to strictly co-vary with.[2] However, one could hold instead that natural indicators represent something only so long as they reliably co-vary with that thing, not perfectly co-vary. For example, one might think that as long as the number of rings in the trunk of a tree frequently or normally co-varies with the ages of a tree, then they represent the age, even if in the occasional year of bad growth some trees do not lay down an extra ring – in which case

---

[2] See, for example, F. Dretske, *Knowledge and the Flow of Information* (MIT Press, 1981).

the number of rings would be misleading with respect to, or would mis-represent, the age of the tree.

What of photographs and pictures? One might think that they do not have accuracy-conditions, for one might think that they do not represent that the world is a certain way.[3] A painting of a chair, for example, might represent a chair, but it may not represent that there is such a chair. It might be a painting of a merely imagined chair which does not exist, or a painting of a chair which once existed but no longer does, and the artist may not intend to represent that this chair exists by painting the image. Similarly, one might think that a photograph of a chair might represent a chair, but does not represent that it exists now. One might retort here that photographs at least represent that a certain state of affairs once existed. For example, a photograph might represent that a chair with a certain look once existed and was in George Square. And the photograph might represent this whether or not this state of affairs ever existed, for the photograph might be misleading in certain respects. Although people say that photographs do not lie, it is true that if they have been digitally altered or if they are taken from a misleading angle they might lead you to believe the world was one way though it was really another. Similarly, one might retort that paintings represent that a state of affairs could exist. And one might think that while most pictures accurately represent things that could exist, some might misrepresent states of affairs that could not exist. For example, a picture of a flying pig would misrepresent that a pig can fly when this is nomologically impossible. M.C. Escher painted what look to be spatially impossible ob-jects, such as the Penrose triangle, in the full knowledge that such an object is a geometrical impossibility. Further moves could be made in this debate. What is certainly true is that if pictures or photographs can misrepresent, one has to give a different account of this from that which one gives of belief misrepresentation.

Another reason why beliefs are held to be representational states is that ascribing such states that represent certain things to subjects helps to explain and predict subjects' behaviour. For example, if I believe that basking sharks swim in the Firth of Clyde, then given that I have certain desires, such as the desire to spot them, this may explain why I frequently look out for them in the Firth of Clyde, and may predict that I shall go to the Firth.

These two reasons for thinking that beliefs are representational states – that they have accuracy-conditions and that attributing them to subjects helps to explain and predict their behaviour – have been cited as reasons that also explain why one should think that perceptual experiences are

---

[3] Note that Crane (in this volume) holds that pictures can be accurate or inaccurate, but not true or false. He therefore claims that the content of pictures is not propositional.

representational states. Let us consider each in turn. Why think that perceptual experiences have accuracy-conditions? Suppose I have a visual experience I would describe as being a visual experience as of a basking shark on the shore. One might think that this type of experience could be accurate or inaccurate. This is because there may really be a basking shark on the shore or there may not. There may be a seal on the shore, which I mistake for a basking shark, or there may be no shark and no object mistaken for a shark, for I may be having a hallucination. (Note that hallucinations are such that although as a matter of contingent fact they tend to be inaccurate, they need not be, and can be accurate – these are called veridical hallucinations.) If this is correct, then the type of experience that I undergo has accuracy-conditions, and can represent accurately or inaccurately (that is, misrepresent) depending on whether those accuracy-conditions obtain. (Philosophers use this 'as of' locution in 'as of a basking shark', as opposed to just saying 'of a basking shark', simply to signal that there need be no basking shark in the world which the experience is of – it may merely appear to be of a particular basking shark that exists in the world.)

There are some dissenting voices, however. Some philosophers – disjunctivists – think that if one sees a basking shark and if one has a hallucination of a basking shark, then one has perceptual experiences that differ in important mental respects, to the extent that we should think of them as being different fundamental types of state – that is, as differing in their most important nature.[4] Such philosophers hold different views of what the mental differences are between the states. For example, some think that they differ because the one is involved in perceptually experiencing a basking shark and the other simply cannot be distinguished from that state just by reflection on the nature of the experience itself by the subject of the experience; some think that they differ in their phenomenal character; some think that they differ in their epistemological status. Some of these philosophers think that you can only have the same fundamental type of perceptual experience that you have when you see a basking shark accurately, when you see it accurately. You cannot have this type of experience when you either misperceive the seal as being a basking shark or if you just have a hallucination as of a basking shark. On account of this fact, some of these philosophers think that the question of whether I could have the type of experience that I have when I accurately see a basking shark on the beach in other circumstances, circumstances in which there is not a basking shark on the beach, should be answered in the negative. I

---

[4] Disjunctivists include M.G.F. Martin, John McDowell, Bill Brewer and William Fish. The various types of disjunctivism are discussed in A. Haddock and F. Macpherson, 'Introduction: Varieties of Disjunctivism', in our *Disjunctivism: Perception, Action, Knowledge* (Oxford UP, 2008).

believe that they hold this because they reason as follows: perceptual experiences of the fundamental type had when seeing a basking shark on the beach accurately are partly composed of the basking shark on the beach. If there is no basking shark on the beach then it cannot partly compose whichever experience the person is having, such as a hallucination of a basking shark or an illusory experience as of a shark caused by a seal. Thus the person cannot be having the same fundamental type of experience. Because there is no possibility of having that fundamental type of experience in those circumstances, there is no possibility of the experience misrepresenting, on this view. And if one thinks that for a state to be representational there has to be the possibility of it misrepresenting, then this line of thought would entail that this type of experience is not representational. The jargon sometimes used to express this is that these experiences 'present' the world as being a certain way; they do not represent it as being that way.[5]

However, this argument has recently been replied to by Susanna Siegel.[6] She argues that even if the type of perceptual experience as of a basking shark had when accurately seeing a basking shark could not be had inaccurately, this does not mean that this type of experience does not represent. She claims that this type of experience can still have accuracy-conditions, and in virtue of this fact alone it is representational. One can accept that one is unable to have this same fundamental type of mental state inaccurately, but nevertheless accuracy-conditions can be specified by comparing the conditions in which one can have the perceptual experience with the conditions that might exist in other possible worlds. The experience is clearly accurate with respect to this world, but it is inaccurate when we compare it with other possible worlds in which the conditions required in order for us to have the experience in the actual world do not obtain. In this way, she argues, we can claim that the experience has accuracy-conditions, and in this minimal sense at least is representational, even though the experience cannot be had inaccurately and so cannot misrepresent. Philosophers are currently debating whether this minimal sense of representation is the sense of representation that people care about when they claim that experiences represent, and if it is not, what exactly that sense is. But recall the example discussed above – that of necessarily true beliefs. It seems that these beliefs cannot be false, but nevertheless they each represent certain things (that two plus two equals four, that vixens are female foxes or that David Hume is David Hume). If this is right, then it seems that the fact that certain types of

---

[5] Versions of this view are defended in C. Travis, 'The Silence of the Senses', *Mind*, 113 (2004), pp. 57–94, and B. Brewer, 'Perception and Content', *European Journal of Philosophy*, 14 (2006), pp. 165–81.

[6] S. Siegel, 'Do Visual Experiences Have Contents?', in B. Nanay (ed.), *Perceiving the World* (Oxford UP, 2010), pp. 333–68.

experience cannot be had inaccurately should not tell in favour of their not being representational.

Let us turn now to the second reason for thinking that experiences are representational – that attributing perceptual states with representational contents to subjects helps to explain and predict their behaviour. Is this true? It can seem so. If I have a visual experience that represents a basking shark, it may explain why I keep looking in the direction I do (perhaps at it swimming up and down the coast). It may explain why I utter 'I see a basking shark', or why I jump up and down with excitement. According to those who reject disjunctivism, and hold that one can have the same funda-mental type of experience when accurately perceiving the world or when inaccurately perceiving the world or when having a hallucination, it is because my experience represents that there is a basking shark that I behave as I do, and do so whether or not there is a basking shark there. You may also be able to make accurate predictions of my behaviour based on my having an experience with that representational content together with other things you know about me – perhaps my desire to swim close to the second largest living shark in the northern hemisphere's most southerly fjord.

However, that this explanation is available to non-disjunctivists does not mean that a similar sort of explanation is not available to disjunctivists who think that experiences do not represent the world but rather present it. They give explanations and predictions of the behaviour of subjects based on what the subjects' experience presents when they are accurately perceiving, and based on what the subjects think that their experiences presents when they are not accurately perceiving.

It lies beyond the scope of this introduction to argue as to which view – representationalism or forms of disjunctivism that reject representationalism – is the right one. For our purposes I need only note that the debate about the admissible contents of experience takes place among those who think that experiences do represent the world. However, it seems to me that a similar debate could take place among those who think experiences present the world rather than represent it. They could debate about which features of the world are presented by experience. However, in practice there has been no such debate, primarily, I believe, because those who endorse this view are very liberal about what experience can present, whereas those who think experiences are representational have tended to fall into two camps: liberals, who believe experiences can represent low-level and high-level properties, and conservatives, who believe that experiences can only repre-sent low-level properties. With the assumption in place for the rest of this introduction that perceptual experiences do represent, I shall now explain the debate about the admissible contents of experience.

II. INTRODUCING THE DEBATE

Let us suppose that visual experiences represent objects and represent them as having certain properties. The range of properties that objects can have is vast. There are the properties of being a certain colour, shape, size, temperature, having a certain smell or taste, having certain causal properties, emitting certain sounds, having a certain texture. An object might also have the property of being a certain individual such as your brother, or the first man on the moon. An object might be one of a certain man-made kind, such as being a knife or a chair, or it might be a natural kind such a being a tree or a sycamore tree, or being an amphibian or a natterjack toad.

It seems obvious that visual experiences represent some of these properties and not others. Most people would agree that visual experiences represent the shape, size, colour and position of objects – properties to do with the visual appearance of things (low-level properties). And most people are agreed that vision does not and could not represent every property. There are two reasons for thinking this.

The first is that there are some properties that the visual system simply is not and could not be sensitive to. Which properties those are is controversial, but I speculate, although it is only speculation, that most people would agree that visual experiences cannot represent the following: the proper sensibles of senses other than vision – sounds in the case of hearing, temperature in the case of touch and so on – and properties such as being radioactive, emitting an electric field, being six hundred years old.

The second reason is that there is often a distinction between what our visual experiences represent and the beliefs we form on the basis of those experiences. This distinction may be masked by the fact that we often claim to see what we strictly speaking, on reflection, would hold that we only believe or know. (Perhaps this occurs in part because in English we often use the word 'see' to mean 'know'.) Here is an example. My mother comes into the kitchen in the morning. There are muddy footprints on the floor. She might say 'I see Fiona came home late last night'. She certainly believes that I did. But does she strictly speaking see that I came home last night? Does she have a visual experience that represents my coming home late? I am strongly inclined to say that she does not. She sees the muddy footprints. What exactly she has a visual experience-as-of is debatable. One might think that it is as of muddy footprints, or that it is as of dark objects on a lighter background. At any rate, it seems obvious that she does not have an experience as of me coming home late. She merely believes this on the basis of inferring from what she does strictly speaking does see – the muddy footprints. On reflection on such cases we might come to think that the properties that our experiences do represent are somewhat restricted.

There are a large class of properties over which there is a fierce dispute concerning whether visual experiences do or can represent them. These include being an artificial kind, being a natural kind, being a specific individual, causation, the nature of the backsides of objects, the nature of the occluded parts of objects, directionality (high-level properties).

It would be good if we could clearly delineate those properties that everyone agrees visual experiences can represent and those that are subject to debate, and those which everyone is agreed that they cannot. Unfortunately, this is difficult to do, and there is no agreed way to do it. Listing properties, as I have done thus far, is the typical way.

We should note that what people's experiences represent may differ. Extreme examples include the colour-blind, whose experiences may represent fewer colours compared to the normally sighted, and people with perfect pitch, who may represent more specific information about pitch than people with relative pitch. So when people ask what the admissible contents of experience are, they are typically either asking about what the normal person's experience represents, or asking what it is possible for anyone's experience to represent.

It might seem odd, on reflection, that there is a debate about what the admissible contents of experience are, at least among people who have normal perceptual experiences. One might think that all we need to do in order to determine the answer is to introspect and see what our experience is like. Our experiences purport to inform us about the way the world is, so why can we not just report how they inform us, and thereby report what they represent? And why do we not find agreement?

There are a couple of reasons why this may be the case. One is that we may ourselves find it hard to tell apart perceptual experience from belief. So perhaps some people mistakenly report belief content as being the content of experience, or *vice versa*. Another reason is that perhaps what our experiences represent is not always available to us as subjects of those experiences. For example, there are some theories of representation that claim that what an experience represents depends on what it is caused by and co-varies with in the world. But what it co-varies with may not be a matter available to the subject of that experience – at least, not just by introspection. Another example is that some philosophers hold that what our experiences represent is not what we typically think they represent. For example, some philosophers think our experiences do not represent colours – which are surface properties of objects, as philosophers typically think – but closely related properties, such as colours in specific illuminations, or mental properties which our experiences have when we look at objects.

III. REASONS TO BE A LOW-LEVEL THEORIST

Low-level theorists are motivated by the thought that if two experiences are different in what they represent then they must have different phenomenal characters. That is to say that 'what it is like' to have the experiences for the subject must be different.[7] This seems plausible, for it is a common assumption (although not among certain disjunctivists) that two experiences are different if and only if they have different phenomenal characters. A second reason to hold this arises if one accepts one of the most popular theories of phenomenal character in philosophy of mind today, namely, representationalism. According to this view, phenomenal character supervenes on representational content; according to a stronger form of the view, the two are identical.[8] In fact, as I shall in due course show, many theorists who argue for high-level content also accept the idea that if two experiences are different in what they represent, they must have different phenomenal characters, and *vice versa*. Whether representationalism is true or not is a topic that lies outwith the scope of this introduction. However, it is plausible to think that at least in a very large number of cases, perhaps within a subject over some specified period of time, differences in phenomenal character supervene on differences in representational content, and *vice versa*.[9]

So, starting with the thought that two experiences have different contents only if they have different phenomenal characters, low-level theorists mount a series of arguments case by case. They try to argue that two experiences, which a high-level theorist might claim have different contents, have the same phenomenal character, and therefore represent the same thing. And they argue that the content which both share is a low-level content. For example, Colin McGinn argues that we should restrict the content of visual experiences to propositions whose content can be specified in general terms, and not particulars.[10] He asks you to imagine seeing your bible. He claims that the experience which you have cannot represent that your bible is in

---

[7] This phrase was introduced into the philosophical lexicon in T. Nagel, 'What is it Like to Be a Bat?', *Philosophical Review*, 83 (1974), pp. 435–50.

[8] Prominent representationalist works include M. Tye, *Ten Problems of Consciousness: a Representational Theory of the Phenomenal Mind* (MIT Press, 1995); F.I. Dretske, *Naturalising the Mind* (MIT Press, 1995); W.G. Lycan, *Consciousness and Experience* (MIT Press, 1996).

[9] See F. Macpherson, *Representational Theories of Phenomenal Character*, PhD Thesis, University of Stirling (2000), available online in STORRE, The University of Stirling's digital repository, at http://hdl.handle.net/1893/25.

[10] C. McGinn, *The Character of Mind* (Oxford UP, 1982), pp. 38–9.

front of you, because you would be having an experience with the very same phenomenal character if you were not seeing your bible but a bible that looked *exactly* similar in all respects. For example, if your bible had a dog-ear, the other bible would have one too. McGinn is thinking that different objects can have the same appearance and thus can cause the same experience in me. Therefore I cannot represent that a particular object is present: I can only represent that there exists a certain sort of object in front of me, one with a certain look. Of course, if I have a visual experience which represents an object with a certain look – a look that my bible shares – and if I believe that my bible has that look and is the only one around with that look, then no doubt I come to believe that my bible is present, on account of the experience that I have. But according to the low-level theorist this content is solely the content of belief. It is not the content of the experience.

One could extend this type of reasoning to natural and artificial kinds. For example, suppose you have a visual experience that you might naturally describe as being one as of a toad on a rock. Perhaps your experience, on reflection, does not really represent a toad on a rock; for would one not have an experience with the same phenomenal character if one were not looking at a toad on a rock but merely a toad skin enclosing a supportive wire framework, or if one were looking at a waxwork of a frog which was so realistic that one could not tell it apart by sight from a real toad? Likewise, one might naïvely think that one's experience could represent that a Geiger counter was present. But could one not have the very same visual experience if an object with the mere look of a Geiger counter was present but did not have the property of being able to detect radiation?

If one accepted this kind of reasoning, then it would be reasonable to hold that the contents of visual experience should be restricted to general contents and observable properties – that is, properties that one can tell an object has just by looking such as shape, size, colour and position.

IV. REASONS TO BE A HIGH-LEVEL THEORIST

Before the chapters in this volume were published, the main arguments against the low-level view were advanced by Susanna Siegel.[11] She claims that some natural-kind properties, such as being a pine tree, can feature in the content of perception. She asks us to imagine that we are novices at identifying trees. While still novices, we look at a particular tree that is in fact a pine tree and have a visual experience. We then become tree experts.

[11] S. Siegel, 'Which Properties are Represented in Perception?', in T.S. Gendler and J. Hawthorne (eds), *Perceptual Experience* (Oxford UP, 2006), pp. 481–503.

We can tell what kind of tree each tree is by looking. She claims that the overall phenomenal character of one's mental life will be different when one looks at a pine tree when one is an expert, and can identify the pine tree as such, compared with when one looks at a pine tree when one is a novice, and cannot identify the tree. She claims that this difference in the overall phenomenology is due to a difference in the phenomenology of the visual experiences had in each case. She also claims that if two experiences differ in phenomenal character then they differ in representational content. Finally, she claims that if there is a difference in content here then it is best explained by the natural-kind property *being a pine tree* being represented in the second but not the first visual experience. The example is of a type now known as 'contrast cases'.

There are two main replies that one can give to this argument. The first is to question whether the difference in the phenomenology of your conscious mental life is a difference in the phenomenology of experience, rather than in other phenomenal states. A plausible claim would be that when you are a novice you consciously believe that a tree is in front of you. When you are an expert you consciously believe that a pine tree is in front of you. One could claim that what it is like to have these two different beliefs is not the same. Thus the difference in phenomenal character is attributable to the different beliefs you have. Thus the phenomenal *difference in experience* required in order for there to be a difference in visual content is not there.

A second reply accepts that there is a difference in the phenomenology of your experience when you are a novice and when you are an expert, but does not accept that the difference shows that a natural kind like 'pine tree' is represented in your experience. Rather, it is argued, a certain outline shape (perhaps of the leaves or of the whole tree) or pattern on the bark or colour of the leaves or bark becomes salient to you when you are an expert; and this is to say that this feature is represented only when you are an expert or represented in more detail in your experience when you are an expert. Perhaps this is because you pay attention to the feature when you are an expert, or perhaps it is because your eyes foveate on this feature when you are an expert more than they did when you were a novice.

Another argument one might give for certain experiences having high-level content puts the question why, when we think that we have identified two visual experiences with the same phenomenal character, we should always think that what they represent is that which is in common to the world in front of the observer on both occasions when having the experiences. For example, take your experience of a toad and your experience of the toad husk that looks like a toad. Let us agree that these two objects cause in a subject visual experiences with the same phenomenal character. The low-level theorist says that both represent an object with certain shape, size and position properties, and that the property of being a toad is not represented. But high-level theorists could question why low-level theorists are so confident that the accuracy-conditions for this experience are simply that a toad-looking object is present, and hence that both experiences are accurate. Rather, they might claim that both experiences represent that a toad is present, and this is the accuracy-condition. On this view, the visual experience of the toad would be accurate, but the visual experience of the toad husk would be inaccurate. It would misrepresent that a toad was there when there was merely a toad husk. But, the argument would continue, this reflects the way our experience strikes us. One would be surprised were one to find out that there was merely a toad husk in front of one.

This second argument shows that it is often very difficult to determine what the accuracy-conditions of a type of experience are. And the former argument shows that determining whether a change in the phenomenal character of one's mental life is a change in the phenomenal character of an experience or of some other aspect of mental life may be very difficult. In addition, knowing what the changes in phenomenal character of an experience signal about the difference in representation is tricky. In short, determining what the admissible contents of experience are is a hard task.

V. WHY IS THE DEBATE IMPORTANT?

The debate as to what the admissible contents of experience are is important for many reasons. One reason is that there are many different theories of how an experience gets to have the content that it does. For example, there are functional-role accounts that say that the role of the experience in the subject's mental life determines its content, and there are causal co-variation accounts where what an experience represents is determined by what it is caused by and co-varies with, and many more accounts. Whether any of these theories are plausible will depend on their ability to account for the forms of representation which, it is alleged, can and cannot occur. Thus having an independent grasp on this issue will be crucial.

The debate is also important for assessing whether representationalism is true. This theory claims that there can be no differences in phenomenal character without differences in content and *vice versa*. Whether this is plausible or not may depend on the representational resources to which one has access in order to explain differences in phenomenal character.[12]

---

[12] See, for example, Macpherson, 'Ambiguous Figures and the Content of Experience', *Noûs*, 40 (2006), pp. 82–117.

Any issue in philosophy of mind where what is at stake is whether a person has a belief or an experience of a certain sort will be influenced by this debate. This is because it may help to determine that a belief is present rather than an experience if the content of the state in question is not one that an experience could have. Thus, for example, it may help in determining whether cognitive penetration has occurred, for it may determine that certain contents could not be contents of experience.[13]

The debate also has links to various epistemological questions. This is because what the content of perceptual experiences can be will affect what we should think concerning whether and how experiences justify beliefs – and thus one's epistemological theory.

VI. THE CHAPTERS IN THIS VOLUME

Each of the chapters in this volume addresses one or more of the issues discussed above.

Tim Bayne argues that high-level contents can feature in perceptual experience. He focuses on associative agnosia, a deficit in which subjects' form perception is intact, but they do not recognize objects as belonging to kinds that they are familiar with. He claims that the best explanation of such subjects is that they are missing high-level phenomenology.

Stephen Butterfill, relying on Michotte's psychological experiments, which provide interesting cases of contrast cases, argues that we can perceive causation. He claims that perception of causation is one instance of categorical perception. At the same time, he holds that causation is not represented in perceptual experience.

Alex Byrne spends some time in his chapter arguing that perception involves representational content. But he does not think that it involves having perceptual experiences with representational content, for he eschews the very idea of experience as philosophers conceive of it. He thus opposes the view that perception does not involve representation, but endorses the view that it does not involve experience. He then claims that the content of perception is not very rich, and that this fact vindicates one claim of those who believe that no content at all is involved in perception. The claim is that perceptual errors are due to false beliefs, not false experience.

In his contribution, Tim Crane argues that perceptual experiences have content, but that this content is of a specific kind. It is not propositional, and thus is not like the content of belief, even though it has accuracy-conditions.

[13] See Macpherson, 'Cognitive Penetration of Colour Experience: Rethinking the Issue in the light of an Indirect Mechanism', *Philosophy and Phenomenological Research* (forthcoming).

He relates these claims to his long-standing view that the content of perceptual experience is non-conceptual.

The idea that there are elements of experience beyond the facing surfaces of unoccluded parts of objects is explored by Alva Noë. These phenomenally 'present as absent' elements, he claims, are represented in my experience in virtue of deployment of my knowledge of the ways in which my movements produce sensory change. Noë goes on to compare and contrast perceptual experience and belief. They are both methods of access to objects and properties, but involve the employment of different access skills.

Adam Pautz's chapter identifies three conceptions of experiential content. A debate about whether experiences have content must concern the identity conception, he argues, for only this makes the debate non-trivial. According to this conception, an experience has content when its subject stands in a special relation, 'sensorily entertaining', to a proposition. He argues that experiences do have this kind of content, as it best explains certain experiential features. He claims these contents are general, not singular, mainly on grounds of simplicity. Finally, he discusses which properties feature in the contents of experience, using which beliefs our experiences can ground as a guide.

Richard Price argues in favour of a low-level view. He claims that several contrast cases which are cited in the literature as showing that high-level properties must be represented are unconvincing, and, at the very least, that natural-kind properties need not be posited as part of the content of experience.

Like Butterfill, Susanna Siegel focuses on whether causation can feature in the content of visual experience. She argues that the Michotte experiments are suggestive but not conclusive. She then develops interesting contrast cases to support her claim that causation can be represented in experience. Finally, Siegel defends the idea that experience may nevertheless remain silent about, that is, may not represent, certain properties of causation.

In the concluding chapter, Michael Tye discusses whether experiences have existential contents, singular contents, gappy contents or multiple contents. According to Tye, content has a structure with a place for an object to fill. In veridical perception it is filled, and one gets a singular content. In hallucination it is unfilled, and one gets a gappy content.

These chapters form an exciting body of work. Diverse opinions are forcefully argued for. The chapters suggest new and exciting directions for research and from which I believe future work on the admissible contents of experience will flow.[14]

[14] Thanks to Michael Brady for his helpful comments.

2

PERCEPTION AND THE REACH OF PHENOMENAL CONTENT

By Tim Bayne

The phenomenal character of perceptual experience involves the representation of colour, shape and motion. Does it also involve the representation of high-level categories? Is the recognition of a tomato as a tomato contained within perceptual phenomenality? Proponents of a conservative view of the reach of phenomenal content say 'No', whereas those who take a liberal view of perceptual phenomenality say 'Yes'. I clarify the debate between conservatives and liberals, and argue in favour of the liberal view that high-level content can directly inform the phenomenal character of perception.

I. INTRODUCTION

What is it like to look at a tomato? You experience yourself as facing an object that occupies a certain region of space and has a particular shape. You are likely to experience the tomato as being a certain colour – say, a particular shade of red. If the tomato happens to be in motion, you may also experience it as being in motion. Each of these features of your perceptual experience involves particular phenomenal properties. Do these phenomenal properties (and others like them) exhaust what it is like to look at a tomato?

Some say they do. Proponents of what I shall call the *conservative view* hold that the phenomenal character of visual experience is exhausted by the representation of low-level properties – colour, shape, spatial location, motion, and so on. Conservatives give similar accounts of other perceptual modalities: the phenomenal character of audition is exhausted by the representation of volume, pitch, timbre, and so on; the phenomenal character of gustation is exhausted by the representation of sweetness, sourness, and so on. The phenomenal world of the conservative is an austere one.[1]

---

[1] Strictly speaking, it is representations of properties rather than properties themselves that are low-level or high-level. Nevertheless, it is very convenient to refer to represented properties as low-level and high-level, and I shall help myself to this convenience on occasion.

This conservative view of perceptual phenomenality can be contrasted with a liberal view according to which the phenomenal character of perception can include the representation of categorical ('high-level') properties, such as being a tomato.[2] We perceive objects and events as belonging to various high-level kinds, and this, the liberal holds, is part and parcel of perception's phenomenal character. What it is like to see a tomato, taste a strawberry or hear a trumpet is not limited to the representation of 'low-level' sensory qualities but involves the representation of such 'high-level' properties as being a tomato, a strawberry or a trumpet.

The debate between these two positions is of no little significance, for getting a fix on the admissible contents of perceptual phenomenality would provide us with an important set of conditions which any adequate theory of consciousness must meet. Some accounts of phenomenal consciousness entail that high-level content is phenomenally inadmissible, other accounts leave the possibility of high-level phenomenal content open, and still other accounts require that high-level representations are phenomenally admissible. However, my goal here is not to explore the potential impact of this debate on theories of phenomenal consciousness, but to present a defence of phenomenal liberalism.

II. THE REACH OF PERCEPTUAL PHENOMENALITY

First in the order of business is the task of clarifying the contrast between conservatism and liberalism. I shall begin with the notion of phenomenal consciousness. Phenomenal states are states which it is 'something it is like' to instantiate.[3] What differentiates one phenomenal state from another is a function of what it is like to have the states in question. What it is like to have a phenomenal state is a function of the state's representational content, at least when it comes to those phenomenal states associated with perception. Indeed, we typically identify phenomenal states by invoking the properties they represent: we talk of what it is like to see the yellow of sunflowers, to hear middle C on a trumpet, and to feel the texture of sandpaper. So phenomenal properties and representational contents are intimately related. The notion of *phenomenal content* puts these two notions together. As I am thinking of it here, phenomenal content is that component of a state's representational content which supervenes on its phenomenal

---

[2] I use the phrase 'perceptual phenomenality' rather than the more common 'perceptual phenomenology', on the ground that 'phenomenology' is best reserved for a discipline rather than a certain type of mental state or property. Those who find talk of 'phenomenality' off-putting can simply replace it with talk of 'phenomenology'.

[3] See T. Nagel, 'What is it Like to Be a Bat?', *Philosophical Review*, 83 (1974), pp. 435–50.

character. There are important debates concerning the kind of supervenience relation that holds between phenomenal character and representational content, but I leave them to one side here. My concern is not with the
nature of phenomenal content but with its *range*.[4]

As I have remarked, the literature presents us with a striking lack of
agreement on the question of what kinds of properties can be phenomenally represented, that is, on the admissible contents of perceptual
phenomenality. On the one hand, there are those who take a conservative
approach to this issue. For example, Tye claims that the features
represented in perceptual phenomenality are limited to the output of
sensory modules, and conjectures that for us these features include such
properties as 'being an edge, being a corner, being square, being red'. In a
similar vein, Prinz holds that only the content of intermediate-level representations (which I am here classing as 'low-level representations') enters
into perceptual phenomenality, and that ordinary kind properties are not
represented in phenomenal consciousness. Lyons argues that although
perceptual learning can expand the range of perceptual contents one can
enjoy, it does so without having any impact on the phenomenal character of
perceptual experience. On his view, learning to perceive the difference
between a melodic minor scale and a diminished scale, between male chicks
and female chicks, and between copperhead snakes and their close relatives,
does not enrich the kinds of phenomenal states the subject is capable of
having.[5]

On the other hand there are those who advocate a rather more liberal
conception of the admissible contents of perceptual phenomenality. According to van Gulick, 'seeing a telephone *as a telephone* is not something that
accompanies visual experience; it is part of one's visual experience'. In a
similar vein, Siegel argues that natural-kind properties such as being a pine
tree can be represented in visual experience. Even Fodor, who famously
describes the outputs of perceptual modules as 'relatively shallow', appears

---

[4] For discussion of the nature of phenomenal content, although not always under that
label, see U. Kriegel, 'Phenomenal Content', *Erkenntnis*, 57 (2002), pp. 175–98; D. Chalmers,
'The Representational Character of Experience', in B. Leiter (ed.), *The Future for Philosophy*
(Oxford UP, 2004), pp. 153–80; C. McGinn, 'Consciousness and Content', *Proceedings of the
British Academy*, 74 (1988), pp. 219–39; T. Horgan and J. Tienson, 'The Intentionality of Phen-
omenology and the Phenomenology of Intentionality', in D. Chalmers (ed.), *Philosophy of Mind:
Classical and Contemporary Readings* (Oxford UP, 2002), pp. 520–33; C. Siewert, *The Significance of
Consciousness* (Princeton UP, 1998).

[5] M. Tye, *Ten Problems of Consciousness* (MIT Press, 1995), p. 141; J. Prinz, 'A Neurofunc-
tional Theory of Consciousness', in A. Brook and K. Akins (eds), *Cognition and the Brain* (Cambridge UP, 2005), pp. 381–96, and 'The Intermediate Level Theory of Consciousness', in
M. Velmans and S. Schneider (eds), *The Blackwell Companion to Consciousness* (Oxford: Blackwell,
2007), pp. 247–60; J. Lyons, 'Perceptual Belief and Nonexperiential Looks', in J. Hawthorne
(ed.), *Philosophical Perspectives*, 19: *Epistemology* (Malden: Blackwell, 2005), pp. 237–56.

to have liberal tendencies, for he suggests that perceptual phenomenality is pitched at the level of what Rosch *et al.* call 'basic categories', and that one can visually experience something as a dog.[6]

The contrast between the conservative and liberal positions is not a precise one, and the distinction is intended to capture two general approaches to perceptual phenomenality rather than cleanly demarcated positions.[7] One respect in which the distinction is vague concerns the fact that there is no precise line between low-level and high-level perceptual content. Perception contains multiple levels of content, and it is doubtful whether there is any principled line to be drawn between low-level content on the one hand and high-level content on the other. (Indeed, it is doubtful whether there are any principled lines to be drawn between low-level, intermediate-level and high-level perceptual content.) Perceptual processing involves a cascade of increasing levels of abstraction, but it is by no means obvious that any two points in any single cascade, let alone any two points belonging to different perceptual cascades, can be ordered with respect to 'levels of content'. Talk of 'high-level content' and 'low-level content' is convenient, but it should be taken with a grain of salt.

A second respect in which the contrast between conservative and liberal views is open-ended concerns modal issues. One type of conservative might deny that *we* are capable of enjoying perceptual states with high-level phenomenal content, but hold that it is entirely possible that creatures of some other kind could enjoy such states. Another type of conservative might hold that there is something deeply problematic in the very notion of high-level phenomenal content, and hold that no possible creature could enjoy such states. Similarly, one can distinguish two kinds of liberal. One kind of liberal holds that high-level perception necessarily has phenomenal character, whereas another kind of liberal holds only that our high-level perceptual states enjoy phenomenal character, and that it is an entirely open question

---

[6] R. van Gulick, 'Deficit Studies and the Function of Phenomenal Consciousness', in G. Graham and G.L. Stephens (eds), *Philosophical Psychopathology* (MIT Press, 1994), pp. 25–49, at p. 46; S. Siegel, 'Which Properties are Represented in Perception?', in T.S. Gendler and J. Hawthorne (eds), *Perceptual Experience* (Oxford UP, 2005), pp. 481–503; J. Fodor, *The Modularity of Mind* (MIT Press, 1983), pp. 94–7.

[7] Theorists who appear to be sympathetic towards conservatism include A. Clark, *A Theory of Sentience* (Oxford UP, 2000); R. Jackendoff, *Consciousness and the Computational Mind* (MIT Press, 1987); H. Langsam, 'Experiences, Thoughts, and Qualia', *Philosophical Studies*, 99 (2000), pp. 269–95; J. Levine, 'Materialism and Qualia', *Pacific Philosophical Quarterly*, 64 (1983), pp. 354–61; E. Lormand, 'Nonphenomenal Consciousness', *Noûs*, 30 (1996), pp. 242–61. Theorists who appear to be sympathetic towards liberalism include P. Carruthers, *Phenomenal Consciousness* (Cambridge UP, 2000); A. Goldman, 'The Psychology of Folk Psychology', *Behavioural and Brain Sciences*, 16 (1993), pp. 15–28; Horgan and Tienson; D. Pitt, 'The Phenomenology of Cognition, or, What it is Like to Think that P', *Philosophy and Phenomenological Research*, 69 (2004), pp. 1–36; Siewert; G. Strawson, *Mental Reality* (MIT Press, 1994).

whether conservatism might be true of other types of creatures. (The liberal could also think that only some of our high-level perceptual states enjoy phenomenal content.) In order to keep the discussion manageable, I shall focus on the debate between conservatism and liberalism in so far as it applies to human experience: does the kind of perceptual experience that *we* enjoy admit of high-level phenomenal content?

One final issue which must be raised before I proceed concerns the question of whether this debate is really substantive. It certainly *looks* substantive. Liberals and conservatives seem to take themselves to be at odds with each other; on the face of things they have a shared notion of phenomenal content but simply disagree about its extension. But there is reason to think that this debate might be less substantive than appearances suggest. Although Tye denies that perceptual phenomenality includes high-level content, he does allow that high-level content enters into perceptual experience, for he takes it that we see objects as coins, telescopes and so on.[8] In saying this, he is committed to a distinction between experiential content and perceptual phenomenality which many of his liberal opponents are likely to find puzzling. I take it that when van Gulick and Siegel claim that the representation of an object as a telephone or a pine tree can be part of visual experience, they mean to equate experiential content with phenomenal content. Further, there are questions about how the various parties to this debate understand the phrase 'what it is like'. Tye defends a conservative account of the reach of perceptual phenomenality, but he does allow (*Ten Problems*, p. 302, n. 3) that there may be 'a very broad use of the locution "what it's like" in ordinary life which concedes a difference in what it is like whenever there is any conscious difference of any sort whatsoever'. Tye is at pains to emphasize that this is not his usage of 'what it is like', but it might well be the usage of his liberal opponents. If conservatives and liberals are putting the 'what it is like' locution to different uses, then we might have a relatively straightforward dissolution of this debate: conservatives and liberals differ in their accounts of the admissible contents of perceptual 'what-it-is-likeness' because they mean something subtly different by 'what it is like'.

Although the prospects of a terminological dissolution of the debate between the conservative and liberal seem to me to be well worth pursuing, I shall proceed on the assumption that removing the various layers of terminological confusion that surround this issue will reveal a real dispute about the reach of perceptual phenomenality, even if the form of that dispute is not quite what it might have seemed at first. I turn now to the question of how this dispute might be resolved.

[8] Tye, *Consciousness, Color, and Content* (MIT Press, 2000), pp. 73–6.

III. THE ARGUMENT FROM AGNOSIA

Direct appeals to introspection have not proven to be particularly effective in resolving this debate: liberals claim that introspection reveals clear instances of high-level perceptual phenomenality, whereas conservatives deny that this is so. Look at a tomato, the liberal says, is there not something it is like to see it as a tomato? The conservative shakes his head in puzzlement.

In the light of the impotence of direct appeals to introspection, liberals have tended to rely on indirect appeals to introspection in the form of *contrast arguments*. Contrast arguments are so called because they involve contrasting two scenarios which supposedly differ in phenomenal character but not in low-level perceptual content.[9] There is, intuitively, a difference between what it is like to hear the sentence 'il fait froid' when one does not understand French and what it is like to hear the same sentence after having learnt French, despite the fact that both involve the same auditory input. In a similar vein, liberals argue that what it is like to hear the sentence 'visiting relatives can be boring' depends on whether one takes the 'boring' to qualify the relatives or the visiting, and that what it is like to look at the young woman/old woman figure depends on whether one perceives the figure as a young woman or as an old woman. The liberal argues that high-level perceptual representations must enter into phenomenal content because each of these scenarios involves a phenomenal contrast unaccompanied by low-level representational differences.

My concern here is not to examine the prospects of these relatively familiar contrast arguments, but to present a novel contrast argument based on agnosia.[10] Agnosia involves impairment in perception which is not due to elementary sensory malfunction.[11] Following Lissauer,[12] most theorists distinguish two main forms of agnosia, apperceptive agnosia and associative agnosia. Apperceptive agnosia, also known as 'form agnosia', involves inability to perceive spatial form. Patients with this condition cannot group the

---

[9] See Goldman; Horgan and Tienson; Pitt; Siewert; Siegel. See Kriegel, and Siegel, 'How Can We Discover the Contents of Experience?', *Southern Journal of Philosophy*, 45 (2007) Suppl., pp. 127–42, for discussion of the contrast methodology as such.

[10] Of course, the argument is not completely novel. See van Gulick for an embryonic presentation of the case.

[11] See, for useful overviews of agnosia, M.J. Farah, *Visual Agnosia*, 2nd edn (MIT Press, 2004); G.W. Humphreys and M.J. Riddoch, *To See But Not to See* (Hillsdale: Erlbaum, 1987).

[12] H. Lissauer, 'Ein Fall von Seelenblindheit nebst einem Beitrage zur Theorie derselben' [1890], tr. J.M. Lissauer, *Cognitive Neuropsychology*, 5 (1988), pp. 155–92.

various parts of overlapping objects into unitary percepts, and are unable to produce accurate copies of pictures that are presented to them. In pure associative agnosia, form perception remains unimpaired but patients are unable to recognize objects as belonging to familiar categories. In Teuber's oft-quoted words, associative agnosia involves 'a normal percept stripped of its meaning'.[13] Here is a particularly striking case study:

> For the first three weeks in the hospital the patient could not identify common objects presented visually and did not know what was on his plate until he tasted it. He identified objects immediately on touching them. When shown a stethoscope, he described it as 'a long cord with a round thing at the end', and asked if it could be a watch. He identified a can opener as 'could it be a key?'. Asked to name a cigarette lighter, he said, 'I don't know', but named it after the examiner lit it. He said he was 'not sure' when shown a toothbrush. Asked to identify a comb, he said, 'I don't know'. When shown a large matchbook, he said, 'It could be a container for keys'. He correctly identified glasses. For a pipe, he said, 'Some type of utensil, I'm not sure'. Shown a key, he said, 'I don't know what that is; perhaps a file or a tool of some sort'. He was never able to describe or demonstrate the use of an object if he could not name it. If he misnamed an object his demonstration of its use would correspond to the mistaken identification.... Remarkably, he could make excellent copies of line drawings and still fail to name the subject.... He easily matched drawings of objects that he could not identify, and had no difficulty in discriminating between complex non-representational patterns differing from each other only subtly. He occasionally failed in discriminating because he included imperfections in the paper or in the printer's ink. He could never group drawings by class unless he could first name the subject.[14]

Associative agnosia provides a tool with which to develop a potent contrast argument for liberalism. Although we have no direct access to the patient's phenomenal state, it is extremely plausible to suppose that the phenomenal character of his visual experience has changed. But what kind of perceptual content has the patient lost? He has not lost low-level perceptual content, for those abilities that require the processing of only low-level content remain intact. The patient's deficit is not one of *form* perception but of *category* perception. Hence high-level perceptual representation – the representation of an object as a stethoscope, a can-opener or a comb – can enter into the contents of perceptual phenomenality.

Associative agnosia can occur across a wide range of categories and modalities. Visual agnosia can take the form of a broad impairment to object-recognition in general or a more circumscribed impairment in the

---

[13] H.-L. Teuber, 'Alteration of Perception and Memory in Man', in L. Weiskrantz (ed.), *Analysis of Behavioural Change* (New York: Harper and Row, 1968), pp. 268–375, at p. 293.

[14] A.B. Rubens and D.F. Benson, 'Associative Visual Agnosia', *Archives of Neurology*, 24 (1971), pp. 305–16, at pp. 308–9.

recognition of particular types of objects, such as faces (prosopagnosia) or words (alexia).[15] Auditory agnosia can occur as a general impairment in the recognition of sounds, or as a more specific impairment in the recognition of non-verbal sounds or music.[16] The desert phenomenality of the conservative will need to be significantly enriched if, as seems plausible, each of these forms of agnosia involves the loss of high-level phenomenal content which is normally present in perceptual experience.

IV. THE CONSERVATIVE RESPONSE

Conservatives have two strategies available to them in responding to contrast arguments. The most popular strategy is to attempt to account for the phenomenal contrasts present in these scenarios in purely low-level terms. Tye provides a particularly clear example of this strategy:

> Consider ... phenomenal differences in what it's like to hear sounds in French before and after the language has been learnt. Obviously there are phenomenal changes here tied to experiential reactions of various sorts associated with understanding the language (e.g., differences in emotional and imagistic responses, feelings of familiarity that weren't present before, differences in effort or concentration involved as one listens to the speaker). There are also phenomenal differences connected to a change in phonological processing. Before one understands French, the phonological structure one hears in the French utterance is fragmentary. For example, one's experience of word boundaries is patently less rich and determinate. This is because some aspects of phonological processing are sensitive to top-down feedback from the centres of comprehension.... Still, the influence here is causal, which I am prepared to allow. My claim is that the phenomenally relevant representation of phonological features is non-conceptual, not that it is produced *exclusively* by what is in the acoustic signal.[17]

We should certainly allow that low-level perceptual content can be subject to top-down modulation. Even colour perception can be modulated in this way. In one study, subjects were presented with photographs of fruit that could be manipulated so as to make the fruit in question appear to be any arbitrary colour. When subjects were instructed to manipulate the image of

---

[15] For achromatopsia, see M.F. Beauvois and B. Saillant, 'Optic Aphasia for Color and Color Agnosia', *Cognitive Neuropsychology*, 2 (1985), pp. 1–48; C.A. Heywood and A. Cowey, 'Cerebral Achromatopsia', in G.W. Humphreys (ed.), *Case Studies in the Neuropsychology of Vision* (London: Plenum, 1999), pp. 17–39; R.W. Kentridge *et al.*, 'Chromatic Edges, Surfaces, and Constancies in Cerebral Achromatopsia', *Neuropsychologia*, 42 (2004), pp. 821–30. For akinetopsia, see S. Zeki, 'Cerebral Akinetopsia (Visual Motion Blindness)', *Brain*, 114 (1991), pp. 811–24.

[16] N. Motomura *et al.*, 'Auditory Agnosia', *Brain*, 109 (1986), pp. 379–91; I. Peretz, 'Brain Specialization for Music', *Trends in Cognitive Sciences*, 9 (2001), pp. 28–33.

[17] Tye, *Consciousness, Color, and Content*, p. 61: see also *Ten Problems*, p. 140.

a banana so that it appeared grey (that is, achromatic), they actually made it slightly bluish, compensating for the fact that they knew that bananas are normally yellow. At the point where the banana was actually achromatic, subjects reported that it looked yellowish.[18] So there is no doubt that high-level content can have a causal impact on low-level representations. But it seems to me highly implausible to suppose that we shall be able to find such low-level differences in *all* contrast cases. Suppose you are looking at a dog in the distance. The light is poor, and you have difficulty identifying the seen object. Suddenly, recognition dawns. Contrast the visual experience that you have immediately prior to the act of recognition with that which you have immediately after recognition. Must there be low-level differences between these two percepts? I do not see why.

The thought that the contrast cases can always be accounted for in low-level terms is particularly hard pressed when confronted with associative agnosia. Although associative agnosia is often impure in the sense that the patient also has some degree of impairment to low-level perception, it can also take a pure form.[19] The patient described in the previous section is a case in point. Although he could not group objects by category, he could match them to visually identical objects, and his performance on tests of immediate visual recall tests was excellent.

Even when contrast cases do involve top-down modulation of low-level perceptual content, it is doubtful that the role of high-level categorization is *merely* causal. It seems plausible to suppose that the phenomenal differences brought about by learning French involve both (low-level) changes in phonological structure *and* (high-level) semantic differences. Similarly, the phenomenal contrast between seeing an object as a stethoscope and failing to recognize it as such might involve both low-level changes in perceptual focus *and* high-level changes associated with kind representation. High-level representations might impinge on phenomenal content in two ways at once, indirectly by means of causally restructuring low-level phenomenal content, and directly in virtue of the fact that they themselves can feature in phenomenal content.

[18] T. Hansen *et al.*, 'Memory Modulates Color Appearance', *Nature Neuroscience*, 9 (2006), pp. 1367–8.

[19] Although pure cases of associative agnosia are relatively rare, one does not need pure cases to show that associative agnosia is not merely a matter of low-level visual impairment: see G. Ettlinger, 'Sensory Deficits in Visual Agnosia', *Journal of Neurology, Neurosurgery, and Psychiatry*, 19 (1956), pp. 297–301; A. Cowey *et al.*, 'Ettlinger at Bay', in A.D. Milner (ed.), *Comparative Neuropsychology* (Oxford UP, 1998), pp. 30–50. Instead, one need only find patients with associative agnosia whose low-level visual impairments are no more serious than those of patients without associative agnosia, and such cases have indeed been found: see Farah; E.K. Warrington, 'Agnosia', in R. Vinken *et al.* (eds), *Handbook of Clinical Neurology* (Amsterdam: Elsevier, 1985), pp. 333–49.

In fact, the liberal could grant that it is impossible for high-level perceptual phenomenality to change without this change being accompanied by some low-level phenomenal change. Consider the experience of causal relations. On one intuitively plausible view, the experience of causal relations is nomologically (if not constitutively) dependent on the experience of spatio-temporal relations, and so in this sense is not autonomous. The liberal might argue that what holds of the experience of causation might hold more generally, and that high-level phenomenal content supervenes on low-level phenomenal content, so that any change to high-level phenomenal content requires a change of low-level phenomenal content. I myself do not find any such view particularly attractive, but I can see nothing in the liberal commitment to high-level phenomenal content which rules it out. It is one thing to posit high-level phenomenal content; it is quite another to hold that high-level phenomenal content is independent of low-level phenomenal content.

If conservatives cannot account for the phenomenal contrast present in cases of (pure) associative agnosia in terms of low-level changes, how *are* they to account for such cases? So far as I can see, conservatives must deny that associative agnosia involves any loss of phenomenal content at all. On this view, associative agnosia does not involve any disruption to the phenomenal looks of objects. This might seem implausible, but conservatives will be at pains to point out that there are different senses of 'looks', and that to deny that associative agnosia involves any alteration to how objects look in the phenomenal sense of the term is perfectly consistent with allowing it to involve alterations to the epistemic and/or comparative look of an object.[20] No doubt agnosia *does* alter the way that objects look in the comparative and epistemic senses of the term, but why deny that it also alters the way that they look (or sound, or feel, etc.) in the *phenomenal* sense of the term? It would clearly be illegitimate to argue that associative agnosia cannot involve changes to how things phenomenally look on the ground that phenomenal-looks talk involves locutions of the form '*x* looks F to *S*', where 'F' expresses a sensory property (Tye, *Consciousness*, p. 54), for any liberal worth his salt will reject this constraint on phenomenal-looks talk. According to liberals, '*x* looks F to *S*' can capture a genuine phenomenal-looks claim even when 'F' expresses a property that is not sensory in any natural sense of that term. In sum, it seems to me that there is every reason to think that associative agnosia is no less a disorder of perceptual phenomenality than is apperceptive agnosia: both conditions involve the loss of a 'layer' of phenomenal content.

[20] Cf. Lyons, 'Perceptual Belief'; Tye, *Consciousness, Color, and Content.*

There is a further lesson to be learnt from associative agnosia. Lying behind some versions of conservatism is a doxastic model of object recognition, as in the following passage from Tye (*Ten Problems*, p. 215):

> Object or shape recognition in vision ... is a matter of seeing that such and such a type of object is present. Seeing that something is the case, in turn, is a matter of forming an appropriate belief or judgement on the basis of visual experiences or sensations.... there are two components in visual recognition, a belief component and a looking component.

On this model, object recognition is not strictly speaking perceptual; instead, it belongs on the cognitive side of the perception–cognition divide. One might argue that if this model were right, then associative agnosia could not bear on questions regarding the admissible contents of perceptual phenomenality, because it is not really a perceptual deficit. Further, if object recognition were a matter of appropriately formed belief, and if belief lacks any proprietary phenomenal character, as many assume it does, then object recognition would also lack proprietary phenomenal character.

It is controversial whether thought does lack proprietary phenomenal character. According to some liberals, phenomenal consciousness pervades not only high-level perception but also cognition. But I shall leave that point to one side here and focus on the question of object recognition. Is it a matter of perception, as I have been assuming, or is Tye right to think that it is doxastic?

There may be no straightforward answer to this question, for different accounts may be needed for different forms of object recognition. But there are good reasons to take object recognition of the kind that is disrupted in agnosia to be perceptual. For one thing, object recognition of this kind resists doxastic penetration. It does not matter what one believes about an object; it still looks like a pipe, a stethoscope, or a cigarette lighter. Perhaps a more potent reason for regarding object recognition as perceptual is that it cannot be *restored* by the insertion of the relevant belief. Suppose a patient with associative agnosia, who fails to recognize a pipe as a pipe, is told that he is looking at a pipe, and on that basis judges – that is, forms the belief – that he is looking at a pipe. (He will be able to do this, for associative agnosia does not involve any conceptual loss.[21] Patients with visual agnosia can both reason about pipes and recognize them via other modalities, such as touch.) The patient now has the two things Tye regards as constitutive of visual recognition, the belief component and the looking component. Would he now recognize the perceptual object as a pipe? Perhaps so, at

---

[21] It should be noted that there is some evidence that conceptual knowledge of a domain is not entirely unaffected in associative agnosia (see Farah, pp. 152–3).

least in some cases, as a further passage from Rubens and Benson (p. 308) suggests:

> When told the correct name of an object, he usually responded with a quick nod and said, 'Yes, I see it now'. Then, often he could point out various parts of the previously unrecognized item as readily as a normal subject (e.g., the stem and bowl of a pipe, and the laces, sole and heel of a shoe). However, if asked by the examiner, 'Suppose I told you that the last object was not really a pipe, what would you say?', he would reply, 'I would take your word for it. Perhaps it's not really a pipe.' Similar vacillation never occurred for tactilely or aurally identified objects.

However, this remission is not reflected in other reports of associative agnosia, and even in this case it seems to have been only temporary. Although the patient (presumably) retained the *belief* that he was looking at a pipe, he seems not to have retained his *experience* of it as a pipe. Perceptual recognition is not simply a matter of believing that such and such a type of object is present whilst enjoying low-level visual experience.

Of course, Tye's account of object recognition involves the claim that one must form the appropriate belief *on the basis of* visual experience, and in Tye's defence the critic might point out that this grounding relation is absent from the case just described. But this omission is easily rectified. Suppose the patient suffers from a freak neurophysiological condition that causes him to believe that every object he is looking at is a pipe. This case satisfies Tye's causal condition on visual recognition, but it seems doubtful whether it suffices to reinstate the missing experiential content. Furthermore, it is far from clear that any such grounding condition for perceptual experience is really warranted. Associative agnosia involves the loss of a certain type of *occurrent* state and not simply the loss of a capacity or causal relation. As I argued above, this occurrent state cannot be identified with a belief or a judgement.

Consider again Teuber's suggestion that associative agnosia involves a 'normal percept stripped of its meaning'. It seems to me that there are two ways in which this claim might be read. One might think that a percept's 'meaning' is external to it, and hold that a percept could remain normal even when stripped of its meaning. This seems to be Tye's view. I have defended a rather different picture, according to which a percept's 'meaning' is to be located within the percept itself, and hence that a percept stripped of its meaning is no longer normal. It seems to me that it is this description which best captures what it would be like to have associative agnosia, and hence provides a reason to endorse the liberal conception of the reach of perceptual phenomenality over the conservative alternative.

V. INDISCERNIBILITY AND INDUBITABILITY

Together with other versions of the contrast argument, the argument from associative agnosia provides a strong *prima facie* case for the liberal view. But if the case for liberalism is so compelling, why do many theorists find the conservative position so appealing? The aim of this section and the next is to explore some possible answers to this question.

One potential route to conservatism proceeds via the notion of indiscernibility. It might be argued that high-level properties cannot be phenomenally represented because objects with different high-level properties can be perceptually indiscernible. In the relevant sense, gin is perceptually indiscernible from water; suitably disguised raccoons are perceptually indiscernible from dogs; and the German word 'Lieder' is perceptually indiscernible from the English word 'leader'. One might take these facts to indicate that perception cannot represent liquids as gin, animals as dogs or utterances as tokens of the word 'leader'.

Tye seems to have an argument like this in mind when he claims (*Ten Problems*, p. 141) that nothing looks like a tiger to us in the phenomenal sense of the term because 'there might conceivably be creatures other than tigers that look to us phenomenally just like tigers'. It is certainly true that non-tigers (ligers, for instance) could look to us phenomenally just like tigers. But this fact counts for little here, for one can also mistake blue things for green things, hot things for cold things and heptadecagons for enneadecagons. Presumably Tye's point is that non-tigers could look just like tigers without being *misrepresented*. This too is true. There might be planets inhabited by tiger-like creatures that look just like tigers. Does it follow from this that tigerhood cannot be phenomenally represented? I think not. To show why not, a short excursion to twin earth is needed.

Twin earth scenarios are routinely employed to put pressure on the link between phenomenal content and perceptual indiscernibility. It seems conceivable that there are worlds in which some property other than yellow looks (in the phenomenal sense) just like yellow, or that there are worlds in which some property other than sourness tastes (in the phenomenal sense) like sourness. The point is not restricted to secondary qualities. It is conceivable that there are worlds in which cracks might look (again in the phenomenal sense) the way shadows look.[22] Nevertheless, it does not follow that

---

[22] See T. Burge, 'Individualism and Psychology', *Philosophical Review*, 95 (1986), pp. 3–45; M. Davies, 'Externalism and Experience', in N. Block *et al.* (eds), *The Nature of Consciousness* (MIT Press, 1997), pp. 309–28.

being yellow, being sour or being a shadow is not phenomenally repre-sented. In short, one cannot employ the fact that an object with property P might be perceptually indiscernible from one lacking property P as a reason for thinking that P is phenomenally inadmissible.

I suspect that Tye is tempted to take indistinguishability as a guide to phenomenal content because he has a Russellian conception of phenomenal content. The Russellian identifies phenomenal contents with represented properties. On this view, phenomenal states of the same kind (that is, with the same phenomenal content) could not be directed (in the relevant sense) towards different types of objects without misrepresenting at least one of those objects. For example, a non-yellow object could not be indistinguish-able from a yellow object (with respect to hue) without one of the two objects being misrepresented. To take another example, a non-tiger that phenomenally looked just like a tiger must be misrepresented if, as the liberal suggests, being a tiger is the kind of property that is phenomenally admissible. But, the conservative might continue, non-tigers could look just like tigers without phenomenal content being guilty of any kind of misrepre-sentation. Of course, one is guilty of some kind of misrepresentation if one takes a non-tiger to be a tiger, but according to this view the phenomenal character of one's perceptual experience is innocent of any mistake.

The Russellian conception of phenomenal content might be able to preserve the link between phenomenal content and indistinguishability, but the Russellian account is problematic. For one thing, it is unable to account for the thought that a single type of phenomenal state might represent dif-ferent properties in different contexts. Intuitively, the phenomenal proper-ties associated with the representation of yellow could have been associated with the representation of blue and *vice versa*; the phenomenal property associated with the representation of shadows could have been associated with the representation of cracks and *vice versa*, and so on. If this is right, then accounts of phenomenal content need to be Fregean.[23] We need to allow that phenomenal content might involve 'senses' or 'modes of presentation'.

Conservatives might press the argument from indiscernibility from another angle. They might argue that if the property of being a tiger were phenomenally admissible, then it would be possible for two objects to look identical apart from the fact that one looks (in the phenomenal sense) to be a tiger but the other does not. But, the objection goes, this is not possible. Hence the property of being a tiger is not phenomenally admissible.

Is it possible for two objects to look identical, apart from the fact that only one of them looks like a tiger? Consider not tigers but chickens.

---

[23] See Chalmers, 'The Representational Character of Experience'; B. Thompson, 'Senses for Senses', *Australasian Journal of Philosophy*, 87 (2008), pp. 99–117.

Chicken-sexers can distinguish male chicks from female chicks, but they typically cannot tell you how they do it.[24] Chicken-sexers employ low-level cues to differentiate male chicks from female chicks, but it is an open question whether these low-level cues are phenomenally represented. Perhaps male and female chicks are phenomenally indistinguishable apart from the fact that male chicks 'seem to be male' whereas females 'seem to be female'. We should not assume that the low-level representations in virtue of which high-level phenomenal content is fixed must themselves be phenomenally conscious. We are often sensitive to the mental states of others without being aware of the basis of our sensitivity. No doubt the detection of others' mental states involves complex computations of their behavioural dynamics, but it may be that these representations are no more consciously available than are the representations which underlie, e.g., experiences of colour constancy or motion. In short, we might want to allow that it is possible for two objects to look identical apart from the fact that only one of them looks like a tiger.

A second and perhaps rather more plausible response to the objection is to challenge the assumption that high-level phenomenal content must be independent of low-level phenomenal content. As I noted above, the liberal need not accept this assumption. The liberal could hold that any two objects that are phenomenally represented as having the same low-level properties must also be phenomenally represented as having the same high-level properties, and thus must be phenomenally indistinguishable. Arguably, the phenomenal representation of causation is supervenient on the phenomenal representation of certain types of spatiotemporal relations between the events or objects involved; even so, it clearly would not follow from this that causation is not phenomenally represented.

A rather different line of argument for the conservative position makes use of indubitability rather than indiscernibility. Consider the following well known passage from H.H. Price:

> When I see a tomato there is much that I can doubt.... One thing however I cannot doubt [in reflecting on my experience is] that there exists a red patch of a round and somewhat bulgy shape, standing out from a background of other colour-patches, and having a certain visual depth, and that this whole field of colour is directly present to my consciousness.... This peculiar and ultimate manner of being present to consciousness is called *being given*, and what is thus present is called a [sense-]*datum*.... The term is meant to stand for something whose existence is indubitable (however fleeting), something from which all theories of perception ought to start, however much they may diverge later.[25]

---

[24] I. Biederman and M.M. Shiffrar, 'Sexing Day-old Chicks', *Journal of Experimental Psychology: Learning, Memory, and Cognition*, 13 (1987), pp. 640–5.

[25] H.H. Price, *Perception* (London: Methuen, 1932), pp. 18–19.

Price does not commit himself to a conservative conception of phenomenal consciousness, but the tenor of this passage certainly points in that direction. The perceived object is 'given' as red, bulgy, and occupying a particular spatial location, but there is no suggestion here that it is also given as a tomato. The passage also suggests that one might be led to this view by considerations deriving from indubitability: one can doubt that one is presented with a tomato, but one cannot doubt that 'there exists a red patch of a round and somewhat bulgy shape, standing out from a background of other colour-patches, and having a certain visual depth'.

I do not know what role this argument might have played in tempting theorists towards conservatism, but I do know that whatever appeal it may have had is ill deserved, for the argument is highly implausible. First, we must ask what exactly it is that is indubitable. Is it a claim about how the object *is* or a claim about how the object *appears*? Surely it is only the latter claim that might be thought indubitable. But there is no asymmetry between being red and being a tomato on this score, for the thought that one experiences the object as a tomato seems to be as immune to doubt as the thought that one experiences the object as red. High-level perceptual content seems to be just as indubitable as low-level perceptual content. We have yet to identify any crucial asymmetry between low-level perception and high-level perception that might bring with it a phenomenal divide.

VI. THE KNOWLEDGE ARGUMENT AND THE EXPLANATORY GAP

I turn now to another potential source of support for conservatism. At first sight, some of the deepest puzzles surrounding phenomenal consciousness suggest a conservative conception of its reach. Jackson's Mary is an expert neuroscientist who has never experienced red but knows everything there is to know about the perception of red.[26] Intuitively, Mary learns something when she first sees red, something she could not have learnt as a neuroscientist. Therefore, the argument goes, facts about what it is like to see red are not physical facts. The knowledge argument may not be sound, but the immense literature it has spawned bears clear witness to its intuitive forcefulness. This forcefulness is something which an account of the reach of perceptual phenomenality must reckon with. Does the knowledge argument generalize to high-level phenomenal content, or is there a good reason why Jackson's argument centres on low-level perceptual features such as colour?

---

[26] F. Jackson, 'Epiphenomenal Qualia', *The Philosophical Quarterly*, 32 (1982), pp. 127–36.

Consider a variant of Jackson's case, in which Mary is an expert in object recognition. She knows everything there is to know about how tomatoes are recognized, but she has never seen a tomato. Does Mary learn anything when she first recognizes a tomato? Arguably not. At any rate, the intuition that she does is *much* weaker than is the intuition that she learns something when she first sees red. Why should this be? Perhaps, the conservative might suggest, Mary does not learn anything when she first recognizes a tomato because there is no phenomenal property distinctive of recognizing a tomato – there is no phenomenal fact here to be learnt.

But the argument is too quick. There is no doubt that it is much harder to construct a plausible version of the knowledge argument around high-level perception than it is to construct a plausible version of the argument around the experience of colour, but we cannot infer from this fact alone that high-level content is phenomenally inadmissible. Suppose Mary is an expert in the perception of space. However, she has never seen, or indeed experienced in any modality, a square. Does Mary learn anything when she first sees a square? Perhaps, but the claim that she does is *much* less intuitively compelling than is the claim that she learns something when she first sees red.[27] Should we conclude from this that primary qualities such as being a square are not phenomenally admissible? Surely not; it is beyond doubt that one can phenomenally represent squares as such. So we cannot take the fact that a property does not easily lend itself to the construction of a plausible version of the knowledge argument as a reason for thinking that it cannot enter into phenomenal content.

We might, at this point, ask why it is harder to construct the knowledge argument around some features than others. I suspect that the answer to this question has something to do with what we might call 'phenomenal distance'. Suppose Mary has experienced red_{27}, but has never seen red_{28}. Does she learn anything when she first sees red_{28}? Perhaps, but this version of the knowledge argument is not particularly compelling. (There is a reason why Jackson restricted Mary to a black and white room.) Intuitively, red_{27} and red_{28} are 'close enough' in phenomenal space for one to be able to 'work out' what it would be like to experience the one from having experienced the other, as with Hume's missing shade of blue. In contrast, there is much to be said for the thought that experiences of red are too far apart from achromatic experiences for one to be able to work out what it would be like to experience red without having experienced colours.

---

[27] I am not claiming that one *cannot* construct a compelling version of the knowledge argument centring on the representation of an object as a square. Rather, my claim is only that it is much more difficult to construct square-based versions of the knowledge argument than it is to create a red-based version of the argument.

Arguably, the square-based version of the knowledge argument has little plausibility because there is insufficient phenomenal distance between the phenomenal property distinctive of seeing something as square and the various spatial phenomenal properties with which Mary will be acquainted in her squareless room.

In the light of the foregoing, we are now in a position to see why it might be difficult to create a plausible version of the knowledge argument for high-level perceptual content. I shall call the phenomenal property associated with recognizing an object as a tomato 'P_t'. To construct a plausible tomato-based version of the knowledge argument, we would need to ensure that Mary could learn about the neurophysiology of high-level perception without being acquainted with phenomenal properties sufficiently close to P_t for her to be able to work out, from within her room, what it is like to instantiate P_t. Can that be done? Perhaps, perhaps not. It is difficult to tell, for it is difficult to measure phenomenal distance when confronted by high-level phenomenal properties. We have some grip on what phenomenal distance might involve when it comes to structured domains such as colour experience, but the notion of phenomenal distance becomes problematic once we leave the realm of sensory spaces. If we do not know how to measure phenomenal distance when it comes to high-level content, we are unlikely to have a firm intuition that Mary must learn something new when she first perceives a tomato as such.

This account of why it is difficult to construct a plausible version of the knowledge argument for high-level content is somewhat speculative, and it may well turn out to be false. But the central point, which is independent of that analysis, is that there is no straightforward knowledge argument objection to phenomenal liberalism. One cannot conclude that high-level content is phenomenally inadmissible on the ground that it is difficult to construct a plausible knowledge argument for such content, for any such argument threatens to commit one to a highly implausible form of *über*-conservatism according to which even primary qualities such as shape and motion are not phenomenally admissible.

So much for the knowledge argument; what about the explanatory gap?[28] Could one appeal to features of the explanatory gap to make a case for conservatism? I doubt it. There is, it seems to me, an explanatory gap between the experience of a tomato's colour and the various neurophysiological states underlying the experience, but there is also an explanatory gap between the experience of the tomato as a tomato and the various neurophysiological states underlying *that* experience. Maybe this gap can be

---

[28] J. Levine, 'Materialism and Qualia: the Explanatory Gap', *Pacific Philosophical Quarterly*, 64 (1983), pp. 354–61.

closed, maybe not; either way, the gap is not restricted to low-level perception. Indeed, one cannot even use the *appearance* of an explanatory gap to separate high-level perception from low-level perception, for high-level perception poses as much of an appearance of an explanatory gap as does low-level perception. It is gaps, or at least the appearance thereof, all the way up.

VII. CONCLUSION

I have done three things in this chapter. I began by distinguishing two approaches to phenomenal content, a conservative approach which would limit phenomenal content to low-level features, and a liberal approach which sees phenomenal content as reaching all the way into high-level perception. In the second part of the chapter I argued that associative agnosia provides the tools with which to construct a particularly potent contrast argument against phenomenal conservatism. In the final two sections of the chapter I examined a number of arguments against liberalism: some of these arguments appealed to a supposed link between phenomenal content on the one hand and indiscriminability or indubitability on the other; others supposed a link between phenomenal content on the one hand and the knowledge argument and the explanatory gap on the other. I argued that none of these arguments is convincing. The roots of resistance to a liberal treatment of perceptual phenomenality are deep and complex, and it is clear that much more needs to be said by way of addressing them than I have been able to say here. None the less I hope that what I have said suffices to dislodge the assumption, dominant in some quarters, that the student of phenomenal consciousness need have no direct interest in high-level perception.

Suppose some form of liberalism is true; what might follow from this? The debate between conservative and liberal treatments of perceptual phenomenality is part of a wider debate about the reach of phenomenality more generally. Some theorists hold that phenomenal consciousness is restricted to perception, bodily sensations and certain kinds of affective states, others hold that cognitive states, such as desires, judgements and intentions, have a distinctive (proprietary) phenomenal character over and above what they may inherit from whatever sensations or images accompany them. Engaging with this debate, the 'cognitive phenomenality' debate, is beyond my present brief, but I shall conclude by noting one potential point of contact between that debate and the one on which I have focused.

There may be an argument from the claim that high-level perception possesses a proprietary phenomenal character to the claim that thought possesses a proprietary phenomenal character. Suppose, as many do, that high-level perception is conceptual. If that thought is right, then there cannot be any objection to cognitive phenomenality on the ground that cognitive states have conceptual content, because it has already been granted that concepts can enter into phenomenal content in the form of high-level perception. On the other hand, if one thinks of high-level perception as having (only) non-conceptual content, then the route from perceptual liberalism to cognitive phenomenality might not be so smooth, for one could embrace high-level perceptual phenomenality but resist cognitive phenomenality on the ground that phenomenal content is exclusively non-conceptual. But even those who advocate a non-conceptual view of perceptual content, as I am inclined to, might think that perceptual liberalism provides the proponent of cognitive phenomenality with some encouragement. After all, even if high-level perceptual phenomenality is not fully conceptualized, it is surely cognitive in some genuine sense, and we have at least broken the identification of the phenomenal with the sensory. It is, I think, no accident that those who are sympathetic with the thought that high-level perception enters into phenomenal content tend to be sympathetic with the thought that the contents of cognition can also enter into phenomenal content.[29]

[29] This chapter was originally presented as a paper at a workshop on the Admissible Contents of Experience at the University of Glasgow organized by Fiona Macpherson, and I am grateful to Fiona and the other participants in that workshop for their comments on the original paper. I have also benefited greatly from the comments of Uriah Kriegel and David Chalmers.

3

SEEING CAUSINGS AND HEARING GESTURES

BY S. BUTTERFILL

Can humans see causal interactions? Evidence on the visual perception of causal interactions, from Michotte to contemporary work, is best interpreted as showing that we can see some causal interactions in the same sense as that in which we can hear speech. Causal perception, like speech perception, is a form of categorical perception.

Which properties and happenings can humans see? It is fairly uncontroversial that we can see the shapes of things and their movements. It is also reasonably uncontroversial that we cannot see properties like market value or processes like radioactive decay. People may sometimes talk about seeing these things, but it seems plausible that what they strictly and literally see are only characteristic visual indicators of market value or radioactive decay.

What about simple causal interactions like launchings, burstings, blockings and supportings – can we see these things? When two balls collide, what do we see? Do we see only one motion followed by another, or do we see some kind of causal interaction?

David Hume appears to have held that we perceive only one motion followed by another: 'When we consider these objects with the utmost attention, we find only that one body approaches the other; and that the motion of it precedes that of the other, but without any sensible interval' (*Treatise* I iii 2). Albert Michotte, on the other hand, held that we can see certain types of causal interaction in the same sense as that in which we can see shape or movement:

> There are some cases ... in which a causal impression arises, clear, genuine, and unmistakable, and the idea of cause can be derived from it by simple abstraction in just the same way as the idea of shape or movement can be derived from the perception of shape or movement.[1]

Several philosophers and psychologists agree with Michotte that causal interactions are visible in the same sense as shape and motion are. Among

[1] A. Michotte, *The Perception of Causality*, tr. T. Miles (London: Methuen, 1946), pp. 270–1.

the philosophers are David Armstrong[2] and Peter Strawson, who says

> In a great boulder rolling down the mountainside and flattening the wooden hut in its
> path we see an exemplary instance of force ... these mechanical transactions ... are
> directly observable (or experienceable).[3]

The psychologists Brian Scholl and Patrice Tremoulet agree that we can see causal interactions:

> ... just as the visual system works to recover the physical structure of the world by
> inferring properties such as 3-D shape, so too does it work to recover the causal ...
> structure of the world by inferring properties such as causality.[4]

While agreeing that we can see some causal interactions, Michotte, Strawson and Scholl adopt different approaches to thinking about perception. Scholl is driven by David Marr's question 'What kind of information is vision really delivering?'.[5] Strawson focuses on descriptions of perceptual content which describe how the world is presented to the perceiver. Michotte is concerned with perception as a source of causal concepts.

The variety of approaches to perception can easily complicate the task of answering questions about what we can perceive. What could ensure that in making claims about what can or cannot be seen, we are genuinely agreeing with or contradicting others who make similar sounding claims, rather than merely using terms like 'see' in a way which fails to connect with other positions? Michotte, Strawson and Scholl all hold that we can see causal interactions in the same sense as we can see shape, whatever sense that is. The appeal to shape perception ensures genuine agreement, despite any differences about the nature of perception.

In this chapter I argue that we can see some causal interactions in the same sense as we can hear speech, whatever sense that is. I shall also tentatively suggest that speech perception is importantly different from shape perception. To see the shapes of things is, in a wide range of naturally occurring conditions if not always, to be aware of those shapes and to be in a position to know things about them; but hearing speech and seeing causings are not similarly related to awareness of the things perceived. If so, Michotte, Strawson and Scholl are right that we can see some causal interactions, but wrong that we can do so in the same sense as we can see shape.

[2] D.M. Armstrong, 'Going through the Open Door Again', in J. Collins *et al.* (eds), *Causation and Counterfactuals* (MIT Press, 2004), pp. 445–58.

[3] P.F. Strawson, 'Causation and Explanation', in his *Analysis and Metaphysics* (Oxford UP, 1992), p. 118.

[4] B.J. Scholl and P.D. Tremoulet, 'Perceptual Causality and Animacy', *Trends in Cognitive Sciences*, 4 (2000), pp. 299–309, at p. 299.

[5] D. Marr, *Vision: a Computational Investigation into the Human Representation and Processing of Visual Information* (San Francisco: W.H. Freeman, 1982), p. 35.

I shall only consider visually presented stimuli. Some researchers hold that we perceive causal interactions through touch or experiences of agency. These views will not be considered here. Following common use, I adopt 'causal perception' as a label for whatever perceptual experiences are associated with visual stimuli involving or standing in for causal interactions. Understood in this way, my first question is whether the objects of causal perception are causal interactions or just movements.

I

Although we have quite a lot of data on causal perception, the interpretation of these data is not straightforward.

I shall take Albert Michotte's experiments on launching as my starting-point. The launching sequence is illustrated schematically in Figure 1.[6] When seeing this sequence, most subjects describe their experiences in causal terms as the experience of a collision or launching. They also distinguish this experience from the experience of seeing one movement followed by another. (The latter experience is reported when

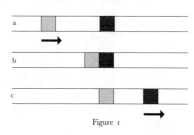

Figure 1

there is a delay between the two movements.) Michotte studied launching in great detail, and I shall discuss his findings below.

Peter White and Elizabeth Milne showed subjects various other kinds of schematic animation (see Figure 2). They found that subjects reliably reported seeing pulling, disintegration and bursting.[7] There is no doubt, then, that people have distinctive experiences for a range

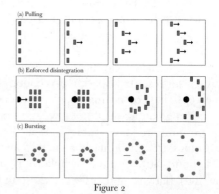

Figure 2

---

[6] A video is available on Brian Scholl's website, http://pantheon.yale.edu/~bs265/demos/causality.html. The figure is from G. Thines, A. Costall and G. Butterworth (eds), *Michotte's Experimental Psychology of Perception* (Hillsdale: Erlbaum, 1991), p. 69.

[7] P. White and E. Milne, 'Impressions of Enforced Disintegration and Bursting in the Visual Perception of Collision Events', *Journal of Experimental Psychology: General*, 128 (1999), pp. 499–516, and 'Phenomenal Causality: Impressions of Pulling in the Visual Perception of Objects in Motion', *American Journal of Psychology*, 110 (1997), pp. 573–602. The illustration is from Scholl and Tremoulet, 'Perceptual Causality and Animacy', p. 301.

of stimuli which mimic different types of causal interaction, and that people regularly describe these experiences in causal terms.

Elizabeth Anscombe, Curt Ducasse and Peter Strawson have all observed that there are also many everyday situations in which it is natural to describe what we see in causal terms.[8] These include seeing a bird bending a branch by alighting on it and a boulder crushing a hut as it rolls down a mountain-side. Reading these authors, it may seem tempting to conclude from what people unreflectively say about their experiences that we can perceive causal interactions.

I do not think this conclusion follows. When shown an animation involving simple geometric shapes of the sort used by Heider and Simmel, many people report seeing things such as the large triangle intimidating the small one, or the small triangle defending the little circle as the big triangle tries to attack it.[9] (Figure 3 shows one frame from Heider and Simmel's animation.) This suggests that there may be nothing that people will not speak of seeing, given the right condi-

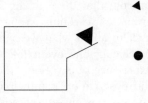

Figure 3

tions. So if there is a substantial question about whether we can see some types of causal interaction, it cannot be correct to answer this question on the basis of what people say they see.

I am not suggesting that people who talk about seeing intimidating or defending are mistaken or confused, only that common sense talk about perception serves a range of practical interests which probably do not include, and are in any case not limited to, answering theoretical questions about the nature of vision. We should not take what people say about their perceptions at face value, any more than what they say about the meanings of their utterances.

In cases like intimidating or defending it seems plausible to say that we see, at most, visible indicators of these things, not the interactions themselves. While there may be special phenomenological effects characteristic of intimidating or defending, it does not follow that we can see these things happen (and of course Heider and Simmel do not claim that we can). This is

    [8] G.E.M. Anscombe, 'Causality and Determination', in E. Sosa and M. Tooley (eds), *Causation* (Oxford UP, 1993), pp. 88–104; C.J. Ducasse, 'Causation: Perceivable? Or Only Inferred?', *Philosophy and Phenomenological Research*, 26 (1965), pp. 173–9; Strawson, *Analysis and Metaphysics*, pp. 109–32.

    [9] F. Heider and M. Simmel, 'An Experimental Study of Apparent Behaviour', *American Journal of Psychology*, 57 (1944), pp. 243–9, figure at p. 244. At the time of writing there is a reconstruction of Heider and Simmel's animation online at http://anthropomorphism.org/img/Heider_Flash.swf.

not to say that future research could not show that subjects really do see intimidating, only that nothing so far considered supports this conclusion. Those who follow Hume in denying that we can perceive causal interactions can say the same thing about findings like Michotte's and White and Milne's. They can admit that various stimuli give rise to characteristic phenomenology which many people unreflectively describe in causal terms, yet deny that we experience causal interactions.

Some philosophers seem to have missed this point. In ch. 4 of his *Intentionality*, John Searle objects to an analysis of causation in terms of regularities on the ground that it 'flies in the face of our common sense conviction that we do perceive causal relations all the time'. Searle may be wrong to suppose that there is any such common sense conviction; for reasons just given he is certainly wrong to suppose that such a conviction would support a claim about what we perceive. Searle then notes that 'The experience of perceiving one event following another is really quite different from the experience of perceiving the second event as caused by the first'.[10] By itself, this observation is unhelpful, because something similar is true of experiences of perceiving intimidating or defending. Searle's final point is that 'the researches of Michotte and Piaget would seem to support our common sense view'. As I shall show by taking a closer look at Michotte, this is not exactly straightforward. Michotte himself acknowledges this. At one point (*The Perception of Causality*, p. 256) he imagines Hume learning about his experiments, and writes 'it is probable that his philosophical position would not have been affected in the least'. In short, neither Michotte's nor more recent research (more of which is considered below) straightforwardly shows that we can see causings. In order to defend the claim that we can see causal interactions, one needs a way of getting beyond what some people unreflectively say about their experiences.

II

How can one get past disagreement over unreflective descriptions of visual experiences? By finding something that needs explaining.

Susanna Siegel suggests considering carefully matched pairs of experiences. For example, she imagines two ways of experiencing a situation in which a ball lands in a plant pot just before the lights go out.[11] You might find it compelling to suppose that the ball's landing causes the lights to go

---

[10] J.R. Searle, *Intentionality: an Essay in the Philosophy of Mind* (Cambridge UP, 1983), pp. 114–15.
[11] S. Siegel, 'The Visual Experience of Causation', *The Philosophical Quarterly*, 59 (2009), pp. 519–40 (this book, pp. 150–71).

out (even though you would presumably not judge this to be so), or you might experience the two events as unconnected. Siegel claims that these are two distinct experiences to which the same stimuli can give rise. Her question is then what explains the difference between the two experiences. She argues that the difference is best explained by supposing that the two events are experienced as causally connected in one case, but not in the other.

Siegel's 'matched pairs' approach looks promising because it identifies something that needs explaining, a difference between two experiences. But can Siegel's approach be applied to Michotte's launching stimulus? There would have to be a pair of occasions on which a subject saw the same type of launching sequence, experiencing successive movements on one occasion and experiencing launching on the other. Unfortunately, it seems there are no such pairs, because in the case of launching and similar stimuli, the characteristic phenomenology described as causal appears to be mandatory if you are paying attention. So one cannot apply Siegel's approach here.

This problem relates to a defect of Siegel's approach: it does not distinguish perceptual phenomenology from the non-perceptual phenomenology associated with the feeling of being struck by an idea. When a ball drops just as a light goes out, are we struck by the thought that the one caused the other, or do we somehow perceive this? Siegel's approach does not distinguish these two possibilities, which undermines her claim to have shown that 'causation is represented in visual experience'. When Michotte (p. 257) discusses the sort of cases Siegel focuses on, he denies that causation is perceived, but notes that 'a causal interpretation is urgently called for'. This seems at least as plausible as Siegel's claim that we perceive a causal interaction when a ball lands in a plant pot just before the lights go out. Indeed, it is tempting to think that genuinely perceptual phenomenology is always mandatory for subjects attending to the relevant aspects of stimuli. If so, the only phenomenological effects Siegel's 'matched pairs' approach can discern are non-perceptual, because the required pairs of experiences do not exist when the phenomenology is mandatory.

My aim is to support the claim that some causal interactions can be seen by finding something that needs explaining. If Siegel's matched pairs of experiences do not provide a suitable target for explanation, what else might?

Brian Scholl and Ken Nakayama offer a promising candidate which needs explaining: illusory crescents.[12] Shown a display just like Michotte's launching stimulus, except that the two objects completely overlap before the second starts to move,[13] almost all subjects report seeing a single object

[12] B.J. Scholl and K. Nakayama, 'Causal Capture: Contextual Effects on the Perception of Collision Events', *Psychological Science*, 13 (2002), pp. 493–8.

[13] A video is available on Scholl's web site referred to in fn. 6 above.

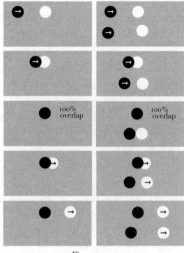

Figure 4

moving in front of or behind a stationary object; some report that the moving object changes colour (for a standard overlap event, see the left-hand side of Figure 4). However, it is possible to enhance this display so as to induce subjects to report seeing the overlap event as a launching event rather than as the movement of a single object (as in the overlap event with contextual launching event on the right-hand side of Figure 4). Here is the fact to be explained: when subjects report seeing the overlap event as launching, they also report seeing an illusory crescent, as if the shapes did not completely overlap; and they systematically underestimate the degree of overlap between the two objects.[14]

Does explaining this fact require conceding that we can see some types of causal interaction? I shall allow that as Scholl and Nakayama claim, subjects are seeing illusory crescents, and that the experience characteristic of launching affects the perception of shape.[15] Given this, Scholl and Nakayama offer (p. 466) 'a simple categorical explanation for the causal crescents illusion':

> ... the visual system, when led by other means to perceive an event as a causal collision, effectively 'refuses' to see the two objects as fully overlapped, because of an internalized constraint to the effect that such a spatial arrangement is not physically possible. As a result, a thin crescent of one object remains uncovered by the other one – as would in fact be the case in a straight-on billiard-ball collision.

If this is the best explanation of the illusory crescents, then we can indeed see at least one type of causal interaction.

This argument appears to be a promising way of attacking the idea that the experience characteristic of launching involves only some special phenomenological effect indicative of collisions. After all, why would such a phenomenological effect be associated with the illusory perception of crescents? Scholl and Nakayama's position is well supported in so far as

[14] Scholl and Nakayama, 'Illusory Causal Crescents: Misperceived Spatial Relations Due to Perceived Causality', *Perception*, 33 (2004), pp. 455–69, at p. 458.

[15] Cf. Scholl and Nakayama, p. 467: 'the perception of causality can also affect other types of visual processing – in this case the perception of spatial relations among moving objects'.

explaining the association between seeing launchings and seeing crescents requires appeal to some state with causal content.

But must that state be perceptual? On the face of it, Scholl and Nakayama's finding is equally well explained by either of two hypotheses: (a) there is a visual perception of a collision; or (b) there is some non-doxastic but also non-perceptual cognition of a collision. Since there may well be ways to exclude (b), I do not claim that Scholl and Nakayama's argument is incorrect. But I cannot make use of this argument here without ruling out (b), and that seems to require understanding how perception is distinct from and relates to other forms of cognition. Also, Scholl and Nakayama's strategy may not generalize to cases other than the launching stimuli. It would be better to be able to say more generally which types of causal interactions can be perceived, rather than just that at least one type is perceived (for examples, see White and Milne's stimuli above). For these reasons I shall introduce and then pursue a third and final approach to showing that we can see some types of causal interaction. (The illusory crescents finding will be useful later.)

Michotte's work provides the most promising candidate for a fact in need of explanation. The first phase of his work involves discovering the precise conditions under which the launching effect occurs, such as the relative speeds of the two objects, the delay between the first and second objects' movements, and the trajectories of the two objects. For instance, what happens if there is a pause between the first object's movement and the second object's movement? How long can the pause be before the launching effect vanishes? Michotte's findings are presented in the adjoining table.[16]

The Launching and Triggering Effects
Breakdown of stages according to time-interval
(30 readings at each interval)
Speed of A = 40 cm/s; speed of B = 11 cm/s. Ratio 3.6:1

Intervals (ms)	Direct launching
14	100%
28	100%
42	100%
56	100%
70	83%
84	58%
98	50%
112	17%
126	3%
140	0
154	0
168	0
196	0
224	0

Contemporary philosophers and psychologists sometimes write as if all Michotte did was study, in minute detail, the conditions under which the launching effect occurs. But this is to ignore the crucial second phase of Michotte's work. He was not directly concerned to know that pauses longer than 70 ms dramatically reduce the impression of launching. His question was *why* the launching impression occurs under precisely these conditions and not others. He writes that after identifying conditions under which the

---

[16] Michotte, *The Perception of Causality*, p. 115, part of table IX.

launching effect occurs, '... we were confronted with a second task, that of "understanding" the phenomenon, of ... seeking to find out why such and such conditions were necessary for its production, and why it possessed such and such properties' (p. 18).

Michotte's idea, then, is that we can get past superficial ideas about the perceptual experiences characteristic of launching by first (a) identifying the precise conditions under which these experiences occur, and then (b) explaining why they occur under these conditions. If it turns out that the best explanation at stage (b) requires the claim that we see causal inter-actions, that will constitute an argument for this claim.

The key fact to be explained, then, is that the experience characteristic of launching occurs under certain conditions. Having come this far with Michotte, I propose now to deviate from his views. To develop the argu-ment that we can see causal interactions, I shall compare causal perception with speech perception.

III

One of the questions set for this symposium is what methods we can use to determine the admissible contents of experience. One way to answer this question is to study cases where researchers have been successful, and speech is one of those cases.

According to Liberman and Mattingly's 'motor theory' of speech per-ception, when we encounter speech we perceive not sounds but gestures. More exactly, we perceive 'the intended phonic gestures of the speaker'.[17]

In the case of causation, the question is whether we perceive merely a sequence of movements, or causal interactions. In the case of speech, the parallel question is whether we perceive sounds or intended phonic gestures.

Naturally, not everyone accepts the motor theory of speech perception.[18] For my purposes, it is most important that Liberman and Mattingly have a

---

[17] What does 'intended' mean here? It is used to indicate that what are perceived are motor commands which produce gestures rather than gestures themselves. See A.M. Liberman and I.G. Mattingly, 'The Motor Theory of Speech Perception Revised', *Cognition*, 21 (1985), pp. 1–36, at p. 23: 'gestures do have characteristic invariant properties ... though these must be seen, not as peripheral movements, but as the more remote structures that control the movements. These structures correspond to the speaker's intentions.' So far these 'remote structures' are hypothetical: see A.M. Liberman and D.H. Whalen, 'On the Relation of Speech to Language', *Trends in Cognitive Sciences*, 4 (2000), pp. 187–96, at p. 195.

[18] A review of objections and some recent supporting evidence can be found in S. Pinker and R. Jackendoff, 'The Faculty of Language: What's Special About It?', *Cognition*, 95 (2005), pp. 201–36, §2.2. Liberman and Mattingly themselves emphasize that arguments for the theory are not conclusive and further research is needed: Liberman and Mattingly, 'A Specialization for Speech Perception', *Science*, 243 (1989), pp. 489–94, at p. 493.

valid argument for the conclusion that the objects of speech perception are intended gestures; whether the premises of this argument are true is less important. After all, even if their claims about speech were false, parallel claims might be true of causal perception.

Liberman and Mattingly's argument starts from the premise that speech perception is categorical. To illustrate, Figure 5 represents thirteen sounds spreading across *ba, da, ga*.[19] Each sound differs from its neighbours by the same amount as any other sound, at least when difference is measured by frequency. Most people would not be able to discriminate two adjacent sounds, except for two special cases (one around –3 to –1 and one around +1 to +3) where discriminating is easier: here people hear the sound change from *da* to *ga* or from *ga* to *ba*. This pattern of heightened discrimination is the defining characteristic of categorical perception.[20] Small changes to stimuli can make large differences to perception, large changes to stimuli can make small differences to perception, and the stimuli can be ordered and sorted into categories; discriminating nearby pairs of stimuli on either side of a category boundary is dramatically easier than discriminating pairs from within a category.

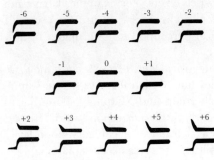

Figure 5 ba-da-ga

The existence of these category boundaries is specific to speech perception as opposed to auditory perception generally. When special tricks are used to make subjects perceive a stimulus first as speech and then as non-speech, the locations of boundaries differ between the two types of perception.[21] Speech perception also exhibits constancy (otherwise called invariance): the location of the category boundaries changes depending on contextual factors such as the speaker's dialect,[22] or the rate at which the speaker talks;[23] both factors dramatically affect which sounds are produced.

[19] Ba-da-ga, from http://www.columbia.edu/itc/psychology/rmk/T2/T2.2b.html.

[20] S. Harnad, 'Psychophysical and Cognitive Aspects of Categorical Perception: a Critical Overview', in S. Harnad (ed.), *Categorical Perception: the Groundwork of Cognition* (Cambridge UP, 1987), pp. 1–28.

[21] See Liberman and Mattingly, 'The Motor Theory of Speech Perception Revised', pp. 20–1.

[22] B.H. Repp and A.M. Liberman, 'Phonetic Category Boundaries Are Flexible', in Harnad (ed.), *Categorical Perception*, pp. 89–112.

[23] L.C. Nygaard and D.B. Pisoni, 'Speech Perception: New Directions in Research and Theory', in J. Miller *et al.* (eds), *Speech, Language and Communication* (London: Academic Press, 1995), pp. 72–5.

This means that in two different contexts, different stimuli may result in the same perceptions, and the same stimulus may result in different perceptions.[24]

Later I shall defend a distinction between categorical and other forms of perception. It is essential for drawing this distinction that I have characterized categorical perception in terms of abilities to distinguish stimuli, and not in terms of how stimuli appear to perceivers. For example, I have not talked about pairs of sounds being perceived as similar. In my view, which I take to be the standard view, categorical perception is not a matter of how things appear at all.[25]

Given that speech perception is categorical and exhibits constancy, we can ask where the category boundaries fall. Which features of the stimuli best predict category membership? Liberman and Mattingly show that in the case of speech, category boundaries typically correspond to differences between intended phonic gestures. The existence of category boundaries and their correspondence to intended phonic gestures needs explaining.

Following Liberman and Mattingly, one can explain this by postulating a module for speech perception. Anything which is potentially speech (including both auditory and visual stimuli) is passed to the module, which attempts to interpret it as speech. It does this by attempting to replicate stimuli by issuing the same gestures as are also used for producing speech (this is the 'motor' in 'motor theory'). Where a replication is possible, the stimuli are perceived as speech, further auditory or visual processing is partially suppressed, and the module identifies the stimuli as composed of the gestures which were used in the successful replication. Accordingly one can say that the stimuli are perceived as a sequence of phonic gestures.

One line of response to this argument involves attempting to show that the category boundaries correspond to some acoustic property of speech at

---

[24] Liberman and Mattingly, 'The Motor Theory of Speech Perception Revised', pp. 14–15. Constancy in speech perception is a complex phenomenon; we should be wary of assuming that speech perception exhibits constancy in just the sense in which colour perception does. For one thing, changes in how phones are produced can increase the amount of cognitive effort required to comprehend speech and can hinder or facilitate learning in different situations: Nygaard and Pisoni, 'Speech Perception', pp. 69ff. Constancy in speech perception may sometimes rely on limited cognitive resources such as attention and working memory.

[25] See Harnad (ed.), *Categorical Perception*. There is controversy over exactly how categorical perception should be defined (see B. Schouten *et al.*, 'The End of Categorical Perception as We Know It', *Speech Communication*, 41 (2003), pp. 71–80), and even on whether speech perception is categorical (e.g., D.W. Massaro and M.M. Cohen, 'Categorical or Continuous Speech Perception: a New Test', *Speech Communication*, 2 (1983), pp. 15–35). It would be a major undertaking to give a rigorous, plausible and useful characterization of the phenomenon; the present rough characterization (like that of Schouten *et al.*) is inadequate because it refers to discriminability of stimuli outright rather than to discriminability by means of a particular perceptual modality.

least as well as to intended phonic gestures. If such a correspondence were found, it might be possible to give an explanation better than Liberman and Mattingly's for the existence of categories corresponding to intended phonic gestures.[26] Reasons for doubting any such explanation exists include the constancy effects already mentioned, and also co-articulation, the fact that phonic gestures overlap (this is what makes talking fast).

In outline, Liberman and Mattingly's argument for the claim that the objects of speech perception are intended phonic gestures has this form:

1. There are category boundaries
2. These boundaries correspond to intended phonic gestures
3. Facts (1) and (2) stand in need of explanation
4. The best explanation of (1) and (2) involves the claim that the objects of speech perception are intended phonic gestures.

This illustrates how one might establish claims about the objects of perception without relying too directly on what people say they perceive, and without presupposing very general theoretical claims about what it means for something to be perceived.

I am not suggesting that the case of speech perception can be taken as a model for understanding perception generally. In my view, speech perception, like other forms of categorical perception, is importantly different from ordinary, non-categorical perception. By contrast, some philosophers have developed general accounts of perception which appear to be supported primarily by cases of categorical perception such as speech and colour. For instance, both Fred Dretske and Jerry Fodor have taken speech perception as a paradigm case for very general theories about what it is for something to be an object of perception.[27] Mohan Matthen has recently gone even further by supposing that all perception is a matter of assigning stimuli to categories.[28] For reasons tentatively outlined later, these authors may be mistaken to take categorical forms of perception as paradigm cases of perception generally. The suggestion I develop next is only that the categorical perception of speech is a reasonable model for causal perception of visual stimuli.

---

[26] See Nygaard and Pisoni, 'Speech Perception', pp. 83–4, for a compact summary.
[27] F. Dretske, *Knowledge and the Flow of Information* (Oxford: Blackwell, 1981), pp. 166–7; J. Fodor and Z. Pylyshyn, 'How Direct Is Visual Perception? Some Reflections on Gibson's "Ecological Approach"', *Cognition*, 9 (1981), pp. 139–96, at p. 176.
[28] M. Matthen, *Seeing, Doing and Knowing* (Oxford: Clarendon Press, 2005).

IV

Is speech perception a good model for causal perception? I suggest that it is, and that an argument like (1)–(4) above can be used to show that we perceive causal interactions.

The first step is to show that causal perception exhibits the key features of categorical perception. As already mentioned, whether or not the experience characteristic of launching occurs depends on interactions among various factors including the relative speeds of the two objects, the delay be-

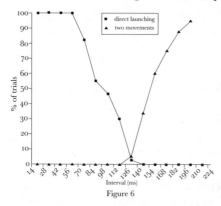

Figure 6

tween the first and second objects' movements, and the trajectories of the two objects. Importantly, the difference between an experience characteristic of launching and an experience of two distinct motions often depends on small changes to parameters, changes smaller than can normally be discerned in perception. Figure 6 shows the effect of the interval between movements on whether subjects report experiencing direct launching or two distinct movements.[29] Subjects would not normally be able to distinguish stimuli between trials when the stimuli differ only in that the gap between movements is 28 ms longer on one of them; but they can easily discriminate stimuli in the special case where 28 ms make the difference between the experience characteristic of launching and the experience characteristic of two movements. As in the case of speech, then, there are points around which exceptionally fine-grained discriminations are possible. This is the key indicator that causal perception is categorical.

As well as such things as relative trajectories and speeds, the experience of launching also depends on high-level features of stimuli. For example, Michotte found (exp. 21, pp. 74ff.) that if the second ball in a launching sequence is initially seen moving backwards and forwards on its own account, then the experience distinctive of launching does not occur. So the experience characteristic of launching depends not only on simple spatial and temporal parameters but also on more complicated structural features

---

[29] Redrawn from Michotte, *The Perception of Causality*, p. 93, table IV.

of the stimuli.[30] Further, Scholl and colleagues have shown that in some situations the experience characteristic of launching depends on how events unfold shortly after the moment of collision.[31] This suggests that the relation between experiences and visual stimuli is complex in the same way as the relation between speech experiences and speech stimuli is: in both cases there is no simple mapping from features of the stimuli to features of the experience unless one characterizes the stimuli in terms of gestures or causes.

In short, the experience characteristic of launching involves both the heightened discriminability and the sensitivity to complex features of stimuli which are characteristic of categorical perception. Research on other causal stimuli such as pulling and bursting is less well developed, but also provides some evidence that causal perception may be a form of categorical perception.[32]

To say that perceptual experiences characteristic of launching and other causal stimuli are categorical is not yet to say where the category boundaries fall. The experimental findings advanced so far rely on what subjects say about their experiences only as a way of distinguishing whether on two occasions they have the same or different types of experience. At this point, what the experiences are experiences of is an open question.

One can take a first step to answering this question by finding things the categories correspond to, that is, by enquiring which features of stimuli reliably predict whether they will be assigned to a given perceptual category. Of course this is only a first step. Facts about what perceptual categories correspond to do not straightforwardly determine what those categories are categories of.

Michotte argued (p. 223) that the conditions under which the experience characteristic of launching occurs correspond to physical laws governing collisions. In fact, he thought the correspondence so close that at one point (p. 228) he even suggested that it would be possible to learn about the physics of collisions by studying their perception:

---

[30] Saxe and Carey treat such findings as showing that subjects make judgements about whether an object is animate or inanimate: R. Saxe and S. Carey, 'The Perception of Causality in Infancy', *Acta Psychologica*, 123 (2006), pp. 144–65. Michotte, by contrast, argues (p. 68) that the effect is due to disrupting polarity, that is, disrupting the appearance of the first object approaching the second or the second object moving away from the first. Here I am supposing that Michotte is right to understand the effect as narrowly perceptual rather than as depending on judgements.

[31] See the contrast between 'dumbbell' and 'removal' conditions in Hoon Choi and B.J. Scholl, 'Effects of Grouping and Attention on the Perception of Causality', *Perception and Psychophysics*, 66 (2004), pp. 926–42, at p. 930.

[32] White and Milne (p. 512) cautiously advance the possibility that causal perception is categorical, noting that the experiments they conducted do not establish this.

... anyone not very familiar with the procedure involved in framing the physical concepts of inertia, energy, conservation of energy, etc., might think that these concepts are simply derived from the data of immediate experience.

Opposing Michotte, Peter White and Elizabeth Milne suggest that the conditions under which the perceptions occur do not correspond to conditions required for actual pulling or bursting. Rather, White and Milne suggest (p. 515) that they may correspond to laws implicit in our naïve conceptions of causal interactions.

Evaluating these hypotheses requires painstaking empirical research on category boundaries (just as in the case of speech). To illustrate, Michotte found that the experience of launching occurs when there is a pause between two objects' movements of around 80 ms or less. How is this consistent with the laws of mechanics? Surely no pause can be tolerated? Ingeniously, Michotte (pp. 91–8, 124) compares launching with the movement of a single object. The single object moves half-way across a screen, then pauses before continuing to move. Michotte found that the longest pause between the two movements consistent with subjects' experiencing them as a single movement is around 80 ms, exactly the longest pause consistent with experiences characteristic of launching. Accordingly, the experience characteristic of launching appears to require that the two movements must be experienced as uninterrupted; this is why they can be separated by a pause of up to but no longer than 80 ms.

This is the kind of detailed investigation needed to support (or refute) claims that conditions for experiences characteristic of launching correspond to conditions for a certain kind of collision. Such research may eventually lead to fine-grained distinctions between competing hypotheses about which causal interactions are perceived and how they are perceived. As things stand, it is already reasonable to conclude that there is some correspondence between the conditions under which experiences characteristic of various types of causal interaction occur and conditions under which the causal interactions themselves occur.

This needs qualification, because few of the stimuli used in experiments on causal perception involve real causal interactions. Strictly speaking, then, it is false that conditions for experiences characteristic of launching correspond with conditions under which collisions occur. I need to hedge this claim by restricting it to the perceiver's natural environment, and excluding factors to which the relevant perceptual systems are insensitive.[33] In case this hedge seems like a fudge, exactly the same considerations apply in the case of speech. Earlier I mentioned that category boundaries in speech

---

[33] Michotte's 'paradoxical cases' may require further hedging (experiments 17, 70).

perception correspond to differences in intended phonic gesture. But as speech perception is reliably fooled into treating all kinds of synthetic sounds as speech, this is not strictly true. As in the causal case, it is at best true taking into account the limits of perceptual systems, their natural environments and the types of information they are concerned with processing.

If a simple co-variational or causal theory of perceptual content were correct, the need to hedge claims about correspondence would show that we do not perceive causal interactions (and that we do not perceive intended phonic gestures). I am assuming that such theories are false, and I am pointing to correspondence not as a necessary or sufficient condition for perception but only as something to be explained. Given this, hedging would only be objectionable if done to such an extent that the correspondence in question were no longer a fact that needed explaining. After all, even imperfect correspondences need explanation (for example, correspondence between weather forecasts and actual weather conditions).

So far, then, I have covered the first three steps of an argument about causal perception parallel to the one about speech:

1'. There are category boundaries
2'. These boundaries correspond to certain types of causal interaction
3'. Facts (1') and (2') need explanation.

This brings me to the fourth and final step of the argument:

4'. The best explanation of (1') and (2') involves the claim that the objects of perception are causal interactions.

In defence of (4'), I conjecture that the perceptual experiences characteristic of causal interactions are best explained as by-products of perceptual mechanisms whose function is to track three-dimensional objects and their movements. Causal perception is part of object perception.

At least three pieces of evidence suggest that perception of objects is closely linked to causal perception. First, Michotte argued for such a link on the basis of his finding that launching occurs when there is a conflict between cues to object identity: good continuity of movement suggests a single object, whereas the existence of two distinct surfaces indicates two objects.[34] It is plausible that other types of causal interaction also involve conflicts between cues to object identity. Secondly, as I pointed out above, Scholl and Nakayama have shown that when a sequence involving complete overlap between two objects is perceived as a launching event, the subject perceives an illusory crescent as if the overlap were only partial. They

---

[34] 'Visual acuity favours, at one and the same time, the segregation of the objects and the unification of movements with the objects performing them' (Michotte, p. 51).

conclude (p. 467) that 'the perception of causality can also affect other types of visual processing – in this case the perception of spatial relations among moving objects'. Thirdly, Krushke and Fragassi have shown that the object-specific preview effect vanishes in launching, but not in various spatio-temporally similar sequences.[35] Since the object-specific preview effect is diagnostic of feature binding, this is evidence that in launching sequences, features of the second object (such as motion) remain bound to the first object for a short time after the second object starts to move. (I do not have space to explain the object-specific preview effect here, but it is very clearly explained by Krushke and Fragassi.) These three pieces of evidence indicate that causal perception interacts with object perception. It is not that we first see sequences of events involving objects and then assign them causal significance. Rather, the perception of something as a causal interaction is bound up with what we perceive as objects in the first place.

This suggests a simple explanation for the correspondence between the perceptions characteristic of various kinds of causal interaction and conditions under which those causal interactions occur. The correspondence exists because given contingent facts about how it actually works, the perceptual system responsible for identifying objects must also concern itself with certain kinds of causal interaction in order to reconcile conflicting cues to object identity. In slightly more detail: one function of our perceptual systems is to identify and track objects; this is done by means of various cues; sometimes the visual system is faced with conflicting cues to object identity which need to be resolved in order to arrive at a satisfactory interpretation; when certain types of causal interaction occur there is a conflict among cues to object identity; these conflicts must be treated differently from other conflicts because they do not indicate failures of object identification, and so do not require resolution or further perceptual processing. So object perception depends on sensitivity to certain types of causal perception, and this is why perception of those types of causal interaction is categorical.

If this explanation is correct, one can conclude that causal interactions are objects of perception in the same sense as intended phonic gestures are. But this explanation is not as satisfying as the one offered in the case of speech: that explained *how* intended phonic gestures could be perceived, whereas this only says that causal interactions *need to be* perceived, given how object perception works.

Where can a deeper explanation be found? If, as I have been suggesting, object perception and causal perception are one and the same process, a

[35] J.K. Krushke and M.M. Fragassi, 'The Perception of Causality: Feature Binding in Interacting Objects', in *Proceedings of the Eighteenth Annual Conference of the Cognitive Science Society* (Hillsdale: Erlbaum, 1996), pp. 441–6.

theory about how object perception works might also explain how causal interactions are perceived. Elizabeth Spelke's theory is that object perception is best understood as an inference where the premises are descriptions of stimuli in terms of surfaces and their layout; conclusions about objects are inferred from these premises by means of a set of principles describing how objects behave. Here, for example, are two of Spelke's four principles of object perception:

Boundedness. Two surface points lie on distinct objects only if no path of connected surface points links them ... the boundedness principle implies that ... two distinct objects cannot interpenetrate

No action at a distance. Separated objects are interpreted as moving independently of one another if such an interpretation exists.[36]

These principles bear not only on object identity but also on causal interactions between objects. In the case of launching, the no-action-at-a-distance principle is clearly relevant; for example, it would explain why there is no launching effect without spatial contact. The boundedness principle is also relevant, as it explains why the experience characteristic of launching is typically absent when there is complete overlap between two objects. In general, Spelke holds (p. 51) that 'object perception reflects basic constraints on the motions of physical bodies'.[37] Developing this idea, Renee Baillargeon, Su-hua Wang and their colleagues have argued that a single set of principles is responsible for object segmentation and for the perceptual identification of certain events as physically possible or impossible.[38] If this is right, the principles which explain object perception also explain how causal perception works.

This completes my argument for the claim that we can perceive certain types of causal interaction. This argument was outlined in (1′)–(4′) above. Clearly the argument is far from decisive, since it depends on a complex mix of theoretical and empirical issues. Even so, the argument demonstrates how to respond to Hume's claim that we do not perceive causal interactions. Given the evidence we have so far, it is more plausible that we perceive causal interactions than that we do not. Equally importantly, the comparison with

---

[36] E. Spelke, 'Principles of Object Perception', *Cognitive Science*, 14 (1990), pp. 49–50.

[37] See also S. Carey and E. Spelke, 'Domain-Specific Knowledge and Conceptual Change', in L. Hirschfeld and S. Gelman (eds), *Mapping the Mind: Domain Specificity in Cognition and Culture* (Cambridge UP, 1994), pp. 169–200, at p. 175: 'A single system of knowledge ... appears to underlie object perception and physical reasoning'.

[38] R. Baillargeon, 'Infants' Physical Knowledge: of Acquired Expectations and Core Principles', in E. Dupoux (ed.), *Language, Brain, and Cognitive Development: Essays in Honor of Jacques Mehler* (MIT Press, 2001), pp. 341–62; Su-hua Wang *et al.*, 'Detecting Continuity Violations in Infancy: a New Account and New Evidence from Covering and Tube Events', *Cognition*, 95 (2005), pp. 129–73.

speech perception provides some insight into what it means to perceive causal interactions: they are perceived categorically, and they are objects of perception in the same sense as intended phonic gestures are.

Strictly speaking, this argument establishes only that we perceive causal interactions when presented with visual stimuli, not that we see them. Causal perception may be amodal, as speech perception is sometimes held to be.[39] Even so, I shall continue to write about seeing causes and hearing gestures for simplicity. Nothing said here contradicts David Marr's view (p. 36) that 'the quintessential fact of human vision – [is] that it tells about shape and space and spatial arrangement'.

V

So far I have argued that we can see some causal interactions, and that seeing causal interactions is part of seeing objects (seeing objects move is interdependent with, not prior to, seeing causal interactions). The argument followed a well understood model from the case of speech perception. First I pointed to a feature of causal perception in need of explanation, the existence of categories and their correspondence with situations in which causal interactions occur. Then I argued that the best explanation for this feature involves the hypothesis that we perceive causal interactions: the feature occurs because given how they actually work, perceptual systems responsible for identifying and tracking objects must also discriminate certain types of causal interaction.

As I mentioned at the start, many of those who agree that we can perceive causings also claim that we perceive causings in the same sense as we perceive shape, whatever sense that is. Full evaluation of this further claim would involve considering issues about perception beyond the scope of this

---

[39] The evidence on this point is controversial. Sekuler and colleagues show that when subjects observe an ambiguous visual display consistent with either a collision or a passing event, the timing of a tone can control whether subjects report seeing a collision or passing, and argue that this is a multisensory phenomenon: R. Sekuler *et al.*, 'Sound Alters Visual Motion Perception', *Nature*, 385 (1997), p. 308. Watanabe and Shimojo extend this finding by showing that not any event (or non-event) which draws attention at the moment of a collision will disambiguate the display; they argue that the tone's effect on the perception of a collision is a 'genuine audiovisual effect, not an audiovisual effect that results from auditory effects': K. Watanabe and S. Shimojo, 'When Sound Affects Vision: Effects of Auditory Grouping on Visual Motion Perception', *Psychological Science*, 12 (2001), pp. 109–16. Guski and Troje, on the other hand, show that features which carry no information about causation, such as a blink, can also influence whether subjects report seeing a collision or a passing. These authors conclude that auditory influences on the perceptual of collisions are 'no true cross-modal phenomenon': R. Guski and N.F. Troje, 'Audiovisual Phenomenal Causality', *Perception and Psychophysics*, 65 (2003), pp. 789–800, at p. 799.

chapter. On the other hand, some evaluation of this claim is necessary for understanding what it means to perceive causings. In a preliminary and tentative way, I suggest that the further claim is false, and I conclude with some considerations distinguishing causal and speech perception from shape perception.

Here are two claims about shape perception. First, in a wide range of naturally occurring circumstances, perceiving an object's shape is a way of being aware of its shape, that is, of being in a position to think about and act on its shape.[40] Secondly, to describe what someone perceives as including a particular shape is to describe a characteristic of their experience which is, often enough, introspectable.[41] I assume that these claims are true and constitutive of shape perception, and I argue that parallel claims about causal or speech perception are false. If these claims are indeed constitutive of shape perception but false of causal perception, then we do not perceive causal interactions in the same sense as we perceive shape.

When it comes to the relation between facts about the objects of speech perception and its introspectable character, not even the best trained, most conceptually sophisticated experts can use introspection to resolve conflicts about whether the objects of speech perception are sounds or gestures. The issues that determine the conflict concern the nature of the stimuli (what invariants are there?) and processes (does passive speech perception involve the motor cortex?). I suspect introspection tells us nothing about what we perceive when we perceive speech; certainly it has no bearing on conflicts about the objects of speech perception. So speech and shape perception differ with respect to introspection.

The parallel point about causal perception is less clear, because some philosophers and psychologists seem to have held that introspection can reveal what we perceive when we perceive causal interactions. While in principle there might also be perceptual experiences about whose objects facts are knowable through introspection, the type of perceptions which Michotte studied and which have been the focus of this chapter are not like this. As in the case of speech perception, discerning the objects of causal perception depends on careful investigation of the conditions under which they occur and the reasons why they occur under these conditions. Introspection is inessential.

[40] M.G.F. Martin, 'Perception, Concepts and Memory', *Philosophical Review*, 101 (1992), pp. 745–63, at p. 761: 'Perception and experience ... are a matter of the world making itself apparent to us'.

[41] 'Describing [Mary's experience] as being as of a dodecahedron ... is ... normally intended to describe its introspectable character, that it is of how the physical world appears to be' (Martin, p. 762).

What about the relation between perception and awareness? In the case of speech, researchers distinguish categorical perception of phonemes from 'phonological awareness', the ability to manipulate phonemes intentionally and reason about them. Phonological awareness is measured by a range of tasks that require sorting words according to their initial phoneme, segmenting or completing words, and blending or eliding phonemes.[42] Although these tasks might seem to test obscure abilities, phonological awareness has practical value in acquiring literacy.

Several factors jointly make it necessary to distinguish perception from awareness of phonemes. Most importantly, infants from four months or earlier enjoy categorical perception of phonemes, but it takes them until around four years before they can think or reason about phonemes.[43] Infants and younger children who hear 'sat' or 'bat' can distinguish the words by virtue of perceiving distinct intended phonic gestures but cannot act on or think about this difference.[44] Perception and awareness also differ with respect to the way they develop and the factors that influence their development. Unlike phoneme perception, children's acquisition of phonological awareness develops gradually over several years, varies systematically depending on their oral language (e.g., Turkish vs French), and is facilitated by learning a writing system where some types of writing system help more than others (e.g., syllabaries vs alphabets). Furthermore, children find certain types of phoneme harder to distinguish in thought than others (e.g., those

[42] There is a short review in J.L. Anthony and C.J. Lonigan, 'The Nature of Phonological Awareness: Converging Evidence from Four Studies of Preschool and Early Grade School Children', *Journal of Educational Psychology*, 96 (2004), pp. 53–5. While children typically pass different tests for phoneme awareness at slightly different times, they are collectively taken to measure phonological awareness because longitudinal surveys have shown that success or failure on these tasks is best explained by a single factor: see J.L. Anthony and D.J. Francis, 'Development of Phonological Awareness', *Current Directions in Psychological Science*, 14 (2005), pp. 255–9, at p. 256.

[43] Eimas and colleagues trained infants to suck in order to hear a sound and were then able to identify infants' interest in different sounds by measuring how vigorously they suck in order to hear the next sound. Since novel sounds are more interesting than familiar sounds, this experiment reveals which sounds infants regard as different and which they treat as the same. The headline finding is that four-month-olds have categorical perception of some phonemes: P.D. Eimas *et al.*, 'Speech Perception in Infants', *Science*, 171 (1971), pp. 303–6. Further research established that infants perceive many phonemes much as adults do. See P. Jusczyk, 'Language Acquisition: Speech Sounds and the Beginning of Phonology', in J. Miller *et al.* (eds), *Speech, Language and Communication* (San Diego: Academic Press, 1995), pp. 263–301, at p. 267: 'from a very early age, infants discriminate many, if not all, of the contrasts that are likely to occur among words in the native language. Moreover, at least on a general level, there are some striking similarities between the way that infants and adults respond to the same kinds of speech contrasts.'

[44] This was first noted by I.Y. Liberman *et al.*, 'Explicit Syllable and Phoneme Segmentation in the Young Child', *Journal of Experimental Child Psychology*, 18 (1974), pp. 201–12, at p. 203: 'it does not follow from the fact that a child can easily distinguish *bud* from *bat* that he can therefore respond analytically to the phonemic structure that underlies the distinction'.

that differ only with respect to voicing are harder to distinguish than those differing only with respect to articulation), whereas they have no corresponding difficulties perceiving distinctions between phonemes. In principle there might be several ways of explaining these developmental findings. But there is a natural explanation which is generally taken for granted by researchers in this area: in becoming aware of phonemes we have to rediscover them, lacking access to them as objects of perception; and we become aware of phonemes as things which sometimes differ with respect to their identities and properties from the intended phonic gestures we perceive.

If this is correct, phoneme and shape perception differ in that perceiving phonemes is not a way of being aware of them. What about causal perception? As in the case of speech, there is a long gap between perceiving and the onset of reasoning abilities. Infants enjoy categorical perception of causal interactions from no later than nine months,[45] whereas children are two and a half or three years old before they can engage in even the simplest forms of causal reasoning.[46] As in the case of speech, children's ability to make judgements about visually presented causal interactions appears to improve gradually over several years up to around five years old,[47] and they have difficulty integrating perceptual information with their reasoning.[48] In the causal case, some investigators regard perception and awareness as closely connected despite the developmental gap, arguing that it can be explained by extraneous factors such as methodological deficiencies or task demands.[49] Given the uncertainty in this area, I suggest that the points of comparison

[45] Some of the first experiments with infants appear in A. Leslie and S. Keeble, 'Do Six-Month-Old Infants Perceive Causality?', *Cognition*, 25 (1987), pp. 265–88; L.M. Oakes and L.B. Cohen, 'Infant Perception of a Causal Event', *Cognitive Development*, 5 (1990), pp. 193–207. For more recent surveys see L.B. Cohen *et al.*, 'The Development of Infant Causal Perception', in A. Slater (ed.), *Perceptual Development: Visual, Auditory, and Speech Perception in Infancy* (Hove: Psychology Press, 1998), pp. 167–210; Saxe and Carey, 'The Perception of Causality in Infancy'.

[46] See, e.g., N.E. Berthier *et al.*, 'Where's the Ball? Two- and Three-Year-Olds Reason about Unseen Events', *Developmental Psychology*, 36 (2000), pp. 394–401. Bruce Hood and colleagues directly contrasted causal tasks requiring perceptual responses with parallel tasks requiring simple reasoning: B. Hood *et al.*, 'Looking and Search Measures of Object Knowledge in Preschool Children', *Developmental Psychology*, 39 (2003), pp. 61–70.

[47] A. Schlottmann *et al.*, 'Perceptual Causality in Children', *Child Development*, 73 (2002), pp. 1656–77, at p. 1671.

[48] A. Schlottmann, 'Perception Versus Knowledge of Cause and Effect in Children: When Seeing Is Believing', *Current Directions in Psychological Science*, 10 (2001), pp. 111–15, and 'Seeing it Happen and Knowing How it Works: How Children Understand the Relation between Perceptual Causality and Underlying Mechanism', *Developmental Psychology*, 35 (1999), pp. 303–17.

[49] M. Haith, 'Who Put the Cog in Infant Cognition? Is Rich Interpretation Too Costly?', *Infant Behaviour and Development*, 21 (1998), pp. 167–79; R. Keen, 'Representation of Objects and Events: Why Do Infants Look So Smart and Toddlers Look So Dumb?', *Current Directions in Psychological Science*, 12 (2003), pp. 79–83.

between speech and causal perception make plausible as a contender the alternative hypothesis that the developmental gap between perception and awareness is explained by the fact that causal perception is not a way of being aware of causal interactions.

These considerations indicate that causal perception differs from shape perception with respect to introspection and awareness. The role of categorical perception of causings is only to distinguish events, not to make manifest to us how the events are distinguished or the natures of the events so distinguished. From the point of view of the perceiver, categorical perception is simply a signal of sameness or difference with distinctive phenomenological effects. In this respect, causal perception is comparable to sensation: perceiving causal interactions is no more or less a way of being aware of them than experiencing a distinctive stinging sensation is a way of being aware of a nettle. If this is right, causal perception may also resemble sensation with respect to epistemology: seeing causings is not a way of gaining knowledge about them, and can be a source of knowledge only because we learn to associate characteristic phenomenology with the kind of events which give rise to it. Certainly we should reject the claim that causal perception is a source of causal concepts.[50]

In the philosophy of perception there is a divide between those who take the claims about introspection and awareness as defining the phenomenon and those who offer theories which are at odds with, or at least hard to reconcile with, these claims. Fred Dretske's views illustrate the second school of thought:

> Seeing objects is a way of getting information about them.... What makes it X (rather than Y) that we see is that the information these internal events carry is information about X (rather than Y).[51]

On the face of it, an internal event's carrying information about something does not necessarily involve either our being aware of that thing or the event's having a particular introspective character. Something like Dretske's way of thinking about perception might be true to causal and speech perception, and perhaps categorical perception more generally. But since these forms of perception may differ from shape perception with respect to awareness and introspection, it does not follow that the same approach is true to shape perception. Equally, although the first view cannot be true to causal or speech perception, because on that view it makes no sense to distinguish sharply perception of an object from awareness of it (on this

---

[50] This claim is made by Michotte, pp. 270–1, Ducasse, 'Causation: Perceivable? Or Only Inferred?', p. 177, and Armstrong, 'Going through the Open Door Again'.

[51] Dretske, 'Simple Seeing', in his *Perception, Knowledge and Belief* (Cambridge UP, 2000), p. 112.

view, perceiving something sometimes just is being aware of it), it does not follow that the view is false when restricted to non-categorical forms of perception.

In conclusion, we do perceive causal interactions, and doing so is part of perceiving objects. In this respect Hume was wrong, but he may have been more right than wrong. For perceiving causal interactions may differ from perceiving shape with respect to how such perceptions relate to awareness and introspection. If these relations are defining characteristics of the kind of perception involved in seeing shapes, Michotte, Strawson and Scholl *et al.* are wrong to regard causal and shape perception as of a kind. We see causal interactions in the same sense as that in which we hear intended phonic gestures.[52]

[52] Christoph Hoerl supported every stage of this research: without his input I could not have done it. Thanks for leads, discussion and opposition to Keith Allen, Ian Apperly, Helen Beebee, Bill Brewer, Naomi Eilan, Hemdat Lerman, Guy Longworth, Fiona Macpherson, Tony Marcel, John Mollon, Louise Richardson, Jonny Roberts, Liz Robinson, Johannes Roessler, Anne Schlottmann, Brian Scholl, Nick Shea, David Sobel, Matt Soteriou, Helen Steward, Toni Tochel and an anonymous referee. I am also grateful for discussion at the Admissible Contents of Experience conference organized by Glasgow University's Centre for the Study of Perceptual Experience, York University, London Institute of Education, a Metaphysics of Science Workshop at Nottingham University, a Royal Institute of Philosophy Lecture at Bradford University, a European Society of Philosophy and Psychology meeting at Lund University, and the 'Dispositions & Causes Workshop' at Bristol University.

4

EXPERIENCE AND CONTENT

By Alex Byrne

The 'content view', in slogan form, is 'Perceptual experiences have representational content'. I explain why the content view should be reformulated to remove any reference to 'experiences'. I then argue, against Bill Brewer, Charles Travis and others, that the content view is true. One corollary of the discussion is that the content of perception is relatively thin (confined, in the visual case, to roughly the output of 'mid-level' vision). Finally, I argue (briefly) that the opponents of the content view are partially vindicated, because perceptual error is due to false belief.

In the dark ages perceptual experiences were supposed to consist in direct awareness of sense-data, which are as they appear to be. Perceptual infallibility was the creed, with error blamed solely on the intellect. Eventually these doctrines were swept aside by the reformation. Perceptual experiences were conceived instead as fallible, testifying (sometimes wrongly) about the subject's familiar external environment. The thesis that experiences have representational content was firmly nailed to the seminar-room door. Early reformers took this thesis to consist in subjects' acquisition of dispositions to believe propositions about their environment, but later reformers rejected any such reduction.

Then came the recent (and inevitable) counter-reformation. While conceding that the reformers had a point against sense-data, the reactionary counter-reformers reaffirmed the doctrine of perceptual infallibility. Perceptual experience, they said, despite concerning ordinary physical objects, is not itself capable of error.[1]

This chapter is about the main thesis of the reformation, that experiences have representational content. What does that mean? (part A). Is it true? (part B).

---

[1] Counter-reformers may well claim that perceptual experience is not capable of correctness either: it is not in the business of either truth or falsity, and so 'infallible' is a tendentious label. Whether this position is plausible is briefly discussed in §III.

Part A: What is the view that 'experiences have representational content'?

I. THE CONTENT VIEW INTRODUCED

According to the reformation, 'experiences' (or 'perceptual experiences'), and in particular 'visual experiences', have representational content. Following Brewer, I shall call this the *content view*, hereafter (CV).[2] One of its first explicit statements (restricted to the visual case) is in Searle's *Intentionality*:

> Visual experiences, like beliefs and desires, are characteristically identified and described in terms of their intentional content.[3]

Searle gives an example of looking at 'a yellow station wagon' (p. 37). At 'a first step', he says, his visual experience has the intentional content, or 'conditions of satisfaction', 'that there is a yellow station wagon there' (p. 41).[4] Another well known statement of (CV), published in the same year, is in Peacocke's *Sense and Content*:

> A visual perceptual experience enjoyed by someone sitting at a desk may represent various writing implements and items of furniture as having particular spatial relations to one another and to the experiencer, and as themselves having various qualities.... The representational content of a perceptual experience has to be given by a proposition, or set of propositions, which specifies the way the experience represents the world to be.[5]

These quotations suggest the following picture. There are certain familiar psychological items, namely 'perceptual experiences', for instance, 'visual experiences', and (CV) is simply the view that these items represent that the world is thus and so; they have 'conditions of satisfaction in exactly the same sense that beliefs and desires have conditions of satisfaction' (Searle, *Intentionality*, p. 39). Those who deny (CV), then, are claiming that these items do

---

[2] B. Brewer, 'Perception and Content', *European Journal of Philosophy*, 14 (2006), pp. 165–81, at p. 165.

[3] J.R. Searle, *Intentionality* (Cambridge UP, 1983), p. 43.

[4] Searle later argues (pp. 47–8) that the content of an experience is reflexive, concerning the experience itself.

[5] C. Peacocke, *Sense and Content* (Oxford UP, 1983), p. 5. For some other statements of (CV), see C. McGinn, *Mental Content* (Oxford: Blackwell, 1989), p. 58; G. Harman, 'The Intrinsic Quality of Experience', *Philosophical Perspectives*, 4 (1990), pp. 31–52, at p. 34; M. Davies, 'Individualism and Perceptual Content', *Mind*, 100 (1991), pp. 461–84, at p. 462; M. Thau, *Consciousness and Cognition* (Oxford UP, 2002), p. 74; F. Jackson, 'Mind and Illusion', in P. Ludlow, Y. Nagasawa and D. Stoljar (eds), *There's Something about Mary* (MIT Press, 2004), pp. 421–32, at p. 428; S. Siegel, 'Do Visual Experiences Have Contents?', in B. Nanay (ed.), *Perceiving the World* (Oxford UP, 2010), pp. 333–68. See also W. Sellars, 'Empiricism and the Philosophy of Mind', *Minnesota Studies in the Philosophy of Science*, 1 (1956), pp. 253–329, at §§16–17, on 'experiences as containing propositional claims'.

not have representational content. The existence of the items, the 'experiences', is not in dispute; the contentious issue is whether they have content. As Searle (p. 44) remarks,

> It is a bit difficult to know how one would argue for the existence of perceptual experiences to someone who denied their existence. It would be a bit like arguing for the existence of pains: if their existence is not obvious already, no philosophical argument could convince one.

Is the existence of perceptual experiences obvious? The next section argues that it is not.[6]

II. EXPERIENCES

Michael Hinton's book *Experiences* is not exactly a shining example of philosophical clarity.[7] But buried beneath Hinton's eccentric prose style and unmemorable neologisms are some excellent points that have gone largely unnoticed. In particular, Hinton distinguished the ordinary notion (or notions) of an 'experience' from the 'special philosophical' one, about which he was highly sceptical. Although he did not explain the 'special philosophical' notion in quite the way it will be explained below, his separation of the two was an important insight.

II.1. *'A very special notion'*

What is the 'very special notion' of an experience, which we find in much philosophical writing on perception? Suppose one sees a galah and hears the screech of a cockatoo. Then in the special philosophical sense one has a *visual* experience and an *auditory* experience. It is not mandatory to take these experiences to be different, but certainly this is a natural inference from the terminology. But whether or not the visual experience and the auditory experience are identical, experiences are supposed to be *particulars*: if you and I both see a galah, then there are *two* visual experiences, yours and mine. Granted that experiences are particulars, there is only one plausible basic category under which they fall: they are *events*. Experiences are like flashes, bangs, conferences, cricket matches, parties and races. They are particular things that occur or happen; they are (at least paradigmatically) extended in time, and have a beginning, a middle and an end. As Searle says (p. 45), 'visual and other sorts of perceptual experiences are *conscious mental events*'. Likewise Peacocke speaks in *Sense and Content* of 'particular'

---

[6] §II elaborates on A. Byrne and H. Logue, 'Either/Or', in A. Haddock and F. Macpherson (eds), *Disjunctivism: Perception, Action, Knowledge* (Oxford UP, 2008), pp. 57–94, at pp. 82–3.

[7] J.M. Hinton, *Experiences: an Inquiry into Some Ambiguities* (Oxford UP, 1973).

(p. 20) and 'token' (p. 37) experiences, and of their 'occurrence' (p. 47). Many subsequent writers, while disagreeing with Searle and Peacocke on a variety of fundamental issues in the philosophy of perception, agree with them on these points.[8]

Why think there are such events? The natural answer is that the existence of experiences is introspectively evident, just as the existence of flashes and bangs is extrospectively evident. This is clearly Searle's view, and it also appears to be Lycan's:

> ... introspection does represent our experiences as having properties. In particular, it classifies them; it assigns them to kinds. We are indeed 'made aware of them, as we are of beer bottles, as objects having properties that serve to identify them', though of course experiences are events, not physical objects like bottles.[9]

Sometimes experiences are said to be states, which suggests that they are *properties* or *conditions* of a certain sort, not events. But although in some contexts states are contrasted with events, in philosophy of mind 'state' not infrequently functions as a convenient umbrella word, with 'mental state' meaning 'mental condition, event, phenomenon, or whatever'.[10] The common phrase 'token state' sometimes signals this inclusive way of talking: if the author is not assuming a controversial ontology of tropes or property instances, the charitable interpretation is to take 'token states' to be events.[11]

II.2. *'A very general one'*

Some everyday examples of the use of 'experience' (the noun) are these:

1. I had the experience of swimming the Bosphorus[12]
2. Seeing the Taj Mahal was an unforgettable experience

---

[8] See, e.g., Harman, 'The Intrinsic Quality of Experience', p. 42; A. Millar, *Reasons and Experience* (Oxford UP, 1991), p. 11; C. Siewert, *The Significance of Consciousness* (Princeton UP, 1998), p. 11; B. O'Shaughnessy, *Consciousness and the World* (Oxford UP, 2000), p. 39; A. Byrne, 'Intentionalism Defended', *Philosophical Review*, 110 (2001), pp. 119–240, at p. 203; M.G.F. Martin, 'On Being Alienated', in T. Gendler and J. Hawthorne (eds), *Perceptual Experience* (Oxford UP, 2006), pp. 354–410, at p. 354; Siegel, 'Which Properties Are Represented in Perception?', also in *Perceptual Experience*, pp. 481–503, at p. 484. Sometimes philosophers use 'event' extraordinarily broadly, so that if an object *o* is F at *t* it supposedly follows that there is an 'event' of *o*'s being F occurring at *t*. Hence there is an 'event' of this pen's being straight, etc.; cf. J. Bennett, *Events and their Names* (Indianapolis: Hackett, 1988), p. 6. It is safe to say that almost none of the philosophers referred to above has such an elastic use in mind.

[9] W.G. Lycan, 'Dretske's Ways of Introspecting', in B. Gertler (ed.), *Privileged Access: Philosophical Accounts of Self-Knowledge* (Aldershot: Ashgate, 2003), pp. 15–30, at p. 26; Lycan is quoting from, and disagreeing with, Dretske's paper 'How Do You Know You are Not a Zombie?' in the same volume.

[10] For an example, see Millar, *Reasons and Experience*, pp. 10–11.

[11] On some views (e.g., Bennett, *Events and their Names*) events *are* property instances. Be that as it may, the point is simply that the existence of events (elections, weddings, etc.) is less controversial than the existence of property instances.

[12] From Hinton, *Experiences*, pp. 5–6.

3. I have not had the experience of tasting haggis
4. I had many strange experiences today[13]
5. No prior experience needed [in a job advertisement for house painters; this is a mass occurrence of 'experience'].

(1)–(5) may be, respectively, paraphrased as follows:

1*. I swam the Bosphorus[14]
2*. I saw the Taj Mahal and I shall not forget seeing it
3*. I have not tasted haggis
4*. Many strange things happened to me today
5*. Applicants do not need to have worked previously as house painters.

These examples illustrate, in Hinton's phrase (p. 7), 'the ordinary biographical sense of the word'. Ordinary talk of one's 'experiences' is talk of what happened to one, what one did, what one encountered or witnessed. Although often this concerns events, it is not talk of experiences in the special philosophical sense.[15] If it were, then presumably an utterance of 'I had the experience of seeing a galah for two minutes' (equivalently, 'I saw a galah for two minutes') would report the occurrence of a certain 'visual experience' lasting for two minutes. However, as Vendler pointed out, 'I saw a galah for two minutes' bears no grammatical hint of an event or process unfolding in time – unlike, say, 'I chased a galah for two minutes'.[16]

II.3. *The 'no experience' hypothesis*

Obviously there are experiences: watching the final inning was a thrilling experience, and eating the crackerjack was an unpleasant one, for example. However, to conclude from this that there are 'visual experiences' and 'gustatory experiences' in the special philosophical sense is just to ignore the fact that 'experience' in its philosophical use is not a harmless extension of ordinary usage. As Travis notes, it is 'a far from innocent count noun'.[17] Unexceptional everyday remarks about experiences do not secure the

[13] From M. Tye, *Consciousness and Persons: Unity and Identity* (MIT Press, 2003), p. 97.

[14] As Hinton points out (*Experiences*, pt. I), this paraphrase is not perfect, since having the experience of doing such and such suggests some sort of awareness on the subject's part. If one somehow managed to swim the Bosphorus while fast asleep it would be at least odd to say one had the experience of swimming the Bosphorus.

[15] See Thau, *Consciousness and Cognition*, p. 207; also B. Farrell, 'Experience', *Mind*, 59 (1950), pp. 170–98.

[16] Contrast, for example, 'I deliberately chased ...'/'I was chasing ...' and *'I deliberately saw ...'/*'I was seeing ...'. See Z. Vendler, 'Verbs and Times', *Philosophical Review*, 66 (1957), pp. 143–60, esp. pp. 155–6.

[17] C. Travis, 'The Silence of the Senses', *Mind*, 113 (2004), pp. 57–94, at p. 57.

existence of 'experiences' of the special philosophical sort. But so what? If there are 'visual experiences', they are revealed by introspection, whether or not we talk about them in daily life. Besides, as Searle says, is it not obvious that there are such things?

That it is not obvious is one moral which can be drawn from the much discussed claim, inspired by remarks in Moore's 'The Refutation of Idealism', that experiences are 'transparent'.[18] Statements of the claim vary, but Tye's is representative: 'In turning one's mind inward to attend to the experience, one seems to end up concentrating on what is outside again, on external features or properties'.[19] 'Attend' should not be read too expansively, as something like *consider*, since Tye holds that we can think about our experiences. Presumably his point is that we cannot attend to our experiences in anything like the way we can attend to perceptual stimuli. In attending to a perceived stimulus, one allocates more cognitive resources to processing information about it; according to Tye, in this sense there is no such thing as 'attending to one's experience'.

This claim is surely plausible. (Cognitive scientists have distinguished many different kinds of attention, but have not yet seen the need to suppose that we can attend to our experiences.) More or less equivalently, we do not know of our experiences by 'looking within' – by a *quasi*-perceptual faculty of introspection. How do we know of them, then? Tye's answer is that we know of them by looking without:

> If we try to focus on our experiences, we 'see' right through them to the world outside. By being aware of the qualities apparently possessed by surfaces, volumes, etc., we become aware that we are undergoing visual experiences. But we are not aware of the experiences themselves.[20]

I know that I see a pig, and the suggestion that I know this by looking outwards and spotting the pig seems right (somehow).[21] Although spelling out the details is far from straightforward, suppose for the sake of argument that this model of self-knowledge is basically correct. *If* I am undergoing a visual experience of a pig, then I can know that by attending to the pig. Fine. But why think I *am* undergoing a visual experience of a pig? (In the special philosophical sense of 'experience', this is not a prolix way of saying 'I see a pig'.) There are, of course, numerous events in the causal chain starting from the pig and continuing into my brain. If I am undergoing an experience of a pig, the experience is presumably to be found in that causal

---

[18] G.E. Moore, 'The Refutation of Idealism', *Mind*, 7 (1903), pp. 1–30.

[19] M. Tye, *Ten Problems of Consciousness* (MIT Press, 1995), p. 30.

[20] Tye, *Consciousness and Persons: Unity and Identity* (MIT Press, 2003), p. 24.

[21] See, in particular, G. Evans, *The Varieties of Reference* (Oxford UP, 1982), pp. 227–31; F. Dretske, *Naturalizing the Mind* (MIT Press, 1995), ch. 2.

chain. But since the issue is whether I am undergoing an experience in the first place, this is of no help at all.

Tye, in fact, comes as close as possible to the conclusion that there are no experiences, without actually affirming it. Although looking without tells us unequivocally that we are undergoing experiences, it leaves their number and duration somewhat conjectural (*Consciousness and Persons*, p. 97):

> The simplest hypothesis compatible with what is revealed by introspection is that, for each period of consciousness, there is only a single experience – an experience that represents everything experienced within the period of consciousness as a whole (the period, that is, between one state of unconsciousness and the next).

One experience too many, perhaps: a simpler hypothesis is that there are *no* experiences. Of course, this simpler hypothesis will be obscured without Hinton's distinction between the 'very special' notion of an experience and the 'very general' one, and Tye's otherwise insightful discussion can be faulted on exactly this point. Immediately after the passage just quoted, Tye responds to an objection:

> Admittedly, this hypothesis may seem to be at odds with such everyday statements as 'I had many strange experiences today'. But in reality there is no conflict. Talk of my undergoing many strange experiences no more requires for its truth that there exist multiple strange experiences than does talk of my having a drowning feeling require that there be a feeling that drowns. Just as in the latter case it suffices that I undergo an experience that *represents* that I am drowning, so too in the former it suffices that my experience today *represented* many strange things.

As pointed out in the previous section, 'I had many strange experiences today', as uttered in an ordinary context, may be paraphrased as 'Many strange things happened to me today'. Since this statement is not about experiences in the special philosophical sense, there is no conflict at all with Tye's 'one-experience' hypothesis, and so no paraphrase in terms of re-presentation is needed.[22] By the same token, there is no conflict with the 'no-experience' hypothesis either.

III. THE CONTENT VIEW EXPLICATED

The content view (CV) is not, or should not be, the view that experiences, in the special philosophical sense, have content. It is doubtful that there are such things. What should (CV) be instead?

---

[22] Tye only offers a paraphrase *sufficient* for the truth of 'I had n F-experiences today', not one which is necessary and sufficient. 'I had a single experience today that represented n F-things' would be false if I had a nap at lunchtime after fewer than n F-things had been represented, yet 'I had n F-experiences today' might well be true.

Sticking with vision for simplicity, one *veridically perceives* an object iff one sees it, and it is the way it appears or looks. One *non-veridically perceives*, or *is illuded by*, an object iff one sees it, and it is not the way it appears or looks. No great weight is being placed on the vocabulary of 'sees' and 'appears/looks'. This is merely intended to be an intuitive gloss on a distinction that we can recognize from a range of examples, situations like seeing a lemon on a table in daylight (veridical perception), seeing the Müller–Lyer figure (non-veridical perception or illusion), and so on. *Perception* comprises, by stipulation, veridical perception and illusion; it therefore excludes (what philosophers call) *hallucination*.[23] If one has a hallucination of a yellow lemon, one does not see anything, but one is not in a position to know this: one cannot tell merely by 'introspection' that one is not veridically perceiving a yellow lemon or having an illusion produced by a green lime.[24]

(CV) is (at least) a claim about *perception*; whether or not it also covers the trickier case of hallucination is something that will (mostly) be set aside. Reversing history, it can be thought of as a descendant of, and an ostensible improvement on, the counter-reformation view as expressed by Brewer ('Perception and Content', p. 169):

> ... in perceptual experience, a person is simply presented with the actual constituents of the physical world themselves. Any errors in her world view which result are the product of the subject's responses to this experience, however automatic, natural, or understandable in retrospect these responses may be. *Error*, strictly speaking, given how the world actually is, is never an essential feature of experience itself.

According to Brewer, even in cases of illusion one is 'simply presented with the actual constituents of the physical world themselves': if there is any misrepresentation, it is to be found at the level of belief or judgement, not perception.

What is it to be 'simply presented' with the constituents of the physical world? In an ordinary situation in which one sees a yellow lemon and a red tomato, one is 'simply presented' with the lemon, the tomato, yellowness, and redness – perhaps that amounts to the fact that one sees the lemon and the tomato and sees yellow and red. But that is not all: the lemon is 'simply presented' *as* yellow, not as red. This is not captured by saying that one sees *that* the lemon is yellow – one may see that it is yellow even if only its distinctive lemon-like shape is 'simply presented'. For instance, in very dim light one might recognize that this is a (yellow) lemon by seeing its shape.[25]

---

[23] In vision science, 'visual illusions' include 'philosophical' hallucinations. The Hermann Grid illusion, for instance, is arguably an example: one 'sees' non-existent grey spots.

[24] See Martin, 'On Being Alienated'.

[25] Further, one may see *that* the lemon is yellow even if one does not see *the lemon*.

How does the fact that the lemon is yellow get into the perceptual story? An attractive answer is to take perception constitutively to involve a propositional attitude, specifically an attitude rather like the factive attitude of knowing – *zeeing*, to coin a verb. Like knowing that p, zeeing that p entails that p. When one sees the yellow lemon, one *zees* that it is yellow – this is the sense in which the lemon is 'simply presented' as yellow.

Could zeeing just *be* knowing? It seems not. Suppose one is mistakenly convinced that the lighting conditions are peculiar and that the lemon is really green, despite looking yellow; one believes that the lemon is green and not yellow, and so presumably one does not know that it is yellow. Yet there is nothing perceptually amiss: one zees that the lemon is yellow.

What about illusions? According to the counter-reformation (elaborated with 'zeeing'), an illusion that q is a case where one zees that p and is (mistakenly) inclined to judge that q, or something along similar lines. Offhand, that seems forced, at best. Why strive and struggle when there is an easier route? Namely, take perception to be like *belief*, rather than like knowledge. This brings us to (CV): perception constitutively involves a propositional attitude rather like the *non*-factive attitude of believing, *exing* (meant to suggest 'experiencing'), not zeeing. Then illusions can be accommodated without strain: an illusion that q is simply a case where one exes that q. One may think of the content of the exing attitude as the output of (largely) informationally encapsulated perceptual modules.[26] Sometimes one will be in possession of background information which undermines that q; this will not affect the output, resulting in the subject exing that q while disbelieving it.

(CV), as just explained, is intended as a theoretically fruitful description of the phenomenon of perception, not a piece of unarticulated folk psychology. Fortunately, it carries no commitment to 'experiences' in the special philosophical sense – introspectable events that occur when one sees a galah or hears a screech. (CV) is silent on whether to ex that p is to undergo an event, or whether it is to be in a state or condition. If to ex that p is to be in a state or condition, like believing and knowing, (CV) can be smoothly conjoined with the 'no experience' hypothesis.

Various optional extras can be added as desired: that the relevant contents are 'non-conceptual', that there is a different attitude for each of the different perceptual modalities, and so on. For present purposes, though, we can work with (CV) in skeletal form.

---

[26] Largely encapsulated: if one believes that the lemon before one is white but cleverly illuminated by a yellow spotlight, it will still look yellow. But only largely: for instance, knowledge of the colours of lemons seems to have a slight effect on colour appearance. See T. Hansen *et al.*, 'Memory Modulates Color Appearance', *Nature Neuroscience*, 9 (2006), pp. 1367–8.

Finally, it should be emphasized that the exposition of (CV) here is entirely unoriginal, and merely repeats with minor amendments a characterization that is often found in the literature. For instance, Millikan introduces 'visaging', 'a general term for what stands to perceiving as believing stands to knowing'; to suffer a perceptual illusion is to 'visage falsely'. And Johnston discusses the view that visual experience involves 'a *sui generis* propositional attitude – visually entertaining a content concerning the scene before the eyes'.[27]

Part B: Is the content view true?

Perhaps surprisingly, explicit arguments for (CV) are rather thin on the ground.[28] It is hard not to sympathize with Travis' complaint in 'The Silence of the Senses' (p. 57): 'In no case I am aware of is this view argued for. Rather it is assumed from the outset.' Fortunately all is not lost, because an examination of Travis' argument *against* (CV) in that paper suggests a powerful argument *for* it.

IV. TRAVIS' ARGUMENT AGAINST THE CONTENT VIEW

In the first section of 'The Silence of the Senses', Travis spends some time unpacking the claim that 'a (given) perceptual experience has a (given) representational content' (p. 57). Although his characterization of (CV) differs in various respects from the one just given, his argument equally targets the latter.

How can (CV) be supported? The obvious suggestion was made in the previous section: appeal to perceptual illusions – the 'phenomena of misleading perceptual experiences' (p. 66). One *believes* that the lines in the Müller–Lyer figure are equal, yet they persist in *looking* unequal. Somehow the (mis-)information that the lines are unequal is perceptually available,

---

[27] M. Johnston, 'Postscript: Visual Experience', in A. Byrne and D.R. Hilbert (eds), *Readings on Color*, Vol. 1: *The Philosophy of Color* (MIT Press, 1997), pp. 172–6; R. Millikan, *On Clear and Confused Ideas* (Cambridge UP, 2000), p. 111. Johnston actually characterizes the view as *identifying* 'visual experience' and the '*sui generis* propositional attitude'. But that stronger claim is not needed.

[28] They are also sometimes unconvincing. For instance, Searle (pp. 41–2) notes that 'sees that the F is G' is intensional, whereas 'sees the F' is extensional, and claims that the 'most obvious explanation of this distinction is that the "see that" form reports the intentional content of the perception'. But of course that cannot be *the* explanation, because 'sees that the stock market has crashed' is also intensional, and the explanation can hardly have anything to do with the content of perception. In any case, although 'sees *o*' has a distinctively visual sense, 'sees that *p*' arguably does not.

and (CV) apparently has a neat diagnosis of the situation: one exes that the lines are unequal. Another (connected) suggestion is to turn to the way we talk. Granted, there seems to be no appropriate propositional-attitude verb, but we do speak of the ways things look, smell, sound and so forth. This lemon, for instance, looks yellow and oval. Is such talk not best understood as implicitly reporting the content of the exing attitude, specifically, that this (the lemon) is yellow and oval?[29] In Travis' terminology (p. 63), this is the suggestion that perceptual content is 'looks-indexed'. That is, 'in some sense of "looks"' (p. 63), 'the representational content of an experience can be read off the way, in it, things looked' (p. 69).

Travis' argument against (CV) consists in attacking both suggestions (focusing on the visual case), and may be set out as follows:

1.   Illusions do not show that (CV) is true
2.   There are 'two different notions of looks' (p. 69):
     (a)   examples of the first notion: Pia looks like her sister, it looks as though it were a Vermeer (pp. 70, 75)
     (b)   examples of the second notion: it looks as if Pia's sister is approaching (p. 75)
3.   'Looks on this first notion ... are unfit to index content. For as to that they point in no one direction' (p. 72)
4.   The second notion is a matter of 'factive meaning', and so 'collapse[s] representation into indicating ... [which is] to lose it altogether' (p. 79)
5.   Hence if there is such a thing as 'the representational content of an experience', it is not looks-indexed – that is, there is no 'looks'-construction that is exclusively used to report the content of the alleged exing propositional attitude
6.   (CV) is not needed to account for illusion, and 'looks'-statements do not help, so (CV) is without support.

I shall postpone discussion of the first step of the argument, that perceptual illusions do not show that (CV) is true, and examine Travis' case against 'looks-indexing'.

IV.1. *Against looks-indexing*

It might be too obvious to mention (perhaps this is why Travis does not mention it), but his two 'notions of looks' correspond to Chisholm's 'comparative' and 'epistemic' uses of 'appear words' (of which 'look' is an example), introduced in ch. 4 of *Perceiving*.[30] Chisholm's distinction is an

---

[29] Cf. R. Price, 'Content Ascriptions and the Reversibility Constraint', *Philosophical Perspectives*, 19 (2005), pp. 353–74, at pp. 357–8.
[30] R.M. Chisholm, *Perceiving: a Philosophical Study* (Cornell UP, 1957).

important component of Jackson's argument for the sense-datum theory in *Perception*.[31] In that book (p. 30), Jackson explains the epistemic use as follows:

> Suppose I say, in front of a house whose bell has not been answered and whose curtains are drawn, 'They appear to be away' or, in our standard form, 'It looks as if they are away'; then I am expressing the fact that a certain body of visually acquired evidence – in this case, drawn curtains and an unanswered bell – supports the proposition that they are away.

The comparative use, as in 'That looks like a cow', Jackson plausibly says, can be roughly paraphrased as 'That looks the way cows normally look' (p. 31). As Travis puts it (pp. 69–70), 'On [this] notion, something looks thus and so, or like such and such, where it looks the way such and such, or things which are (were) thus and so, does (would, might) look'. The comparative use is explained *using* 'looks' (the way cows normally *look*), a fact which will be important later.

Does either of these uses index the content of experience?

Travis' main complaint against comparative indexing (step 3 in the argument set out in the previous section), is that 'looks like' points 'in no one direction' (p. 72). Although his elaboration of this point is not easy to follow, one of his basic ideas is straightforward. The comparative construction reports that some things look the same way, *without reporting what that way is*. If I say that Pia looks to me like her sister, I am saying, roughly, that Pia looks to me the (salient) way her sister looks to me. If Pia looks tall and blonde to me and so does her sister, my remark is true. Similarly if Pia and her sister both look short and tired. *How* Pia looks to me (blonde, pink, angry) is not something that can be 'read off' what I have literally said, although my audience might well be able to infer it.

Travis' complaint against epistemic indexing (step 4) is this. Suppose, to take Jackson's example, it looks as if they are away. Then their drawn curtains and unanswered bell must be some sort of *sign* that they are away. As Travis puts it, 'What things look like on this use of "looks" is thus a matter of what things mean factively, or indicate'. This, he continues, 'is precisely not a matter of things being represented as so. Representation simply does not work that way' (p. 78).

But this complaint is not obviously right. On one popular account, representation (and perceptual representation in particular), precisely *is* a matter of what things indicate (under certain conditions).[32] But further

---

[31] F. Jackson, *Perception: a Representative Theory* (Cambridge UP, 1977).

[32] See, e.g., R. Stalnaker, *Inquiry* (MIT Press, 1984), ch. 1. In the course of explaining why the relevant sense of 'represent' has nothing to do with indication (pp. 58–9), Travis actually mentions one of the standard examples used to suggest the opposite, namely, tree rings.

discussion of Travis' argument is not necessary, because his conclusion can be secured much more swiftly.

First, clearly the epistemic use is not used *exclusively* to report the alleged content of perception, since almost *anything* can follow 'It looks as if': they are away, away in Uganda, trainspotters, Obama supporters, fond of dogs, etc. Proponents of (CV) do not typically think that perceptual experience can have the content *that they are away in Uganda*.[33]

Secondly, even if the way something epistemically looks is specified in very restricted visual terms, this still need not be the alleged content of experience. Viewing one's car in an underground parking garage, it might both *look black*, and thereby *look as if it is blue* (epistemic) – that is how blue things look in this light. Evidently in such a situation the alleged content of experience is that the object is black (not blue).

Obvious next question: what about the 'phenomenal use' of 'looks' – 'looks black', and the like – which Travis does not discuss?

IV.2. *'Phenomenal' indexing?*

In *Perceiving*, Chisholm distinguishes a 'non-comparative use' of appear words, in addition to the comparative and epistemic uses. In Jackson's *Perception* (p. 77) this becomes the familiar 'phenomenal use':

> The phenomenal use is characterized by being explicitly tied to terms for colour, shape, and/or distance: 'It looks blue to me', 'It looks triangular', 'The tree looks closer than the house', 'The top line looks longer than the bottom line', 'There looks to be a red square in the middle of the white wall', and so on. That is, instead of terms like 'cow', 'house', 'happy', we have, in the phenomenal use, terms like 'red', 'square', and 'longer than'.

The phenomenal use does seem to be a genuine 'third use'. I observed in the previous section that the comparative use is explained using 'looks': if that sculpture looks like a cow, it looks the (salient) way cows look. So if cows look F, and that sculpture looks like a cow, then that sculpture looks F. Cows look to have a distinctive shape – cow-shaped, for want of a better term. Given contingent facts about the way cows look, to look like a cow (comparative) is to look, *inter alia*, cow-shaped. What is *that* use of 'looks'? Not comparative, on pain of a regress. Apparently not the epistemic one either. In a distorting mirror, something might look cow-shaped but not look *as if* it is cow-shaped.

One might hope that the phenomenal use can be analysed, as Jackson puts it, 'in terms of concepts pertaining to the epistemic or comparative uses'

---

[33] Cf. Siegel, 'Which Properties are Represented in Perception?', p. 481.

(p. 33). Jackson makes a convincing case that it cannot.[34] He goes on to argue that 'It is the analysis of [the phenomenal] use which leads to sense-data' (p. 33). With hindsight, he could have taken it to index the content of perception instead: if o looks$_p$ (the subscript indicating the phenomenal use) F to S then S exes, of o, that it is F.

However, Jackson has not characterized this third use of 'looks' properly. Talk of the 'phenomenal use' or, as Jackson sometimes says, the 'phenomenal sense', is naturally taken as a claim of ambiguity. If 'looks' has a special meaning when followed by 'terms for colour, shape, and/or distance' then, as Thau points out (p. 230), 'It looks red and very old' should seem anomalous, since this construction forces a univocal interpretation of 'looks' (cf. Searle, pp. 76–7). Yet that sentence is perfectly in order. Thau concludes that 'We do not mean two different things by "looks" when we say that something looks red and that something looks old'.

A fair point, as far as it goes. However, Thau's argument is incomplete, because it is targeted at the view that 'looks' when followed by 'red' *only* bears the phenomenal sense. Since 'It looks old' is unquestionably acceptable, and cannot be used phenomenally, its use must be either epistemic or comparative. In fact 'It looks old' can have both uses, as Jackson himself in effect observes.[35] Given that 'looks [adjective]' is sometimes used epistemically, there is no good reason for someone to insist that 'looks' can *never* be interpreted in this way with 'red' as its complement. A defender of the 'phenomenal use' should say that the whole phrase 'looks red' is capable of being used epistemically, comparatively, and phenomenally. If that is right, then 'It looks red and very old' has two straightforward interpretations, and should not (*pace* Thau, p. 230) 'seem ill formed or at best false'. Admittedly, this sentence will have *an* anomalous reading, which offhand it does not seem to, but that might be because it is obscured by the two straightforward interpretations.

Still, even though his argument does not secure the point, Thau is correct that there is no phenomenal use of 'looks', as least as Jackson explains it. Chisholm agrees. One illustration he gives of the 'non-comparative use' is 'The mountainside looks red to me' (*Perceiving*, p. 52), which sounds like Jackson's phenomenal use. But it is not, because Chisholm says later

---

[34] See *Perception*, pp. 37–48. There is a comparative construction that with only mild straining can be read as equivalent to the phenomenal/non-comparative use of 'looks red', namely, 'looks like a *stereotypically* red object'. But this is not the hoped-for analysis, since in order to get the equivalence the intended interpretation of 'stereotypically red object' has to be explained in terms of the phenomenal/non-comparative use: a stereotypically red object is one that would *look* red. (Merely *being* red is insufficient.) This point applies equally to the examples of 'looks centurian', 'looks old', and the like, discussed below.

[35] Jackson's example (*Perception*, p. 33) is 'The dog looks dangerous'.

(p. 116) that 'looks' in 'That animal looks centaurian' can be 'take[n] ... non-comparatively'. Jackson, not surprisingly, is unconvinced (*Perception*, p. 89):

> It seems, in fact, that 'looks centaurian' normally amounts to 'looks like a centaur' or, as there are no centaurs, 'looks like a centaur would'; that is that it is to be understood comparatively.

How would a centaur look? (Let us ignore distractions about whether centaurs have an essentially mythical nature.) Centaurs, going by the usual artists' renditions, share distinctive visible characteristics, which is why they can (in mythology) easily be identified by sight. That is, there is a distinctive centaurian 'visual *Gestalt*': centaurs have a certain kind of body hair, torso, colouring, gait, and so forth. 'Centaur-shaped' does not do it justice. Likewise, 'cow-shaped' is a significantly oversimplified answer to the question 'How do cows look?' (cf. §IV.2 above). On a particular occasion, communicating that a certain animal has that distinctive centaurish look may well be crucial. It might not matter whether the animal looks the way centaurs would look (maybe they would not look much like the illustrations, and instead more like actual horses): what matters is that the animal looks to have those distinctive characteristics that are, as it happens, popularly associated with centaurs. There is an obvious verbal means of conveying the needed information: the animal looks centaurian.

Similar remarks go for 'looks old'. Plausibly, sometimes this phrase is used to convey a thing's distinctive visual appearance, not to make an epistemic or comparative claim. Naked mole rats are hairless, sparsely whiskered, pinkish-grey, and very wrinkled. They look old. A person who sees a naked mole rat and asserts that the animal looks old need not be saying that the rat looks as if it is old: he might think such an inference from its appearance would be nothing better than a wild guess. Neither need he be making a comparative claim: he might have no idea whether the rat looks like an old mole rat.[36] Thus 'It looks red and very old' has a natural reading that is neither comparative nor epistemic, an illustration of Chisholm's non-comparative use. There is no 'phenomenal use' to index perceptual content; could the non-comparative use step in to fill the breach? That is, is this claim true: if o looks$_{nc}$ (the subscript indicating the non-comparative use) F to S then S exes, of o, that it is F? No, because perceptual content, if there is such a thing, goes with the ways things look when they look$_{nc}$ F, which need not include Fness. If a naked mole rat looks$_{nc}$ old to S, then S exes, of the rat, that it is wrinkled, pink, etc. – not that it is old. In other words, naked mole

---

[36] In fact, naked mole rats are exceptionally long-lived: see P.W. Sherman and J.U.M. Jarvis, 'Extraordinary Life Spans of Naked Mole-Rats (Heterocephalus Glaber)', *Journal of Zoology*, 258 (2002), pp. 307–11.

rats can *be* as they look$_{nc}$ (wrinkled, pink, etc.) without *being* old (in principle, anyway).

Similarly, if someone looks$_{nc}$ Scandinavian, and so looks to have the stereotypical Scandinavian bodily features (straight blond hair, small nose, pale skin, etc.), he can *be* as he looks$_{nc}$ without being Scandinavian. Again, that animal, which looks$_{nc}$ centaurian, can be as it looks$_{nc}$ without being a centaur. 'Looks$_{nc}$ F' is therefore idiomatic in the interesting way 'red hair' is. 'Red hair' *does* refer to hair of a distinctive colour similar to red (and so is an example of polysemy), but that orangeish shade is not the semantic value of 'red'. ('Looks$_{nc}$ Scandinavian' and 'red hair' are thus quite different from paradigmatic idioms like 'blue blood' and 'green thumb'.) Although it might seem implausible, one could hold that 'looks$_{nc}$ yellow' is in the same boat as 'looks$_{nc}$ Scandinavian': something can *be* as it looks$_{nc}$ when it looks$_{nc}$ yellow without being yellow. In fact that is (near enough) Thau's view: he accepts (CV), and agrees that lemons look yellow (in every sense), but denies that perceptual content ever includes propositions predicating yellowness.[37]

The upshot is that Travis is in one way right. Perceptual content, if there is such a thing, is not 'looks-indexed', at least as that notion has been explained here. But Travis is wrong to conclude that our ordinary talk provides no support for (CV). On occasion, we use 'looks' to convey information about the non-comparative looks of things. The phenomenon of non-comparative looking is something that (CV) appears well suited to explain.

V. TRAVIS' MODEL OF ILLUSION

A visual illusion is a situation of the following sort: o looks$_{nc}$ F to S and o is not the way it looks$_{nc}$. The phenomenon of illusion and the phenomenon of non-comparative looking are thus intimately connected: to explain one is to explain the other.

(CV) is not a claim about how we talk, and illusions and non-comparative looking are likewise non-linguistic phenomena. If there is direct support for (CV), it is to be found here, rather than in subtleties about our use of 'looks'. 'The Silence of the Senses', however, briskly dispatches illusions early on. Travis starts by observing that one may have one's 'surroundings in view', and yet be misled (p. 67): 'seeing Luc and Pia's flat strewn with broken crockery, one might reasonably suppose there to have been a tiff. For all that there might not have been one.' It appears as if there has been a tiff, but all that amounts to is that the evidence points that way, or that someone

---

[37] For a related view, see S. Shoemaker, 'On the Ways Things Appear', in Gendler and Hawthorne (eds), *Perceptual Experience*, pp. 461–80.

might reasonably take it to point that way. This sort of example does not provide any reason to wheel on the exing propositional attitude, with the content that there has been a tiff.

Travis then tries to extend this treatment to perceptual illusions. The Müller–Lyer lines, he suggests, *epistemically* look unequal to me: it looks to me *as if* they are unequal. That is, my evidence points that way, or someone (perhaps not myself) might reasonably take it to point that way. This does not imply that *I* have some tendency to believe that the lines are unequal: I can comment on what someone might reasonably conclude from the evidence without being inclined to conclude this myself. ('It looks as if there has been a tiff', I might say, even though I know that Luc and Pia would never throw their valuable crockery in anger.)

An immediate problem with this suggestion is the apparent lack of suitable evidence. I see the lines and, as Travis puts it (p. 65), 'simply confront what is there'. I must be aware of a feature of the lines that might reasonably lead someone to conclude that they are unequal. Suppose I am a naïve subject looking at the Müller–Lyer diagram for the first time and I believe that the lines are unequal. What feature of the lines led me to this conclusion? *Not* the arrow heads and tails – why would the fact that the lines have these features suggest that they are unequal? Equal lines could easily have those features.

A less forlorn candidate for the evidence can be extracted in this passage from *Sense and Sensibilia* (p. 43), a book to which Travis acknowledges a debt:[38]

> It is perhaps even clearer that the way things look is, in general, just as much a fact about the world, just as open to public confirmation or challenge, as the way things are. I am not disclosing a fact about *myself*, but about petrol, when I say that petrol looks like water.

Petrol looks like water whether or not these two liquids look similar to any specific individual, and in that sense petrol shares an 'objective look' with water. What is that 'objective look', exactly? Petrol looks clear, and so does water: that is (one of) the 'objective looks' they share. Austin chose the comparative 'looks like', but he could have picked the (non-comparative, non-epistemic) 'looks clear': I am not disclosing a fact about myself, but about petrol, when I say that petrol looks clear. Even if it does not look clear *to me* (I may be blind), petrol still 'objectively' looks clear.

Likewise, the Müller–Lyer lines objectively look unequal. That might seem a much better candidate for the needed evidence. I see the lines for the first time and note that they have that objective look. Mostly, things are as

---

[38] J.L. Austin, *Sense and Sensibilia* (Oxford UP, 1962). See also Travis, 'The Silence', p. 64, fn. 5.

they objectively look – petrol really is clear. So it would be reasonable for me to conclude that the lines are unequal. Similarly, when I am wise to the illusion, I conclude that they look as if they are unequal – someone might reasonably take their objective look to show that they are unequal.

Travis (p. 68) puts this as follows:

> In the Müller–Lyer, two lines are contrived ... to have a certain look. They do not just *seem* to have that look; that is actually the way they look. (Witness the 'robustness' of the illusion.) Two lines may well have that look because one *is* longer than the other ... that look may thus *indicate* that it is two lines of unequal length that one confronts.... *Thus* may someone be misled by a Müller–Lyer. False expectations arise here in the wrong view of what something (a look) means, though perhaps a right view of what it ought to. What one gets wrong is the arrangement of the world: how the misleading seen thing relates to other things. That mistake neither requires, nor suggests, that in this illusion one line is represented to us as being longer than the other.

But what are 'objective looks'? In particular, what is it for petrol to objectively look clear? Surely there is no special mystery here: petrol objectively looks clear iff it looks$_{nc}$ clear to normal people, or something along similar lines. Grass objectively looks green; more specifically, it objectively looks yellowish green. Does light of wavelength 495nm objectively look a unique green, a shade of green that is neither yellowish nor blueish? No: it looks$_{nc}$ a unique green to some, but not to others.[39]

If this is correct, then Travis' treatment of illusions, at least as I am reconstructing it, fails. In effect, he *denies* that the Müller–Lyer lines look$_{nc}$ unequal to individual perceivers. Rather, the lines have a certain 'objective look', and 'that look may thus *indicate* that it is two lines of unequal length that one confronts': one knows that the lines have that look, and thus the lines look *as if* they are unequal. But this account *presupposes* that the lines may look$_{nc}$ unequal to a particular individual; if they cannot, then they cannot objectively look unequal either. Once it is *conceded* that the lines may look$_{nc}$ unequal to someone, it also should be conceded that they may look$_{nc}$ unequal to someone who believes that the lines are equal. This now needs explaining without invoking (CV), and Travis' account does nothing at all to explain it.

Travis would doubtless resist the account of 'objective looks' in terms of non-comparative looking. But that would only bring temporary relief. If one stares at a bright red surface for a minute or so and then looks at a grey surface, it appears tinged with green. A Travis-style explanation of this illusion would involve taking a certain objective look of the grey surface to suggest that the surface is green (or greenish) – specifically, an objective

---

[39] See C.L. Hardin, *Color for Philosophers* (Indianapolis: Hackett, 1988), pp. 79–80.

green look. But *whatever* the account of 'objective looks', an ordinary grey surface does *not* objectively look green, or greenish: it objectively looks grey. Hence a Travis-style treatment does not get off the ground.[40]

VI. THE CONTENT VIEW AS THE BEST EXPLANATION OF ILLUSIONS

According to Travis (p. 65), perception 'simply places our surroundings in view; affords us awareness of them'. As noted in §III above, Brewer agrees. Illusions pose a challenge to this position, as of course Travis and Brewer both recognize. The lines in the Müller–Lyer figure $look_{nc}$ unequal, and this precisely suggests that sometimes perception does *not* 'simply place our surroundings in view'. I have just shown how difficult it is to resist this conclusion.

Still, I have not yet shown why we should embrace (CV). Why not rest with non-comparative looking, stopping short of the $exing$ propositional attitude? (Visual) perception essentially involves the relation o $looks_{nc}$ F to S, not, in addition, an attitude to a proposition. The possibility of strict perceptual error is provided for: that will happen exactly when o $looks_{nc}$ F to S but is not the way it $looks_{nc}$. In other words, why not stick with the good old 'theory of appearing', recently revived by Langsam and Alston?[41]

As Alston explains it (p. 182), the theory of appearing 'takes perceptual consciousness to consist, most basically, in the fact that one or more objects *appear* to the subject *as so and so*, as round, bulgy, blue, jagged, etc.'. The theory's fundamental primitive is the relation o *appears as* F to S (p. 191, changing Alston's schematic letters). This suggests that the terminology for the fundamental primitive is a piece of ordinary English, but appearances (pun intended) are deceptive. In Alston's 'appears' terminology, an illusion is supposed to be a situation in which o appears as F, but is not F. Therefore, because of the point about 'looks old/centaurian/Scandinavian' mentioned at the end of §IV, o *(visually)* *appears as* F to S cannot be identified with the relation conveyed by 'o looks F to S', taken non-comparatively. 'o appears as

---

[40] This also poses a problem for the similar account of illusion in Brewer, 'Perception and Content'. Another quite different counter-reformation account of illusion is that developed in the work of M.G.F. Martin (e.g., 'On Being Alienated'). Martin's constitutive account of the illusion just mentioned in the text is roughly this: one sees the grey surface, but cannot tell by introspection alone that one is not veridically perceiving a surface tinged with green. For references to the main discussions of Martin's view, see Byrne and Logue, 'Either/Or', p. 74, fn. 31.

[41] H. Langsam, 'The Theory of Appearing Defended', *Philosophical Studies*, 87 (1997), pp. 33–59; W.P. Alston, 'Back to the Theory of Appearing', *Philosophical Perspectives*, 13 (1999), pp. 181–203. See also Jackson, *Perception*, ch. 4.

F to *S*' is thus a bit of jargon, not a familiar English expression, and in that respect is on all fours with '*S* exes that *p*'.

Moreover, (CV) has a clear edge over the theory of appearing. First, room must be made for perceptible relations, in addition to perceptible (monadic) properties. To take the simplest example, suppose one sees a red spot ('this') to the left of a brighter red spot ('that'). *This* appears red and *that* appears red, but of course that is not all: *this* appears to the left of *that*, and *that* appears brighter than *this*, facts which an account of 'perceptual consciousness' should not overlook. Without supplementation, they are overlooked: 'F' is supposed to be replaced by a term for a perceptible quality like colour and shape. But if 'brighter than *this*' is allowed to specify the way *that* appears, it is very hard to see why a singular term for a perceived object has to remain in subject position, in the theory's canonical locutions. If '*That* appears as brighter than *this* to *S*' is acceptable (with 'this' in the complement of 'appears'), what is wrong with the more pleasingly symmetrical 'It appears to *S* that *that* is brighter than *this*'? In this formulation, the theory is just a notational variant of (CV).

Secondly, what about hallucinations? If *S* has a hallucination of a lemon, no physical object in *S*'s environment appears yellow to *S*. According to Alston (pp. 191–2), a 'mental image' appears yellow. According to Langsam (pp. 38–41), *nothing at all* appears yellow, and so some other account of hallucinations is required. Plainly the proper treatment of hallucinations is no simple matter, and at least the proponent of (CV) has more options.[42] The matter is too complicated to discuss here, but there should be the suspicion that the theory of appearing founders at this point.

Thirdly, even if we set hallucinations aside, it is not at all obvious that *all* perception is directed on particular objects, as the theory of appearing would have it. Smelling and tasting are ways of perceiving, but when one smells, is there a particular thing that one smells, in the way that there is a particular thing that one sees? Grammar puts 'smells the cheese' and 'sees the cheese' on all fours, but the corresponding perceptual phenomena are quite different: seeing the cheese enables one to entertain singular thoughts about it, smelling the cheese does not. Arguably, smelling the cheese provides no object-dependent information, not even about, in Lycan's phrase, 'vaporous emanations'.[43] This is not a problem for (CV), since quantified propositions of various sorts are there for the taking.

---

[42] See Byrne and Logue, 'Either/Or', pp. 89–90.

[43] W.G. Lycan, *Consciousness and Experience* (MIT Press, 1996), p. 146; see also C. Batty, *Lessons in Smelling: Essays on Olfactory Perception* (MIT: PhD thesis, 2007).

VII. TWO MATTERS ARISING

Suppose (CV) is true, and the preceding defence of it is on the right lines: to see is, *inter alia*, to ex that *p*. Two questions are particularly pressing. First, what are the allowable substituends for '*p*'? That is, what sorts of propositions comprise the content of perceptual experience? Secondly, can the exing attitude be characterized in more detail?

To take the first question first, if (CV) is supported by an inference to the best explanation of illusions, then one might expect perceptual content to be relatively thin. Visual illusions, as the object of study in the visual sciences, concern properties like shape, motion, colour, shading, orientation and the like, not properties like *being tired, belonging to Smith* or *being a lemon*.[44] There is thus no immediate reason to take (visual) perceptual content to include the proposition *that o is a lemon*, and the like. Suppose Alice, a lemon-fancier, is fooled by Austin's lemon-like bar of soap (*Sense and Sensibilia*, p. 50) – 'Lo, a lemon', she says. On discovering that the object is not in fact a lemon, will she insist that the visual impression as of a lemon still persists, in the way that the visual impression as of unequal lines persists in the Müller–Lyer? That seems doubtful: the natural response is either comparative or epistemic. 'Well, it looks exactly *like* a lemon', Alice might say, meaning that it shares its visible characteristics with lemons. (Hence since the soap is not a lemon, *being a lemon* is not a visible characteristic in the relevant sense.) Alternatively, she might say 'It looks exactly *as if* it is a lemon', meaning that it would be reasonable for someone to take the soap to be a lemon.

Siegel demurs, arguing that properties like *being a lemon* figure in the content of perception. Modifying her main example (which concerns pine trees), suppose one has never seen a lemon. On exposure to enough lemons, one develops the capacity to recognize them by sight. Plausibly, lemons now look (non-comparatively, non-epistemically) different from how they did when one saw lemons for the first time. As Siegel puts it (p. 500), 'gaining a disposition to recognize [lemons] can make a difference to visual phenomenology'. She then argues that the best explanation for this difference is that (in my terminology) one can now ex that this is a lemon.

But the following scenario shows that there must be something wrong with Siegel's argument. Suppose lemons grown on Island *A* look like normal lemons, and that lemons grown on Island *B* look like cucumbers (because of the strange soil and climate). One develops a recognitional disposition for

---

[44] Causation, though, is an especially tricky case – *locus classicus*: A. Michotte, *The Perception of Causality* (London: Methuen, 1963); see also S. Siegel, 'The Visual Experience of Causation', *The Philosophical Quarterly*, 59 (2009), pp. 519–40 (this book, pp. 150–71).

the fruit on Island A, and similarly for the fruit on Island B (but does not know that the fruits are identical). If Siegel's argument works, then if one sees an A fruit and a B fruit side by side, they will both be visually represented as lemons. Presumably, then, (a) one will believe that the two fruits are of the same kind, and (b) they will appear *more* visually similar after one has learnt to recognize them by sight than they did before. Clearly neither of these predicted consequences will be borne out.

It might be replied that the property of being a lemon is represented under two different 'modes of presentation', corresponding to the distinctive *Gestalten* of shape, colour and texture that respectively characterize the A and B fruit, and it is the modes of presentation that account for one's beliefs about the fruits and for visual similarities. That the *Gestalten* are represented is plausible, but this point undercuts the case for the conclusion that the property of being a lemon is also visually represented. If learning to recognize A and B fruits involves acquiring perceptual contents concerning different *Gestalten*, the same diagnosis applies to Siegel's original example. On learning to recognize (normal) lemons by sight, one's perceptual contents change, but not by including propositions about lemons as such.

We may provisionally conclude that perceptual content is relatively thin. To that extent, its epistemological importance is lessened. No doubt perceptual content figures in an explanation of how one knows by sight that this is a lemon, but its role cannot be to serve up that proposition in the first place.

Finally, the second question, about the nature of exing. It is supposed to be a non-factive propositional attitude that is constitutively involved in perception, but this to say alarmingly little. If there really is such an attitude, it is puzzling that there is no corresponding propositional-attitude verb.

These vexing issues would vanish if it turns out that exing *is* believing. That happy prospect is usually dismissed, though, on the ground that it fails to account for cases of known illusion. Looking at the Müller–Lyer figure, one exes that the lines are unequal but believes that they are equal. Hence, it is typically concluded, exing is not believing (cf. §III above).

But there is a hole in this style of argument. Inconsistent beliefs are perfectly common. That one believes that the lines are equal need not prevent one from also believing that the lines are unequal. Admittedly, if one has the latter belief, it is not manifest in one's behaviour: one does not assert that the lines are unequal, for example. But it might be, as Armstrong once suggested, that this belief is 'held in check by a stronger belief'.[45] If

---

[45] D.M. Armstrong, *A Materialist Theory of the Mind* (London: Routledge & Kegan Paul, 1968), p. 221; see also A.D. Smith, 'Perception and Belief', *Philosophy and Phenomenological Research*, 62 (2001), pp. 283–309. It is important to note that the claim that perception constitutively involves belief (in particular, that exing is believing) does not imply that perception can be *reduced* to belief.

perception constitutively involves belief, then this neatly explains the commonly agreed fact that in the absence of any reason for thinking otherwise, one believes, in the usual unimpeded way, that the lines are unequal. If exing *is* believing, then the explanation of this otherwise mysterious connection between perception and belief is trivial.

If exing is believing, then the reformers and counter-reformers are not so far apart. The reformers are right in holding that illusion involves perceptual error; the counter-reformers are right in tracing the error to a false belief. The issue is complicated, but let us pray that this present-day schism in the philosophy of perception will have an ecumenical ending.[46]

[46] For advice and assistance which greatly improved this chapter, thanks to David Chalmers, James Genone, Jeff King, Heather Logue, Fiona Macpherson, Adam Pautz, Susanna Rinard, Susanna Siegel, Charles Travis, Michael Tye, an anonymous referee, and audiences at the Australian National University and the University of Glasgow.

5

IS PERCEPTION A PROPOSITIONAL ATTITUDE?

By Tim Crane

It is widely agreed that perceptual experience is a form of intentionality, i.e., that it has representational content. Many philosophers take this to mean that like belief, experience has propositional content, that it can be true or false. I accept that perceptual experience has intentionality; but I dispute the claim that it has propositional content. This claim does not follow from the fact that experience is intentional, nor does it follow from the fact that experiences are accurate or inaccurate. I end by considering the relationship between this question and the question of whether experience has non-conceptual content.

I. INTRODUCTION

It has for a long time been noted by philosophers that we talk about our perceptual experiences in a number of different ways.[1] Sometimes we describe our experiences using perceptual verbs with sentential complements, as when we say that someone can see (or hear) that the bus has arrived. On other occasions we use transitive perceptual verbs whose direct objects are given by noun phrases, as when we say that someone saw (or heard) the bus, or saw (or heard) the arrival of the bus; sometimes what is perceived is given by so-called 'small clauses', as when we say that someone saw (or heard) the bus arrive. The kinds of things which are referred to by these noun phrases and small clauses are varied: complex events, people, sounds and smells are among them. There are other obvious distinctions to be made in our ways of talking about experiences. For example, some ways of talking about experience are factive ('sees that ...') or relational ('sees ...'), while some are not ('seems to see ...'); and then there is the less everyday, more philosophical idiom 'has an experience as of ...'.

Faced with this variety, it is natural to ask whether any of these ways of talking is more fundamental. Is there a way of talking about perception, or perceptual experience, which corresponds more closely with its metaphysics

---

[1] For a classic discussion, see F.I. Dretske, *Seeing and Knowing* (London: Routledge & Kegan Paul, 1969).

or its phenomenology? Opinions differ. In this chapter, I shall examine an answer to this question which has gained some popularity in recent years, the view that perceptual experience is a propositional attitude. According to Alex Byrne, it is widely accepted that

> perceiving is very much like a traditional propositional attitude, such as believing or intending ... when one has a perceptual experience, one bears the perception relation to a certain proposition *p*.[2]

It is natural for someone who takes this view to hold, then, that the canonical or fundamental form which ascriptions of perception should take is one in which perceptual verbs have sentential complements. Since experiencing is a relation to a proposition, the best way to ascribe an experience to someone is to say that they perceptually experience that ..., where the '...' is filled in with a sentence which expresses that proposition.[3] Some philosophers also believe that if the content of experience is propositional, then the content of experience is the kind of thing that can be the content of a belief or judgement, since these are propositional too. This claim has been famously defended by John McDowell. In *Mind and World*, he argues that

> In a particular experience in which one is not misled, what one takes in is that things are thus and so. That things are thus and so is the content of the experience, and it can also be the content of a judgement: it becomes the content of a judgement if the subject decides to take the experience at face value.[4]

McDowell's idea is a specific version of the claim that experience has a propositional content. He thinks that experience can only have this structure if its content is conceptual. Some of those who believe that experience has a non-conceptual content (like Byrne) disagree with this claim: experience can have a propositional content without that content being conceptual. None the less these philosophers agree that experience has propositional content, and in this sense it is a propositional attitude.

In this chapter I shall argue that both Byrne and McDowell are wrong: the content of experience is not propositional, and so it cannot be the kind of thing that can be the content of a belief or judgement. Neither perceptual experience, nor perception proper, is a propositional attitude.

Some assumptions: I assume the now standard terminological distinction between *perceptual experience*, which is non-factive or non-relational, and

---

[2] A. Byrne, 'Perception and Conceptual Content', in E. Sosa and M. Steup (eds), *Contemporary Debates in Epistemology* (Oxford: Blackwell, 2005), pp. 231–50, at p. 232.

[3] For some statements of this view, see J. Searle, *Intentionality* (Cambridge UP, 1983), ch. 3; C. Peacocke, *Sense and Content* (Oxford UP, 1983), ch. 1; M. Tye, *Ten Problems of Consciousness* (MIT Press, 1995); M. Thau, *Consciousness and Cognition* (Oxford UP, 2002).

[4] J. McDowell, *Mind and World* (Harvard UP, 1994), p. 26.

perception, which is both factive and relational. I shall adopt the usual understanding of propositional contents, or propositions, as the bearers of truth-value, the meanings of indicative sentences, the relata of truth-functional logical relations, and so on. However, nothing in particular turns on any particular detail of the theory of propositions assumed.

I shall first introduce one neutral way to understand the idea of the *object* of a mental state, and I shall define one sense in which experiences have *content*. I shall then examine the familiar claim that experience must have a propositional content because experiences can be accurate or inaccurate. I shall argue that accuracy is not the same thing as truth (for example, a picture can be accurate or inaccurate without being true or false). It is undeniable that we do use propositions to describe, express or otherwise give the contents of some of our experiences. But I shall argue that it does not follow from the fact that we give the content by using a proposition that the proposition *is* the content of the experience. I shall conclude by commenting on the connection between this issue and the debate about non-conceptual content.

II. CONTENT AND OBJECT

The terms 'content', 'intentional content' and 'content of experience' are technical terms. So we should not expect to be able to analyse them in terms of the meaning of the ordinary word 'content'. Any discussion of the idea of the 'content' of experience should take place against the background of the theoretical assumptions which should be made about content and experience. It would not, for example, be helpful to start off by assuming that 'content' means *propositional content*, since then I would have to express my thesis by saying that perceptions do not have content at all; but this would be a very misleading thing to say in the context of today's philosophy of perception. In any case, philosophical discussions of intentional content have not always used the term to mean propositional content, so history does not oblige us to take this starting-point.

The notion of content belongs within the theory of intentionality. Intentional mental states fall into different kinds: there are hopes, beliefs, fears, desires and so on. All these mental states exhibit what has been called 'aboutness' or 'directedness': they are about or directed on things. I express this idea in a general way, as follows: for every intentional state of kind ϕ, there is something on which the ϕing is directed. What the ϕing is directed on is the object of the state. This is what I mean by saying that every intentional state has an object. Like many others, I take my lead from a famous remark of Brentano's: 'in presentation, something is presented, in judgement something is affirmed or denied, in love loved, in hate hated, in desire desired, and so on'.[5] Sometimes we can say that what the φing is directed on is what is φed. For example, in a state of desire there is something that is desired: what is desired is the object of the desire. In a state of fear, there is something that is feared; in a state of love, there is something that is loved; and so on. What is φed in each of these cases is the object of the φing. In some cases this need not be true. In the case of the paradigm intentional state of belief, for example, *what is believed* is the propositional content of the belief. But we also need the idea of what a belief is 'about'; so I shall say that the object of a belief is what it is about.

In some cases, the object of a state might be something that does not or cannot exist. I might hope for everlasting world peace, desire a cheap bottle of champagne or fear the ghost under the bed, even though there are not, and never will be, any such things. But in other cases, the object of an intentional state does exist, and when it does, it is an ordinary real thing. So when I am imagining my mother in her kitchen, what I am imagining is my mother herself, the real person, in her very real kitchen. When the object of an intentional state exists, then it is the very same thing as a real existing entity.

We cannot describe the whole nature of every intentional state by describing the kind of state it is (fear, imagination, desire, etc.) and describing its object. For there are many ways to imagine my mother in her kitchen: she might be baking bread, she might be listening to the radio, she might be frying onions, and so on. A particular episode of imagining my mother will present my mother in one way and not in others. These ways need not be determinate in every respect. But every episode of visual imagining will certainly exclude some ways of presenting the object of the episode.

This is where I would introduce the idea of content. There are three distinct reasons for introducing this idea, which I label *aspect*, *absence* and *accuracy*.

(i) *Aspect.* The object of a state of mind can be presented or represented in many ways, even when the states of mind are of the same general kind (desire, fear, etc.). States can have the same objects but differ in the *aspects* under which they represent these objects.[6] In the general framework I am proposing here, that fact that an object is represented under an aspect is

[5] Brentano, *Psychology from an Empirical Standpoint* [1874], ed. L. McAlister (London: Routledge & Kegan Paul, 1973, repr. London: Routledge, 1995), p. 88.
[6] I follow Searle, *The Rediscovery of the Mind* (MIT Press, 1992), p. 131, in this use of the word 'aspect'; for more details, see T. Crane, *Elements of Mind* (Oxford UP, 2001), §6.

what is called the content of that state. There is a further question about whether different objects can be represented under the same aspect. Philosophers who agree with Frege's doctrine that sense determines reference deny this, since they believe that a difference in reference must correspond to a difference in sense. I reject Frege's doctrine, but I shall not pursue the matter here.[7]

(ii) *Absence*. Searle says in *Intentionality* that not all intentional states have objects, since he takes objects of intentional states to be entities. I prefer to say that some intentional states do not have existing objects, or real objects. None the less, whichever of these ways of talking is preferable, there is something real in each intentional state, and that is what we can call its *real content*: there is a representation of an object, whether real or unreal, in every intentional state or act.[8] For some intentional states, their reality can be what it is independently of the real existence of their objects. The state is of a certain kind (belief, hope, whatever) and it also incorporates a representation of its object. This representational aspect of the state is its content.

(iii) *Accuracy*. Some intentional states present their objects in a certain way, but they might not be like that. Some intentional states can be inaccurate. I can fantasize about an inexpensive bottle of champagne, but there is no such thing. In so far as my fantasizing was representing reality, it is not accurate. Intentional states, then, can be accurate or inaccurate. This is a matter of how they represent their objects; and this, again, is what I call content.

These three ideas – aspect, absence and accuracy – are what make necessary the introduction of representational content. They do not all apply to each intentional state; but at least one of them applies to every kind. How should we apply this to the idea of perceptual experience?

Perceptual experiences can be of different kinds – they can be visual, auditory, etc. – and they have objects. The objects of perceptual experiences are *what* is seen, *what* is heard and so on. Since it is plausible that different experiences of the same kind can differ in the aspect under which they represent their objects (*aspect*), they can represent what does not exist (*absence*) and they can be accurate or inaccurate (*accuracy*), then this is why it is plausible to say that experience has content. I realize this is not uncontroversial, but I shall not defend this idea further in this chapter.

The notion of the content of experience, then, is the notion of the way the world is represented in experience. The basic commitment one incurs in saying that experience has content (in this sense) is the commitment that

---

[7] But see K. Farkas, *The Subject's Point of View* (Oxford UP, 2008), ch. 7.

[8] The idea derives from Husserl, *Logical Investigations* [1901], tr. J.N. Findlay (London: Routledge, 1970), No. V, ch. 2.

experiences represent the world. This way of introducing content is in line with most contemporary uses of the term. For those who reject the idea that experiences represent the world tend also to reject the idea that experiences have content.[9] Hence my usage of the term 'content' is not just a stipulation: it corresponds to the way many philosophers use the term.

However, it does not follow from the way in which I have introduced the notion of content that content must be propositional. In the next section I shall consider, and reject, one reason which has been given for thinking that it must be.

III. ACCURACY AND TRUTH

Those who think that perception is a propositional attitude often point to the fact just mentioned that experiences have accuracy- or correctness-conditions.[10] If an experience represents its object in a certain way, then the experience is accurate if and only if it has an actual object which is as the experience represents it as being. The content of the experience then is the proposition which gives how the object or objects of experience are represented to be. I see the grey cat on the mat, it is represented in a particular way in my experience; the experience is accurate (correct) if that is how the cat and the mat actually are. The content of the experience is, then, the proposition that *the cat is on the mat*.

The propositional-attitude thesis (as I shall call it) is not the thesis that perceptual experiences are beliefs, a view famously defended by Armstrong.[11] There are many well known reasons against identifying experiences with beliefs. (More precisely, since experiences are events rather than states, the identification should at most be with the *acquisition* of beliefs.) For example, systematic illusions show that experiences can present the world in a way we know it not to be, but this is not plausibly represented as a case of contradictory beliefs. But the propositional-attitude thesis does not say that perceptions are beliefs, it says only that they have the same kind of *content* as belief. As McDowell says, the content of an experience is 'the sort of thing one can also ... judge'.[12] What one can judge is a proposition,

---

[9] For non-representational views of experience, see B. Brewer, 'Perception and Content', *European Journal of Philosophy*, 14 (2006), pp. 165–81; C. Travis, 'The Silence of the Senses', *Mind*, 113 (2004), pp. 57–94; J. Campbell, *Reference and Consciousness* (Oxford UP, 2003). Brewer explicitly rejects the use of the word 'content' in the theory of perception.

[10] See S. Siegel, 'The Contents of Perception', in E.N. Zalta (ed.), *Stanford Encyclopedia of Philosophy*, http://plato.stanford.edu/entries/perception-contents.

[11] D.M. Armstrong, *A Materialist Theory of the Mind* (London: Routledge, 1968).

[12] McDowell, *Mind and World* (Harvard UP, 1994), p. 36.

something which is true or false. Since propositions are what are true and false, then the propositional-attitude thesis says that the contents of experience can be true or false.

But this claim does not follow from the fact that experiences can be accurate or inaccurate. Accuracy is not truth, since accuracy admits of degrees and truth does not. (The same can be said of correctness.) A picture, for example, can be more or less accurate, but a picture is not true or false. So there is no straightforward deductive inference from the claim that experiences can be accurate and inaccurate to the conclusion that they can be true or false, that they have propositional contents.

The defenders of the thesis can respond that the conclusion is not meant to follow; rather it is the *best explanation* of the fact that experience has accuracy-conditions. It also explains the other two As of §II above: *absence* (so long as the propositions in question are not 'object-dependent') and *aspect* (so long as the propositions in question are not 'Russellian'). This is a possible thing to say. But the comparison with pictures suggests that it is not the best thing to say. Light may be shed if I pursue this comparison further.

Like an experience, a picture can be more or less accurate. A proposition, on the standard understanding at least, cannot be more or less true. Truth and falsehood are all or nothing. It is central to the idea of a proposition that it can be true or false, since truth and falsehood are the crucial semantic concepts of propositional logic. Propositional logic shows how the truth or falsehood of complex propositions depends on the truth or falsehood of others. Truth-functions operate on propositions: propositions can be negated, disjoined, conjoined; they can imply one another or be equivalent. That there are things which stand in these logical relations is one of the reasons for talking in terms of propositions at all (though of course not all philosophers of logic accept this).

None of this is true of pictures. Just as pictures are not true or false, so they do not stand in logical relations.[13] Complex pictures do not stand to their pictorial parts as complex propositions stand to their constituent propositions. Pictures do not imply one another; they cannot be negated or disjoined. In this way they are like experiences.

Perhaps it will be replied that although pictures and experiences do not stand in logical relations, their *contents* might. Just as we should distinguish between a sentence and its content, we should distinguish between a picture and its content. A sentence as such is a thing which can be characterized non-semantically. When a sentence is characterized semantically (interpreted),

[13] *Pace* J. Westerhoff, 'Logical Relations between Pictures', *Journal of Philosophy*, 102 (2005), pp. 603–23.

we say that it *expresses* a proposition. After all, on the standard view it is propositions, not sentences, which stand in logical relations, since the things which stand in logical relations must be the bearers of truth-values.

We can distinguish in a similar way between a picture and its content. Pictures themselves can be characterized non-semantically. When characterized 'semantically', in terms of what it depicts, then we can say that a picture represents something. What it represents (and the way it does so) is the content of the picture. This content, the objection goes, can be affirmed and denied, it can be negated and disjoined, it can imply other contents. So although pictures themselves do not stand in logical relations, nothing has been said to prevent their *contents* standing in logical relations. Therefore nothing has been said to prevent their contents from being propositional.

We should, of course, concede the distinction between a picture (the physical object) and its content. We should also concede that logical relations hold between the contents of sentences. This is illustrated by the fact that just as pictures themselves do not assert anything, so sentences themselves do not assert anything either.

But none the less the analogy between pictures and sentences fails at a crucial point. This can be brought out by considering assertion. As just noted, a sentence itself does not assert anything. Nor does a proposition assert anything. Assertions are speech acts. Speakers use sentences to assert things: what they assert is the proposition some sentence expresses. How can a parallel thing be said about pictures? Pictures themselves do not assert something, but can someone assert something by using a picture? Can someone assert the proposition which the picture allegedly expresses?

It seems to me that someone could assert something by using a picture – but *only* by saying something too. If I take Jacques-Louis David's famous picture of the coronation of Napoleon, and I want to assert what it represents, then I have to *say* 'Napoleon crowned himself' or something of this sort. I cannot simply use the picture itself to assert this. (How could I possibly do this? By holding it up to my audience? But what would make that an assertion?) Similarly, I can only deny what the picture represents by using some words to do so. I can hold up the picture and say 'This is not how it was: Napoleon did not crown himself'. There is no way of simply using a picture alone to deny what it represents. The same applies to the logical operations of negation and disjunction. You can only negate or disjoin the content of a picture by using some non-pictorial symbol. You cannot simply append another picture to a picture and display a logical relation between them.

The upshot is that even though we must distinguish between the picture and its content, and between a sentence and its content, this does not imply that pictures and sentences both have propositional content. For in order to obtain something which one can assert, or to which one can apply logical operations, you need to employ non-pictorial symbols. Without these non-pictorial symbols, it makes little sense to say that the content of the picture can be something which can be asserted, denied, negated or disjoined.

But the propositional-attitude theory can be defended from a different direction. Although it may be conceded that the content of the picture cannot be asserted (nor negated, disjoined, etc.) by using pictures only, could there not be a sentence that has the *same* content as the content of the picture? In other words, may not the following principle (P) be true?

P. For any picture *P*, there is a sentence which gives the content of *P*.

This principle seems undeniable. For given what I mean by the content of the picture – how the object of the picture is represented – then this principle is merely a commitment to the idea that there can always be a sentence which describes what a picture represents and how it represents it. Short of an argument for the conclusion that there are some ineffable aspects of the content of pictures, there seems no reason to deny this.

It might be thought that some pictures are too complex to allow description in language. But where is the argument for this? Principle (P) does not say that the sentence must be short, or that it must be restricted to any one language, or that we cannot make up words for aspects of the content when lacking them in a natural language. In fact, it is easy to show that (P) is true, if we allow that sentences containing demonstratives can give descriptions of pictures, and help to express their content. A sentence of the form 'Napoleon did this and this ...' can express the content of David's picture. It is not an objection to say that someone would not be able to understand this sentence without seeing the picture. Sentences containing demonstratives obviously can express propositions; what it takes to understand an utterance of such a sentence is another question, on which principle (P) is silent.

Principle (P), then, says that there is always a sentence which gives the content of a picture. 'Gives', in this context, means *describes*. But describing the content and *being* the content are not the same thing. The content of a representation, I have stipulated, is how its object is represented. Content in this sense can be described in many ways; the description of this content is not the same thing as the content itself. For example, the content of a picture can be given by asserting 'This is the content of this picture' or 'This is what this picture represents'.

This distinction can be developed by drawing on a recent suggestion by Zoltán Szabó. He argues that there is a distinctive mental state of believing in things, in terms of which the notion of ontological commitment can be explained.[14] Philosophers who think that all intentional states are propositional attitudes reject this: they say that 'believing in' can always be given some kind of propositional analysis – believing in Fs just is believing that there are Fs. But Szabó argues that this approach cannot make sense of a number of perfectly intelligible phenomena: for example, someone can acknowledge that there are things in whose existence they do not believe. One of his examples is based on Hamlet's remark to Horatio: 'There are more things in heaven and earth than are dreamt of in our philosophy'. The speaker is not saying that there are things of this kind, and we do not believe that there are things of this kind. Rather, he is expressing a certain kind of epistemic modesty.

Szabó's view is that 'believing in' is an intensional transitive verb, which can take a singular or plural object. Belief-in has much in common with belief-that; in particular, and most importantly, it aims at a correct representation of the world. This representation Szabó calls (following Russell) a *term*, and he represents the term for the plural object Fs by '[Fs]'. The condition for the correctness of this representation he gives as follows:

> [Fs] is representationally correct iff Fs exist and the conception of Fs is true.

The idea is that it is not enough for your belief in Fs to be correct that Fs merely exist; in addition, you have to have a conception of Fs, and this conception has to be true. I do not need to go into the details of this novel proposal. The point I shall use for the moment is that one can represent the condition for the correctness of a representation in terms of a sentence, the right-hand side of the biconditional quoted above, without the representation itself's being sentence-like. So even if the right-hand side of this biconditional gives the content of the representation [Fs], this is not enough to make this representation propositional.

The thesis that pictures have propositional content cannot, therefore, be the same as the thesis expressed by principle (P). To say that for every picture there is a sentence which expresses a proposition and this sentence gives the content of the picture is not the same thing as saying that pictures have propositional content.

---

[14] Z.G. Szabó, 'Believing in Things', *Philosophy and Phenomenological Research*, 66 (2003), pp. 584–611.

IV. THE CONTENTS OF EXPERIENCE

I shall now apply some of these ideas about pictures to the content of experience. I started by discussing the idea that the fact that a state or representation has accuracy-conditions does not itself imply that it has a propositional content, since propositions are (by definition) true or false, and accuracy is not the same as truth. This is why I introduced pictures: pictures can be accurate or inaccurate but not true or false. Thus presented, this argument was unpersuasive; but it led to arguments which were, I hope, more persuasive.

I shall now argue that a view on which the content of perceptual experience is more like the content of a picture gives a better account of the fact that experiences can be accurate or inaccurate than the propositional-attitude theory does. I do not mean to imply that having a visual experience is like looking at a picture. This is not the right way to think about experience, for many familiar reasons. But the comparison between pictures and experiences is none the less apt because one of the things a painter, for example, is doing when painting a (realistic) picture is portraying *how things look*. The point, then, is not that visual perception is essentially pictorial; it is rather that picturing is essentially visual.

In the previous section I claimed that pictures do not have propositional content because propositions can be asserted or denied, and they can stand in logical relations. The only sense in which pictures stand in logical relations is when someone uses a picture along with some non-pictorial representation to make some claim. Similarly, if a proposition were the content of a perceptual experience, then it should be capable of being negated, disjoined, conjoined, etc. But it seems that just as one cannot do these things to the content of pictures, one cannot do them to the contents of experiences either.

The only literal sense which could be made of negating, disjoining and asserting the content of pictures was in the context of descriptions of pictures. We need to distinguish, then, between the content of a picture and a description of the content (or a description which gives the content). This distinction can apply to intentional states. There is a principle for intentional states which parallels the principle (P) for pictures:

I. For any intentional state *I* there is a sentence which gives the content of *I*.

But just as principle (P) does not imply that pictures have propositional con-tent, so principle (I) does not imply that intentional states have propositional content. One case of an intentional state which is clearly not a relation to a proposition is provided by love. Napoleon's love for Josephine is not a propositional attitude. But none the less there is a sentence which describes the content of Napoleon's love, i.e., describes what he loves and the way in which he represents her, namely, *as Josephine*, and that sentence is 'There is someone who is identical with Josephine'. This is not *who* Napoleon loves, of course: it is a description of whom he loves (the object of his love). It gives or describes the content of his love, without *being* the content of his love.

For perceptual experience, the relevant principle is (E):

E.   For any perceptual experience *E*, there is a sentence which gives the content of *E*.

Principle (E), like (P), is an unexceptionable principle. Of course, it may be difficult in some cases to describe in non-demonstrative ways what the content of the experience is, but we can always do it with a sentence that includes a demonstrative – 'Things are like this', or 'Things look like this', or something of that sort. Again we should not worry that someone would not know what was being said unless they could see what the speaker was seeing; principle (E), like (P), makes no claim about what it is to understand the sentence which gives the content of an experience.

None the less it is clear that (E) cannot be all that is meant by the thesis that perceptual experience is a propositional attitude. As Byrne states the thesis, perceptual experience is a matter of standing in a 'perception relation' to a proposition.[15] Someone sceptical about propositions, and relations to them, can agree with (E) without agreeing with Byrne's thesis. For all that (E) says is that the content of any experience can be given or described by a sentence. As I have shown, this does not imply that the content is propositional.

Nor does principle (E) imply McDowell's thesis that what we 'take in' in experience is also something we can judge, unless all that 'taking in' means is that one can assert a sentence which describes what one experiences. (Certainly, for McDowell, this is necessary for 'taking in', but it is not sufficient.) For whenever we make a judgement and express it in language, we are expressing something which has a sentential form. This is why when we make a *judgement* about how things look, or how they are in the experienced environment, what we *judge* is a proposition: something we judge to be true or the case. Of course; but this is a consequence of making

[15] Byrne, 'Perception and Conceptual Content', in E. Sosa and M. Steup (eds), *Contemporary Debates in Epistemology* (Oxford: Blackwell, 2005), pp. 231–50; cf. D. Stoljar, 'The Argument from Diaphanousness', *Canadian Journal of Philosophy*, Supp. Vol. 30 (2004), pp. 341–90; Thau, *Consciousness and Cognition*.

the judgement, not of having the experience. Or at least, that is all that is implied by principle (E).

It might be said on behalf of McDowell that the essence of his account of perception is that what we take in are *facts*, things' actually being such and such. This is certainly how he originally presented his disjunctive theory of appearance: an appearance of an X is either a *mere* appearance, or it is the fact that there is an X before you making itself manifest.[16] But whatever the merits of that idea, it does not support the claim that what in experience we take in is what we can judge. For we do not judge facts; we judge that something *is* a fact, in other words, that something is true. McDowell clearly thinks that we can withhold judgement on what we 'take in' in experience: that is, we can judge that it is not a fact. The idea that we perceive facts may well be the right description of veridical perception; but it does not fit well with the idea that what we perceive is what we can judge.

The propositional-attitude thesis, then, is more than the anodyne principle (E). It is a claim about the *structure* of experience, and the structure of its content, that is, how experience represents the world, not how those representations can be described. The propositional-attitude theory (in Byrne's formulation) says that experience has a relational structure, as belief does: it is a relation to a proposition. It says that the content of an experience – its objects and the aspects under which they appear – is always that something is such and such, and that the content is true when things are like that, and false when they are not.

One lesson of the comparison with pictures is that just because things are represented in a certain way, this does not mean that the representation is true or false. Another lesson is that although what is represented can be described in a sentence (as principles (P) and (E) say), this is not the *only* way to describe what is represented. What does David's painting represent? 'Napoleon crowning himself' would be an answer; and 'Napoleon crowning himself' refers to an event, not a fact (though of course, if there was such an event, then there is also the fact that there was such an event). So a picture can represent an event; and so can an experience. The content of an experience (what you experience, and how) might be snow falling in the back yard. This is an event (though of course, if there really is such an event, there is also the fact that there is such an event). Shedding the straitjacket of the propositional-attitude theory permits saying that an event, presented in a certain way, can be the content of a perceptual experience.

When we move beyond vision to the other senses, this approach is equally attractive. The objects of the sense of smell, I would claim, are

[16] McDowell, 'Criteria, Defeasibility and Knowledge', *Proceedings of the British Academy*, 68 (1982), pp. 455–79.

smells, represented as such. The object of smell is what you smell. You smell
the cheese by smelling the smell of the cheese, and it is presented to you as
such, not as the cloud of particles which the cheese releases when you
unwrap it. You hear the sound of the coach on the cobbles; you taste the
sourness of the wine; you feel the ferns tickling your leg.... These are what
you hear, what you taste, what you touch. Once we escape from the grip of
the propositional-attitude theory, we can accept these natural idioms at face
value, as giving the obvious phenomenological content of perceptual
experience.

On this alternative picture, what is represented in experience are objects,
properties and events, in what might loosely be called a 'manifold', but
which does not have the structure of judgeable content. We are faced with
the perceptual 'given' in all its complexity, and we make judgements about
how things are or how things look (sound, smell, etc.) on the basis of this. In
attending to some element or elements of what is experienced, we judge that
things look, or are, a certain way. Perceptual judgement (judgement made
on the basis of perception) is normally selective, and the result of attention.
This is, of course, only a starting-point for a description of the relationship
between perceptual experience and judgement. But whatever the exact
account of this relationship, my point in this chapter is that it is a mistake to
read back from the content of a perceptual judgement a hypothesis about
the structure of experience on the basis of which it is made.

V. NON-CONCEPTUAL CONTENT

What is the relationship between the line of thought defended in the
previous section and the recent debate about non-conceptual content? The
idea that the content of perceptual experience is a different kind of thing
from the content of belief and judgement might be thought to be related to
this debate. One might think this, perhaps, because of McDowell's
association of the propositional-attitude thesis with the thesis that experience
has conceptual content. But in fact the question whether the content of
experience is propositional is a different question from whether it is
conceptual, on the correct understanding of the conceptual/non-conceptual
debate, though it is easy to link the two questions. I shall end this chapter
with some comments on this issue.

I agree with Richard Heck that there are two ways of understanding the
thesis that experience has non-conceptual content. One is a view about
the structure or composition of contents themselves, so to speak. On this
view, conceptual contents are contents which are composed of concepts,

where concepts are (for example) entities individuated at the level of sense rather than reference. Non-conceptual contents are therefore contents which are not composed of concepts. I shall follow Heck in calling this way of understanding the idea of non-conceptual content 'the content view'.[17]

On the alternative view, the thesis of non-conceptual content is fundamentally a thesis about types of mental states (so it is not really very well named). The view says that a conceptual state is one to be in which requires the possession of certain concepts, *viz* the concepts which canonically characterize the content of the state. A canonical characterization of a state of mind is one which characterizes it in such a way as to capture the point of view of someone who is in that state. So a state is conceptual when the subject S does have to possess the concepts that are required in order to characterize it from S's own point of view. A non-conceptual state is, then, a state to be in which does not require the possession of such concepts. This view of the non-conceptual is what Heck calls the 'state view'.

In the past I have defended the state view both as a thesis about the way to understand 'non-conceptual' and as a way to understand experience.[18] Given what I have said in this chapter, it follows that I should withdraw my claim in previous work ('The Non-Conceptual Content', §4) that the content of perception can literally be the content of a belief. This is not a consequence of the state view of non-conceptual content, and reflection shows that it is itself of dubious coherence.

My reason for understanding 'non-conceptual' in terms of the state view, as opposed to the content view, is essentially the following. If the content view were the right way of understanding 'non-conceptual', then a Lewis/Stalnaker conception of the contents of beliefs (as sets of worlds or sets of *possibilia*) would be a conception of non-conceptual content, since neither worlds nor individuals are concepts. But a theory which counted beliefs as having non-conceptual contents would miss the point of the original introduction of non-conceptual content, which was to identify a form of mental representation which is in some ways more primitive, more basic than belief.[19] If the purpose of introducing the notion of non-conceptual content is to identify such a form of representation, then we should reject the content view and accept the state view. But what is the relationship between the state view and the view that experience is a propositional attitude?

---

[17] R. Heck, 'Non-Conceptual Content and the "Space of Reasons"', *Philosophical Review*, 109 (2000), pp. 483–523.

[18] See T. Crane, 'The Non-Conceptual Content of Experience', in T. Crane (ed.), *The Contents of Experience* (Cambridge UP, 1992), pp. 136–57, and 'Content, Non-Conceptual', in E.J. Craig (ed.), *Encylopedia of Philosophy* (London: Routledge, 1998).

[19] G. Evans, *The Varieties of Reference* (Oxford UP, 1982).

It seems to me that these views are strictly speaking independent of one another. Suppose you believe that perception has a propositional content. Nothing follows from that about whether you have to possess the concepts which are canonical for the content in question in order to be in that state. That is, nothing follows about whether the state is a conceptual state. Suppose, on the other hand, you believe that perception does not have a propositional content. Likewise, nothing follows about whether in order to be in that state you have to possess the concepts which canonically characterize that content. That is, nothing follows about whether this state is a conceptual state.

Approaching the issue from the other side, suppose you had reason to believe that perceptual states are non-conceptual. Nothing would follow about whether the content in question is propositional or non-propositional. Likewise if you thought that perceptual states are conceptual.

Is this independence an artefact of my commitment to the state view? Suppose for a moment that the content view is the right way of conceiving of the thesis that a state has non-conceptual content. Then if experience had a non-conceptual content as the content view understands this, the question would still be open whether it had a propositional content, so long as propositions can be constituted by things other than concepts. Likewise, if experience had a conceptual content as the content view understands this, then the question would still be open whether it has a propositional content, so long as propositions are not by definition the only kind of content states can have. Of course, I have argued briefly above that the content view is mistaken. But my point here is that even if it were not, then the issues about the propositional content of experience and its non-conceptual content would still be independent.

These issues are conceptually independent, then; strictly speaking, they are not the same issue. But it would be wrong for an investigation into perception to treat them independently. For after all, a theory of perceptual representation needs to take a stand on whether it is conceptual (in the sense of the state view) just as the theory needs to take a stand on whether the representation is propositional. My own view is that perceptual states are non-conceptual as well as non-propositional. By this I mean that in order for S's perceptual state to represent X, S does not have to possess the concepts which canonically characterize X. Although this is a 'state view' conception of non-conceptual content, it does have consequences for what kinds of abstract objects should be employed to model the state best. In particular, the 'canonical characterization' requirement does place a constraint on what kinds of contents perceptual states must have: the contents must be individuated in terms of aspects or *quasi*-Fregean 'modes of presentation'.

Purely 'Russellian' contents will not do. This is because the canonical description of experience describes it in terms of the way it represents the objects of experience to the subject. (Given the way in which I have introduced the idea of content, this is a constraint I willingly accept.[20])

An account of the content of experience which shows how it is both (a) non-propositional, and (b) non-conceptual (in the state view's sense) might look something very similar to Christopher Peacocke's conception of 'scenario content'.[21] Peacocke proposed that we should think of the content of a perceptual experience as given by a set of ways of filling out the space around the perceiver consistent with the correctness of the experience. Such a set he called a 'scenario'. An experience is correct, Peacocke claimed, when the actual space around the perceiver is in this set. On the face of it, Peacocke's theory might seem to be a version of the content view, but properly understood, it is a version of the state view. The reason why a state with scenario content is non-conceptual is because S is not required to possess any of the concepts that canonically characterize the scenario in order for S's state to be canonically characterized in terms of it. Here the distinction made in the previous section, between the content of a state and a description of that content, may be useful: relating the experience to a scenario is a way of giving a description of the content of the state. It is because this abstract object can be used in the description of the experience that the experience might be said to have this object as its content. But it is non-conceptual because of what this attribution requires of its subject, not because of anything to do with the structure of the object itself. Peacocke's proposal is, therefore, congenial to the main conclusion of this chapter.

VI. CONCLUSION

I have argued that experience does not have propositional content. I have not argued for this claim directly, but indirectly, by showing that it does not follow either from the claim that experiences have accuracy-conditions, or from the claim that the content of experience can always be described in a sentence which expresses a proposition. It remains, of course, to give a positive characterization of perceptual content which does not treat it as propositional. But the present chapter has a more general lesson for theories of perception, and if its argument is correct, then this general lesson should

[20] I am especially indebted here to Ian Phillips.

[21] Peacocke, 'Scenarios, Concepts and Perception', in Crane (ed.), *The Contents of Experience*, pp. 105–35. For a discussion of Peacocke, see J.L. Bermúdez, 'The Sources of Self-Consciousness', *Proceedings of the Aristotelian Society*, 102 (2001), pp. 87–107.

form a starting-point for discussions of perception. The general lesson is this: we do not have to choose between a theory which treats perception as propositional (like Byrne, Siegel, Peacocke and Thau) and those which treat it as relational (like Brewer, Campbell and Travis). For there is, it seems, a third way: experience might be representational without being a propositional attitude.[22]

[22] Thanks to an anonymous referee, and to Alex Byrne, Katalin Farkas, James Genone, Hannah Ginsborg, John MacFarlane, Ian Phillips, Murali Ramachandran, Dan Zahavi, and audiences in Berkeley, Copenhagen, Glasgow, Sussex and Zagreb. Special thanks to Susanna Siegel for her detailed and penetrating written comments; I am sure my answers have not satisfied her. I gratefully acknowledge the support of the EU NEST project REFCOM.

6

CONSCIOUS REFERENCE

By Alva Noë

The world shows up to perceptual consciousness in virtue of the deployment of distinct sensorimotor and also conceptual skills. The availability of the world to thought is, in contrast, to be explained in connection with the different sorts of skills put to work in thought. I show that thought and experience are varieties of skilful access to the world. The aim of the paper is to present the outlines of a general theory of access.

It is not controversial that we perceive only what there is. We do so, however, only when a further condition is met: we perceive what there is only when it is there. Perceptual presence, being there for us to perceive, is not merely a matter of existence or proximity. It is a matter of availability. What fixes the scope of what is available, beyond mere existence or proximity, is understanding. By understanding I mean conceptual knowledge, but also more practical forms of knowledge including what I call 'sensorimotor' knowledge. For us to see an object, it must be there for us; and for it to be there for us, we must, in some sense, know it.

I. PRESENCE AS ABSENCE

1. I begin with vision, and with a somewhat paradoxical claim: vision is not confined to the visible. We visually experience what is out of view, what is hidden or occluded.

The metaphor that has guided thought about vision is that of depiction, projection, and the *camera obscura*. I reject this metaphor.[1] We do not see the world in so far as it projects to a point.

Examples of hidden presence are ready to hand.

For example, you look at a tomato. You have a sense of its presence as a whole, even though the back of the tomato (for example) is hidden from

---

[1] I join Gibson, Merleau-Ponty and Wittgenstein in rejecting the pictorial metaphor for seeing. See A. Noë, *Action in Perception* (MIT Press, 2004), ch. 2, for a more developed discussion of this.

view. You do not merely *think* that the tomato has a back, or *judge* or *infer* that it is there. You have a sense, a visual sense, of its presence.

In what does the visual sense of the presence of the hidden parts of a thing consist, if it does not consist in the fact that we see them? This is the problem of perceptual presence – or better, the problem of presence *in* absence. The object shows up for visual consciousness precisely as unseen.

Philosophers may find themselves unconvinced that this is a problem. Some will insist that we do not really experience the visual presence of the occluded parts of the things we see. At best, we think we do. I demur: it is bedrock, phenomenologically speaking, that the tomato looks voluminous, that it looks to have a back. Which is not to say that we take ourselves to *see* the hidden parts of things before us. The thing that needs explaining is not that we mistakenly take ourselves to see something that we do not see. The puzzle is that we take ourselves to have a sense of the presence in perception of something that is manifestly out of view.

Other philosophers have a converse sort of worry; they deny that it is true to say, when you see a thing, that you see only the facing part of it. Such a claim, they urge, distorts the character of visual experience. We see tomatoes, after all, not tomato parts. We live among objects, not sense-data.

A simple observation suffices to meet this worry. To appreciate the phenomenon of perceptual presence, there is no need to insist that we see only the face of the tomato. We need only admit that we cannot see the tomato's back. How can the tomato's back show up in experience when we manifestly do not see it?

Scientists are not nonplussed by this question, and may think they have the answer. We see what the relevant neurophysiology represents. We visually experience the presence of a voluminous furrowed ovoid if that is what the nervous system represents. End of story. But that cannot be the end of our story. It is definitely a relief to know that neurophysiology gets into the act; it would be upsetting if there were no traces in neurophysiology of important differences in our experience. The trouble is this: neurons speak only one language, that of the receptive field. There is no way to say 'present in absence' in the receptive-field idiom. Neurons can modulate the strength of their activity to signify the presence of a feature in their receptive field; they signify the absence of a feature by failing in any way to modulate their activity. What they cannot do, so far as I know, is fire in such a way to signal that a hidden feature is present.

A somewhat more promising line of empirical research is developed by Nakayama *et al.*[2] They turn away from neurophysiology and argue that the

---

[2] K. Nakayama, Z.J. He and K. Shimojo, 'Visual Surface Representation', in D.N. Osherson *et al.* (eds), *Visual Cognition: Invitation to Cognitive Science*, rev. edn (MIT Press, 1990), pp. 1–70.

visual system plays the odds. We see whatever is judged most likely to have produced the image we receive. If you are presented with a cube in such a way that you can only see one of its faces head on, you do not have a visual experience of a cube. The odds are just too low, the system reasons, for your relation to a cube to have projected *that* image. When you take up a low-odds angle on a thing, in this way, the system (the visual system, that is) lets you down. A striking feature of this account is that it lays importance on such facts as that perceivers have a perspective on what they see; that how things look varies as the perspective changes; that how things look carries all sorts of information about what one is looking at. But what a theory such as this does not explain is how the fact that the visual system represents a cube (or *that there is a cube*) causes you to experience the cube in just the way you do, that is, with just the right presence-in-absence structure. It is this fact, a fact that the theory treats as brute, which needs explaining.

2. The problem of perceptual presence is very general. Under this heading we can group the so-called perceptual constancies.

You experience the uniform colour of an unevenly lit wall across the surface of the wall, despite variations in brightness across its surface and despite the fact that variations in brightness make for local differences in colour. The *actual* colour of the wall, like the back of the tomato, is hidden from view, and yet you experience it. It shows up in your experience.

You see the rectangular shape of the window, even though from where you stand the window's profile is not rectangular but trapezoidal. There is a sense, then, in which you *cannot* see the actual rectangularity of the window; it is present, but out of view. You have a visual sense of its presence even though it is hidden from view.

Finally, a different kind of phenomenon is provided by your sense now of the busy detail in the room before you. You have a sense of the presence of lots of people and colour and detail. Of course, it is not the case that you actually see everyone in sharp focus and uniform detail from the centre out to the periphery. We know that is not true. It does not seem as if it is true. You no more directly see all the detail than you see the underlying colour of the wall or the back of the tomato. Yet you have a perceptual sense of its presence.

These features of the world – the tomato's body, the wall's colour, the window's shape, the detailed environment – fall within the scope of your perceptual awareness despite the fact that they are, in a straightforward way, out of view, or concealed, or hidden, or absent. They are present in experience – they are *there* – despite the fact that they are absent in the sense of being *out of view*. They are present precisely *as* absent.

In what does the sense of the presence of these hidden features consist, in what does their visual presence consist, if not in the fact that we actually see them? This *problem of perceptual presence* is a basic and pressing problem for the general theory of perception.

3. What stands in the way of our comprehension of the phenomenon of perceptual presence is our reluctance to admit the deep *amodality* of perceptual consciousness. This amodality is surprising and underappreciated. The back of the tomato, the wall's colour, the detail in the room, the window's shape – these are all hidden from view. They are present *as* absent; they are *amodally present*. We suppose, optimistically, that at least the *face* of the tomato, the wall's *apparent* colours, this or that piece of detail, the window's profile – all these at least are given unproblematically. They are simply *present*.

But stop and look again, for example, at the face of the tomato. You cannot comprehend the whole of it all at once in your visual consciousness. You focus on the colour now, but in doing so you fail to pay attention to the shape, or to the variations in brightness across the surface. You focus now on this portion of the tomato's surface, but only at the price of ignoring the rest of it. You can no more achieve perceptual consciousness of every aspect of the tomato's front side all at once than you can see the tomato from every side at once. Indeed, no perceptual quality is so simple that it can be consumed by consciousness. (The idea of simple *qualia* is a myth.) Experience, in the large, and in the small, is complex and manifold; it is always an encounter with hidden complexity. Experience is fractal in this sense. Perceptual experience extends to the hidden. In a way, for perception, everything is hidden. Nothing is given.

II. PRESENCE AS AVAILABILITY

4. Here is the solution.[3] The fact that we visually experience what is occluded shows that what is visible is not what projects to a point. I propose, instead, that we should think of what is visible as what is *available from a place*. Perceptual presence is availability.

For example, my sense of the presence of the detail in the room before me consists not in the fact that I represent it all in my consciousness in the way a picture might – all the detail spread out at once in sharp focus and

---

[3] I develop these ideas in other work, although not quite in the terms I use here. See esp. my *Action in Perception*, and J.K. O'Regan and A. Noë, 'A Sensorimotor Account of Vision and Visual Consciousness', *Behavioural and Brain Sciences*, 24 (2001), pp. 883–975.

high resolution. It does not even seem as if the detail is present in my mind in that way. It seems as if the detail is present in the world, out there, before me and around me. The detail shows up not as 'represented in my mind', but as available to me. It shows up as present – this is crucial – in that I understand, implicitly, practically, that by the merest movement of my eyes and head I can secure access to an element that now is obscured on the periphery of the visual field. It *now* shows up as present, but out of view, in so far as I understand that I am now related to it by familiar patterns of motor-sensory dependence. It is my basic understanding of the way my movements produce sensory change given my situation that makes it the case, now, even before I have moved an inch, that elements outside focus and attention can be perceptually present.

Likewise, my sense of the visual presence of the tomato's back – in contrast, say, with that of the tomato's *insides* – consists in practical understanding that simple movements of my head and body in relation to the tomato would bring the reverse side into view. It is visually present to me now; but because I understand that, I now have a distinctively *visual* style of access to it. The basis of this access is my mastery of the ways in which my movements produce sensory change.

The proposal, then, is this: perceptual consciousness is a special style of access to the world. But *access* is not something bare, brute or found. The ground of access is our possession of knowledge, understanding and skills. Without understanding, there is no access and so no perception. My emphasis here is on a special kind of understanding which distinctively underwrites our *perceptual* access to objects and properties, namely, sensorimotor understanding. We can see what there is when it is there, and what makes it the case that it is there is the fact that we comprehend its sensorimotor significance. Sensorimotor understanding brings the world into focus for perceptual consciousness.

A surprising consequence of the idea that we need understanding to perceive is that it is impossible to perceive real novelty. Schubert hinted at this when he explained why it is not difficult to write great songs. You simply need to come up with new melodies that sound as if they are familiar. In a way this is a comment about styles; if a work does not make sense against a background of styles, then at best it can only be 'ahead of its time'. But the point is deeper and more general. To perceive something, you must understand it, and to understand it you must, in a way, already know it, you must have already made its acquaintance. There are no novel experiences. The conditions of novelty are, in effect, the conditions of invisibility. To experience something, you must comprehend it by the familiarizing work of the understanding. You must master it. Domesticate it. Know it.

I said before that nothing is given. We might say: if anything is given, everything is. If the front of the tomato is given, then so is the back. The nature of our access to the front is of a kind with that of our access to the back. The thing (front and back) is there for us, present, in reach. Crucially, to be conscious of something is not to depict it, or to represent it. To perceive something is not to consume it, just as it is not a matter of constructing, within our brains or minds, a model or picture or representation of the world without. There is no need. The world is right there, and it suffices. At most we can meet the world. Stand with it, up against it. The tomato is right there, front and back, for us to explore.

5. Once we give up the idea that *real seeing* is having an object or a detailed scene in all its aspects in focal attention, all at once, we can appreciate more fully what is wrong with the philosopher's objection raised at the outset about sense-data. The worry was that we live among objects, not sense-data, and that it is therefore a mistake to think that when we are perceptually engaged with things, we are also aware of how things look from a particular vantage point. In this spirit, Sean Kelly, for example, baulks at the claim that you are aware of the trapezoidal perspectival shape when you see the rectangular window from here.[4] He allows that you can learn to make yourself see the perspectival shapes of things, but he insists that doing so requires detachment and taking up 'the painterly attitude'. Anyway, the fact that we can make the effort to direct our attention to the perspectival shape gives us no reason to think that we are aware of the perspectival shape (how the object looks with respect to shape) *whenever* we see its shape. It is no easier to see the shape and the perspectival shape at once than it is to see the duck in the famous ambiguous duck–rabbit and see the rabbit at the same time. To do that is to commit a nearly impossible feat of divided attention.

Kelly is right that the duck and the rabbit exclude each other; how best to understand this phenomenon is worth careful consideration. It is beside the point here, however. Seeing the window's shape, and how it looks with respect to shape from here, is not like seeing the duck and the rabbit at once; it is like seeing the duck and the lines on paper at once. It is easy to do this. But what makes it easy is not that it is a simpler attentional task. What makes it easy is that it is not an attentional task at all. Seeing the duck, and the lines on paper, is not a matter of dividing attention between them; it is simply a matter of having skilful access to them both at once. The world shows up for perceptual consciousness in so far as it is available in the distinctively perceptual way, i.e., thanks to the perceiver's

---

[4] S.D. Kelly, 'Content and Constancy', *Philosophy and Phenomenological Research*, 76 (2008), pp. 682–90.

knowingly and skilfully standing in the right sort of sensorimotor relation to things. Awareness extends to that to which we have access, and does not require divided attention. We see the duck, and the lines, the window's shape, and its apparent shape, just as we see the object *and* its shape, size, colour, etc.

6. In fact, things are a bit more complicated. It is not enough for perceptual presence that movements of the body can bring now hidden elements into view. After all, movements of the body will bring the hallway outside this room into view, but we would not want to say without further ado that the hallway is visually present. Perceptual presence requires a more complicated two-way relation to the perceptual object. Perceptual consciousness is *transactional*, as Putnam has put it.[5] It must not only be the case that the perceiver's movements produce changes in the character of the standing motor-sensory relation; it must also be the case that changes in the object itself would manifestly perturb the character of the standing relation that the perceiver has to the object.

To put things more generally: an object or quality is perceptually present (i.e., it is an object of perceptual consciousness) when the perceiver understands, in a practical, bodily way, that there obtains a physical, motor-sensory relation between the perceiver and the object or quality, satisfying two conditions:

(i) Movement-dependence: movements of the body manifestly control the character of the relation to the object or quality
(ii) Object-dependence: movements or other changes in the object manifestly control the character of the relation to the object or quality.

In short, an object or quality is present in perceptual experience when it is perceptually available. An object is perceptually available when our motor-sensory relation to the objects satisfies movement- and object-dependence. Intuitively, we are perceptually in touch with an object when our relation to the object is highly sensitive to how things are with the object and to the way what we do changes our relation to the object.

I refer to this account of perceptual consciousness as actionism.[6] This name serves to highlight the importance of sensorimotor understanding for perceptual consciousness.

---

[5] H. Putnam, *The Threefold Cord* (Columbia UP, 1999).

[6] In other work I have spoken of the enactive or sensorimotor approach; in work with Hurley, we speak of the dynamic sensorimotor approach, e.g., S.L. Hurley and A. Noë, 'Neural Plasticity and Consciousness', *Biology and Philosophy*, 18 (2003), pp. 131–68.

7. One upshot of the actionism I am presenting here is that it enables us to appreciate the insights, but also the limitations, of the traditional causal theory of perception.

'The thought of my perception as a *perception* of a continuously and independently existing thing implicitly contains the thought that if the thing had not been there, I should not even have seemed to perceive it.' This is how P.F. Strawson states the basic idea of the causal theory.[7] If I see that things are thus and so, then my visual experience depends, in a fine-grained counterfactual-supporting way, on things being thus and so. I am seeing how things are if things would have looked otherwise had they been significantly different. The challenge faced by the causal theory has been that of placing constraints on the forms which can be taken by this dependence of experience on how things are, so as to rule out deviant forms of so-called veridical hallucination while admitting the possibility of seeing by means of unnatural prostheses. Philosophers have despaired of providing an analysis of the perception relation.

Until now, that is. Perceptual experience has two dimensions of content: it registers not only how things are, but also the perceiver's relation to how things are. If we perceive, then how things look must depend (in a suitably fine-grained counterfactual-supporting way) not only on how things are, but on one's relation to how things are. For this reason, when one is perceptually conscious of a state of affairs, changes in how things look must track both how things are and what one does. As I have argued elsewhere,[8] the hard cases of veridical hallucination that have been the cause of so much concern to Grice, Strawson, Lewis, Sanford and others[9] are one and all cases where there has been a marked failure of appropriate dependence of perspectival aspects of perceptual content on the perceiver's actual and possible movements. I know of no counter-examples to this reformulation of the causal theory.

8. To sum up: I propose that perceptual consciousness requires the joint operation of sensitivity to the object and also what I am calling *sensorimotor understanding*. I think of sensorimotor understanding as a species of understanding in general, and so I think of the ways in which perception depends

---

[7] P.F. Strawson, 'Perception and its Objects', in G.F. MacDonald, *Perception and Identity* (Cornell UP, 1979), pp. 41–60, at p. 51.

[8] See *Action in Perception*, ch. 5, and also Noë, 'Perception and Causation', *Analysis*, 63 (2003), pp. 93–100.

[9] See Strawson, 'Perception and its Objects'; H.P. Grice, 'The Causal Theory of Perception', *Proceedings of the Aristotelian Society*, Supp. Vol. 35 (1961), pp. 121–52; D.K. Lewis, 'Veridical Hallucination and Prosthetic Vision', *Australasian Journal of Philosophy*, 58 (1980), pp. 239–49.

on the operation of sensorimotor understanding as exemplifying the more general phenomenon, invoked at the outset, that understanding discloses the world to us. If you baulk at using the term 'understanding' to refer to a form of practical knowledge which is independent of language-use and which is shared by humans and non-humans, then it can be called something else. Perhaps we could follow Hilary Putnam's example and call it proto-understanding.[10] Call it what you will, sensorimotor skill plays (*inter alia*) the same function as conceptual understanding can play in mature humans, that of bringing the world into focus and enabling us to lock onto it (in both perception and thought).

III. INTENTIONALITY AS A RELATION

9. Perceptual consciousness is a species of intentional directedness. States or acts of consciousness are intentional in so far as they pertain to or are directed towards objects. There is a tension in traditional thought about intentional directedness. On the one hand, intentional directedness purports to be a relation to the intentional object. When I think of my friend Dominic in Berlin, my thoughts pertain to him, and not, say, to an idea of him, or an image of him. Likewise, when I see a tomato, or a crowded room, it is the tomato, or the room, of which I am visually aware. On the other hand, intentional directedness purports to allow for the non-actuality of the intentional object. The tension is very well known: if one can be intentionally directed to a non-actual entity, then, it seems, intentional directedness cannot be a fully fledged relation between a thinker/perceiver and a thing.

In the case of perception, at least, I am inclined to agree with those who hold that we should resolve the tension in favour of relationality (I am thinking of so-called disjunctivists, e.g., Michael Martin, John Campbell and John McDowell). That is, perceptual consciousness is a genuine form of intentional directedness, even though it is a relation that could not obtain without the intentional object.

Actionism aims to do justice to the relational conception of experience (as John Campbell has named it). Perceptual consciousness is access or availability. Crucially, existence is a condition of availability or access. We do not have access to what is non-existent. However, mere existence is not alone sufficient for perceptual consciousness. For consciousness, one needs skills *of* access or, as I think of them, understanding.

[10] See Putnam, *Renewing Philosophy* (Harvard UP, 1995), p. 29, for use of the phrase 'proto-concepts'.

Both the object itself, then, and the understanding or skills of access, play an essential role in perception. When there is no object, there is, at best, something misleadingly like perceptual consciousness going on. Where there is an object, but no understanding, there is nothing that rises even to the level of being misleadingly like perceptual consciousness; there is only blindness.

IV. EXTENDED PERCEPTION

10. Actionism has a far-reaching upshot: it allows us to understand what we can call the continuity of thought and experience. Perception and thought are both ways of achieving access to things. Where they differ is in the methods or skills of access that they each deploy. We can get at this issue by considering a problem that actionism might seem to face. The theory seems to have the embarrassing consequence that we are perceptually conscious of everything. After all, your relation to any existing spatiotemporally located thing is such that were you to make appropriate movements, you would bring it into view, and were it to make appropriate movements, it would perturb your standing dynamic relation to it.

This unwanted consequence is easily avoided, however. Movement- and object-dependence are conditions whose satisfaction can be measured. My relation to the tomato in front of me is *highly* movement-dependent: even the slightest flicker or blink of my eye affects my sensory relation to the tomato. My relation to the back of the tomato is slightly lower on the movement-dependence scale, i.e., I need to move *more* to change my relation to the back of the tomato. My relation to distant objects is only minimally movement-dependent. Object-dependence too admits of measurement. The slightest movements of the tomato on the table in front of me will modulate my relation to the tomato. Only quite enormous changes in the hallway outside this room will make a visual difference to me; and only an unthinkably large event near the Eiffel Tower would be able to capture my visual attention.

From the actionist standpoint there is no sharp line to be drawn between that which is and that which is not perceptually present. The front of the tomato is maximally present; the back a little less so; the hallway even less so. To these gradations in degree of perceptual presence there correspond gradations in the degree to which the motor-sensory relation we bear to the object, quality, or situation, is movement- and object-dependent. In general, an object shows up for distinctively perceptual consciousness when the basis of our access to the object is a relation that scores high on scales of both movement- and object-dependence.

11. From the standpoint of actionism, we are perceptually conscious, at least to some degree, of much more than has traditionally been supposed. This is a feature of the theory, not a bug; it flows from the theory's basic positive claim that presence is availability. Perceptual presence is *one kind* of availability; it is *one kind* of presence to mind. An object is perceptually present when our access to it depends on the exercise of *sensorimotor* skills. Of course, objects can show up for consciousness without being perceived. For example, when I think of Aristotle, Aristotle is present to my mind. But he is not perceptually present. He is *thought* present. That is, he is present thanks to a different battery of skills of access, e.g., descriptive, conceptual, linguistic skills.

Importantly, there are intermediate cases. For example, when I speak of my conscious thoughts of my friend Dominic in Berlin, I do not mean the thought *that* Dominic is in Berlin. I mean something else. When I think of Dominic in this way, he shows up for me in my thinking; he has a certain presence; he is present to mind. Not that he *is* present. He is in Berlin. Nor does it seem to me as if he is somehow here. He is present to my thoughts, now, but not as *here*; my sense of his presence, such as it is, is a sense of his presence as far away, *there*, in Berlin. Sartre calls this kind of intentional act of conscious thought about someone 'imaging consciousness'.[11]

When I think about Dominic in this way, he is present in my conscious thoughts, but he is present as absent. It is just this presence in absence that I have argued is a hallmark of *perceptual* consciousness. Phenomenologically, it certainly seems reasonable to say that an absent friend can show up in one's thoughts in very much the same way that the occluded portions of things we see can show up in perceptual consciousness. Dominic's presence-in-absence is different from that of the objects around me; but the difference, I suggest, is one of degree, not of kind. Of course the actionism I have presented has the resources to explain this: Dominic scores very low on the movement- and object-dependence scales, but the score is not zero.

What I am proposing is that thought is sometimes a kind of extended perception. Thought can be extended perception when one deploys sensori-motor skills (presumably in conjunction with other sorts of skills and know-ledge) to achieve access to something or someone very remote. For example, Dominic shows up for me precisely as standing in a *quasi*-perceptual relation to me, namely, the relation of being *too far away to be seen*.

If this analysis is right, then the actual intentional object of my conscious thinking, no less than the cognitive and sensorimotor skills that enable access

[11] J.-P. Sartre, *The Imaginary* (London: Routledge, 1940/2004), e.g., p. 11.

to it, is an essential constituent of my intentional act. In the way I am now thinking of Dominic, it would not be possible to think of something non-actual. Conscious reference to Dominic is a Dominic-involving act of consciousness rather like a perceptual act. If this is right, then it is not a representational state. In particular, it is not a state in which I represent Dominic *as in Berlin*. Dominic's being in Berlin is a condition of my cognitive/sensorimotor access to him, not something I predicate of him.

12. What takes shape, then, is the idea that *conscious reference* is, in general, an achievement of the understanding. To see something – that is, for something to show up for one in conscious visual experience – or to refer in thought to something – that is, for it to show up in one's conscious thoughts – is a matter of skilful access to the thing.

To repeat, what I am suggesting is that some forms of intentionality or conscious reference are a relation between a skilful person and a really existing thing. Where there is no really existing thing there can be no access or genuine availability; at most there can be the illusion of it. But the mere existence of the intentional object is not sufficient to guarantee that our thought or experience can involve it: for thought or experience to involve the object, the perceiver must be comprehending. He must know how to close the deal, how to reach out and make contact with the intended object.

13. Suppose over time I have lost track of Dominic. It has been years since we have been in touch; I do not know whether he is in Berlin; I do not know whether he is alive or dead. Surely I can still direct my thoughts to him, even in circumstances like this?[12] Yes, of course. But this is a very different way of having someone in mind; it is a different kind of thought, with a different kind of content. It is like the difference between entering a dark room when you know where the light switch is, and entering a dark room when you have no idea where the light switch is. In both cases you may have some good reason to think that there is a light switch. But the fact that you need to search in the one case, but not the other, changes your relation to the room, and the light. So it is with my long lost friend. The manner of his presence to mind is fixed by the extent to which I have or fail to have access to him, and also by the kind of skills of access in virtue of which I manage to have access to him.

I do not claim that *all* thought is extended perception. My claim is that all thought is directed to its object thanks to the thinker's skilful access to the object. In some cases, the skills on the basis of which one has access will be

---

[12] Thanks to Alex Byrne for pressing the challenge to which I respond in this passage.

perceptual skills; in other cases, they will be skills of a different sort (e.g., analytic conceptual skills).

14. What enables objects and their properties to show up for us in experience is the fact that they exist and that we have access to them. A theory of direct perception requires a theory of access.[13] This is what I have been offering here, the sketch of a general theory of access.[14]

[13] J.J. Gibson appreciated this: see *The Ecological Approach to Visual Perception* (Hillsdale: Earlbaum, 1986). He liked to talk of picking up affordances of things. This is usually understood in a *quasi*-information-theoretic way. I think he actually might have had something simpler in mind. We *pick up* affordances as we might pick up pebbles on the beach. Perceiving, on this view, is not representing the world in the mind but exploring the world and achieving hands-on contact with it. This is something we can do thanks to our repertoire of skills.

[14] I am grateful to Alex Byrne, James Conant, Hubert Dreyfus, James Genone, Steven Gross, Susan Hurley, John McDowell, James Stazicker, Hilary Putnam and Dan Zahavi for helpful and challenging comments on an earlier draft.

7

WHAT ARE THE CONTENTS OF EXPERIENCES?

By Adam Pautz

I address three interrelated issues concerning the contents of experiences. First, I address the preliminary issue of what it means to say that experiences have contents. Then I address the issue of why we should believe that experiences have contents. Finally, I address the issue of what the contents of experiences are.

I shall address three interrelated issues concerning the contents of experiences. In §I I shall outline the preliminary issue of what it means to say that experiences have contents. In §II I shall sketch an argument for believing that experiences have contents. As a bonus, the argument for believing that experiences have contents naturally suggests a method for determining what the contents of experiences are. In §III I shall develop this method and apply it to some debates over what the contents of experiences are, including the debate over whether kind properties such as *being a pine tree* enter into the contents of our experiences.

I. WHAT DOES IT MEAN TO SAY THAT EXPERIENCES HAVE CONTENTS?

Past philosophers of perception did not credit experiences themselves with intentional contents, only the beliefs which experiences are apt to cause. In contrast, contemporary philosophers of perception freely credit experiences with intentional contents. Indeed, the notion that experiences have contents figures in some central debates in the philosophy of perception. One is the debate over whether the phenomenal characters of experiences supervene on what contents they have.[1] Another is the debate over what the contents of experience are. Do they, for instance, include singular contents about particular objects? Do they include contents involving kind properties

---

[1] See M. Tye, *Consciousness, Color and Content* (MIT Press, 2000).

such as *being a pine tree*, as well as colour and shape properties?[2] More recently, there has been a debate over whether experiences have contents at all.[3]

These debates are framed in terms of the expression *experience x has content y*. This is a technical expression, not part of ordinary language. Therefore no one can understand these debates until this expression is explained. It may be said that we know what contents are. They are abstract objects which are true or false. But what does it mean to say that a particular experience *has* a particular content? Those involved in the debates cannot answer this question in terms of their favourite naturalistic theories of intentionality. For it is supposed that anyone can understand the expression *experience x has content y* and the debates in which it figures without accepting any particular naturalistic theory.

There are two standard conceptions of the contents of experiences. I call them the *appears-looks conception* and the *accuracy conception*. One interesting feature of these conceptions is that according to them, the claim that experiences have contents is neutral on the issue of whether the phenomenal character of experience is to be explained in terms of content. In other words, it does not entail *intentionalism* about experience. This is reflected in the fact that *qualia* theorists and other philosophers who accept diverse theories of phenomenal character agree that experiences have contents and indeed engage in debates about what they are.[4]

In my view, we should be pluralists about conceptions of 'the contents of experiences'.[5] The appears-looks and the accuracy conceptions provide senses in which experiences can be said to have intentional contents. But in this section I shall argue that we should not employ these theory-neutral conceptions when examining debates about the contents of experiences, since they trivialize those debates. Instead, we should employ a much more theory-laden conception of what it means to say that experiences have contents. On this alternative conception, which I call the *identity conception*, the claim that experiences *have* contents is equated with a version of intentionalism according to which they are *identical with* relations to contents, somewhat as beliefs and desires are identical with relations to contents. The claim, then, concerns the structure or real definition of experiences.

---

[2] See S. Siegel, 'Which Properties are Represented in Perception?', in T.S. Gendler and J. Hawthorne (eds), *Perceptual Experience* (Oxford UP, 2006), pp. 481–503.

[3] C. Travis, 'The Silence of the Senses', *Mind*, 113 (2004), pp. 57–94.

[4] T. Burge, 'Qualia and Intentional Content: Reply to Block', in M. Hahn and B. Ramberg (eds), *Reflections and Replies: Essays on the Philosophy of Tyler Burge* (MIT Press, 2003), pp. 405–17.

[5] D. Chalmers, 'Perception and the Fall from Eden', in Gendler and Hawthorne (eds), *Perceptual Experience*, pp. 49–125, at p. 51.

First, the *appears-looks conception*. For instance, before developing an argument for the thesis that phenomenal character supervenes on content
(differences in phenomenal character entail differences in content), Byrne
explains what it means to say that a particular experience has a particular
content by saying that 'the content of a perceptual experience specifies the
way the world appears or seems to the subject'.[6] (Indeed, this conception is
crucial to the second premise of Byrne's argument, since this premise states
that differences in phenomenal character entail differences in *how things seem*,
which unproblematically entail differences in content only if this conception
is adopted.) Likewise, Byrne and Hilbert say that 'the proposition that *p* is
part of the content of a subject's visual experience if and only if it visually
appears to the subject that *p*'.[7] Occasionally, other philosophers say that an
experience represents that something is F if and only if it *presents* something
as having property F. Since the technical term *presents* is presumably
explainable in terms of *appears* or *looks* (otherwise it is unclear what it means),
these philosophers too are ultimately explaining the notion of the content of
an experience in terms of *appears* or *looks*. These remarks could be taken as
rough glosses or heuristics, rather than as definitions. But then one would
still not understand the technical expression *experience x has content y*, and
hence debates in which this expression figures would not be understandable.
So I shall take these remarks as giving the meaning of this expression;
'experience *e* has the proposition *p* as a content' means that in having *e* it
appears to the subject that *p*. (For visual experiences, one might use 'looks as
if *p*'.) I shall say that *p* is an *appears-looks content* of *e* iff *p* is a content of *e*
as defined by the appears-looks conception. Those who adopt the appears-
looks conception might stipulate that an experience is *accurate* with respect
to a situation if and only if its appears-looks contents are true with respect to
that situation. The appears-looks conception is obviously theory-neutral.

But, equally obviously, the appears-looks conception trivializes debates
concerning the contents of experiences. First, it trivializes the debate over
whether experiences have contents. Given its stipulative definition of what it
means to claim that 'experiences have representational contents', this claim
is equated with the triviality that experiential episodes are associated with
true appears-looks reports. This must be accepted by *qualia* theorists. It must
also be accepted by disjunctivists, such as Brewer, who hold that the phenomenal character of a non-hallucinatory experience is to be given simply by
citing the object of experience,[8] and that hallucination is to be given some

---

[6] A. Byrne, 'Intentionalism Defended', *Philosophical Review*, 110 (2001), pp. 199–240, at p. 201.
[7] A. Byrne and D. Hilbert, 'Color Realism and Color Science', *Behavioural and Brain Sciences*,
26 (2003), pp. 3–21, at p. 5.
[8] B. Brewer, 'Perception and Content', *European Journal of Philosophy*, 14 (2006), pp. 165–81.

different explanation. When Brewer and others deny that experience is to be explained in terms of content, they must have some more theory-laden conception in mind. Secondly, if we adopt the appears-looks conception and then examine the thesis that phenomenal character supervenes on content, we can easily obtain a negative answer prior to examining arguments in its favour. When small children and animals lacking the capacity for conceptual thought have various experiences, it does not seem to them (visually or otherwise) that the world is any way at all. So, on the appears-looks conception, their experiences lack intentional contents. In cases of change blindness (in which a large but unnoticed change in the viewed scene occurs) there is arguably a change in phenomenal character but no change in the truth-values of reports of the form 'It appears that p' or 'It looks as if p'. Thirdly, the appears-looks conception trivializes the debate over what the contents of visual experiences are because it trivially entails that experiences have both singular contents and contents involving kind properties. For instance, in a perfectly ordinary sense, there might appear to you to be a tree there with the property of being a pine tree. So, on this conception, the claim that experiences have contents involving kind properties is trivially true. If these debates are to be both intelligible and non-trivial, the technical expression 'experience e has content p' must be given meaning in some other way.

A different version of the appears-looks conception might avoid triviality. It is plausible that 'it appears to S that p' and 'it looks to S as if p', of which I have made use so far, always mean something doxastic. One view is that they always mean that S's experience gives him an inclination to believe p. (This does not entail that he is inclined to believe p *simpliciter*, given his total evidence.) But some claim that looks-reports of the different form 'o looks F to S' have a special phenomenal sense.[9] So 'e has as a content the proposition that o is F' might be stipulatively defined to mean that in experience e the object o looks F to the subject of e.

But this too trivializes debates about the contents of experiences. On this conception, it is trivially true that non-hallucinatory experiences have contents; it is trivially false that phenomenal character supervenes on content, because on this conception hallucinations lack contents (since 'o looks F to S' is true only if S sees o); and it is trivially false that *being a pine tree* enters into the content of any experience, because 'o looks pine tree to S' is ungrammatical. Indeed, on *any* version of the appears-looks conception, these debates will be uninteresting, because they will amount to debates about the truth-values of appears-looks reports in ordinary English.

[9] F. Jackson, *Perception: a Representative Theory* (Cambridge UP, 1977).

Next, the *accuracy conception* of the contents of experiences. It would be natural to start with the claim that experiences have contents, and then define an accurate experience as one with a true content. In contrast, the accuracy conception starts with the notion that experiences are accurate or inaccurate, and then defines the contents of experience in terms of this notion. For instance, Siegel writes that 'the content of an experience is given by the conditions under which it is accurate', so that if an 'experience is accurate only if there is something fish-shaped and orange at location L ... [then] the contents of the experience include *that there is something fish-shaped and orange at location L'*.[10] Likewise, Byrne and Hilbert write that if 'your experience is veridical only if something is green and square at *L*', then 'your experience may be said to *represent* that there is something green and square at *L*'.[11]

There are at least two ways of elaborating the accuracy conception. First, it might be stipulated that 'experience *e* has the proposition *p* as a content' means that, necessarily, if *e* is accurate, then *p* is true. In other words, in every possible world in which *e* is accurate, *p* is true. But this is problematic, since *e* is a particular token-experience not present in different possible worlds. So a better formulation might be this: in every possible world in which someone has an accurate *phenomenal duplicate* of *e*, *p* is true.

The second way of elaborating the accuracy conception assumes that as with sentences, we can evaluate particular token experiences for accuracy with respect to worlds in which neither they nor duplicates of them occur, as well as worlds in which they do occur. These will be worlds that are centred on a particular location (centred worlds), since we always experience things 'from here'. Given this assumption, one might stipulate that 'experience *e* has the centred proposition *p* as a content' means that *p* is true at every centred world at which *e* is accurate. So, for instance, the centred proposition *that there is a red and round thing before me* might be a content of an experience. I shall say that *p* is an *accuracy content* of *e* iff *p* is a content of *e* as defined by the accuracy conception.

The accuracy conception entails that every necessary proposition is a content of every experience. To avoid this result, the theory might be refined as follows: 'experience *e* has proposition *p* as a content' means that *p* is an accuracy content of *e* and *p* reflects the phenomenal character of *e*.[12] This would require explaining what it is for a proposition to reflect the phenomenal character of an experience. Since this definition explains the content

---

[10] S. Siegel, 'Subject and Object in Visual Experience', *Philosophical Review*, 115 (2006), pp. 355–88, at p. 361.

[11] A. Byrne and D. Hilbert, 'Colors and Reflectances', in A. Byrne and D. Hilbert (eds), *Readings on Color*, Vol. 1: *The Philosophy of Color* (MIT Press, 1997), pp. 263–88, at p. 263.

[12] Siegel, 'Subject and Object in Visual Experience', p. 362, fn. 4.

of experience in terms of phenomenal character, it would rule out reductive versions of intentionalism which attempt to explain phenomenal character in terms of content. But the problems for the accuracy conception which I shall raise below apply even if this problem can be overcome.

Before I develop these problems, I need to clarify the accuracy conception further. The accuracy conception is based on the initial claim that experiences may be classified as accurate or inaccurate. But 'is an accurate experience' and 'is an inaccurate experience' are technical expressions not employed in ordinary language. Of course, the accuracy conception cannot define these notions in terms of the content of experience, because it defines the content of experience in terms of these notions. Those who employ the accuracy conception typically explain the notions in one of two alternative ways.

First, some philosophers attempt to give meaning to 'is an accurate experience' and 'is an inaccurate experience' by giving examples.[13] I shall call this the *way of example*. So, for instance, some say that completely successful experiences (in which the actual properties of objects are perceived) are examples of accurate experiences, while illusory and hallucinatory experiences are examples of inaccurate experiences. This would not distinguish the philosopher's concept of an *accurate experience* from the more ordinary concept of a *successful experience*, an experience in which objects and their properties are perceived. But most philosophers who speak of accuracy in relation to experiences mean something different from success. To pin down what he means by 'is accurate', the philosopher might provide examples of *accurate hallucinations*. Suppose, for instance, a wizard causes S to have hallucinations at random, and by chance at one point the hallucinatory scene exactly matches the actual scene before S. The philosopher might explain that as he uses 'accurate', this hallucination is accurate. It is difficult to deny that by means of such examples 'is an accurate experience' could acquire meaning. I shall use *accurate$_e$* to indicate this meaning. So on one version of the accuracy conception, the accuracy$_e$ conception, 'experience e has proposition p as a content' means p is true in every case in which someone has an accurate$_e$ phenomenal duplicate of e.

If the accuracy$_e$ conception is to be theory-neutral, there is bound to be some indeterminacy concerning which experiences are accurate$_e$, and hence indeterminacy concerning what the contents of experiences are. For instance, there is nothing in how the concept of accuracy$_e$ was introduced to determine whether the experience of a fake pine tree, a tilted penny or the Müller–Lyer diagram are accurate$_e$ or inaccurate$_e$. If experiences have contents in the sense provided by the identity conception, to be introduced

[13] D. Chalmers, 'Perception and the Fall from Eden', p. 50.

below, this indeterminacy can be explained. On the identity conception, experiences have 'phenomenal contents' which are privileged in the sense that they constitute phenomenal character. But content pluralism implies that they can be associated with various appears-looks contents as well. When it is introduced with examples, the predicate 'is an accurate experience' is indeterminate, because the examples do not determine whether it picks out the truth of phenomenal contents or the truth of appears-looks contents. Of course, as part of the accuracy conception of the content of an experience it might be stipulated that by an 'accurate experience' is meant an experience with a true phenomenal content. But then the accuracy conception would no longer be theory-neutral, because it would presuppose the intentionalist thesis that experience is constituted by intentional content. Further, the accuracy conception would now be otiose, because the identity conception would already provide an understanding of what it means to say that a particular experience has a particular content.

There is a second way in which the accuracy conception might explain accuracy, the *way of definition*. For instance, Siegel says (p. 363) that 'an experience is accurate if its object has the properties it looks to have and is inaccurate if not'. I shall stipulate that an experience is accurate$_d$ if and only if its object has the property it looks to have. This yields the accuracy$_d$ conception: 'experience e has proposition p as a content' means p is true in every case in which someone has an accurate$_d$ phenomenal duplicate of e. It will emerge that the accuracy$_e$ conception and the accuracy$_d$ conception yield different verdicts in some cases.

In either version, the accuracy conception, like the appears-looks conception, is theory-neutral. But it trivializes the three central debates concerning the contents of experiences.

First, the accuracy conception trivializes the debate over whether experiences have contents. Some who adopt the accuracy conception say that the claim that experiences have contents requires substantive argument, but this is not so. On this conception, the claim that experiences have contents follows from the claim that they can be classified as accurate or inaccurate with respect to various scenarios in the thin senses provided by the way of example or the way of definition. For on the accuracy conception, the claim that they have contents or accuracy-conditions is reached by definition. But who could deny that experiences can be classified as accurate or inaccurate in these thin senses?

Indeed, even disjunctivists, who often say that they are opposed to the notion that experiences have contents, must recognize that they have contents in the senses specified by the different versions of the accuracy conception. For instance, must they not recognize that experiences may be classified as accurate$_e$ or inaccurate$_e$? After all, when these concepts are introduced to us, we catch on fairly quickly. We can imagine a hypothetical language in which ordinary people use the predicates 'is an accurate experience' and 'is an inaccurate experience', mostly agreeing in how to classify cases. An error theory of such talk would be implausible. Indeed, the disjunctivist can specify a property which is a candidate for what philosophers mean when they use 'is an accurate experience': an experience e is counted 'accurate' iff (i) e is indistinguishable by reflection from seeing the instantiation of a complex profile of sensible properties P by some objects, and (ii) before the subject of e there are in fact objects which have P. The disjunctivist must of course admit that experiences can be accurate$_d$ or inaccurate$_d$. For this is merely to say that in some cases things have the properties they look to have, but in other cases this is not so. Anyone who accepts that experiences are accurate or inaccurate, in one of these thin senses, must admit that in the weak sense specified by the accuracy conception, experiences may be associated with contents or accuracy-conditions. For instance, on one version of the accuracy conception, p is a content of an experience e iff in every world in which someone has an accurate phenomenal duplicate of e, p is true. (The use of phenomenal duplication here should be acceptable to disjunctivists as well as common factor theorists; disjunctivists and common factor theorists simply provide a different analysis of it.) Likewise, sense-datum theorists, *qualia* theorists and everyone else must accept that experiences have contents in the sense provided by the accuracy conception, because on all of these theories experiences can be assessed for accuracy$_e$ or accuracy$_d$ with respect to possible scenarios.

Why then do some disjunctivists deny that experience is the sort of thing that can be inaccurate and that it has contents? They must have in mind more theory-laden conceptions of what these things mean. On one interpretation, when Travis and Brewer deny that experiences can be accurate or inaccurate (as they put it, 'in error'), they have in mind a conception of accuracy and inaccuracy which requires that experiences, like beliefs, are mental states with a *mind to world* direction of fit. (At the end of §II I shall argue that the issue of whether experiences can be in error in this thick sense is orthogonal to the issue of whether experience is to be explained in terms of content.) This is not a requirement of the thinner concepts of accuracy$_e$ and of accuracy$_d$. When Brewer in particular denies that experiences have contents, he may have in mind something like the theory-laden identity conception, to be developed below, rather than the theory-neutral accuracy conception or the appears-looks conception. For he agrees that experiences have contents; what he denies (p. 179) is that contents give experiences their basic natures. What he denies is that the 'subjective character' of perceptual experience is to be given by its representational content.

Secondly, the accuracy conception makes it trivially false that phenomenal character supervenes on content. If one looks at a square pattern of equidistant dots, one can first have an experience e_1 in which the fact that they are arranged horizontally is perceptually salient, and then have a phenomenally different experience e_2 in which the fact that they are arranged vertically is perceptually salient. It would be natural for the proponent of the supervenience thesis to adopt a fine-grained view of propositional contents according to which the propositions *there are rows of equidistant dots arranged horizontally* and *there are rows of equidistant dots arranged vertically* are distinct, even though they are modally equivalent, and then to say that e_1 represents the first proposition but not the second, and that e_2 represents the second proposition but not the first. But on the accuracy conception, since these propositions are true with respect to exactly the same scenarios, both propositions will be counted among the contents of both e_1 and e_2. Indeed, even though they differ phenomenally, since e_1 and e_2 are accurate with respect to the same scenarios they have exactly the same contents, on the accuracy conception. The trouble is that even if propositions are fine-grained, the accuracy conception provides a coarse-grained criterion for when a particular experience has a particular content, one which cannot distinguish between modally equivalent propositions. So if the debate over the supervenience thesis is to be intelligible and non-trivial, another conception of what it is for a particular experience to have a particular content is needed.

Thirdly, the accuracy conception trivializes the debate over what the contents of experiences are. What, for instance, does the claim that the kind property *being a pine tree* enters into the content of some experience t of a pine tree mean? On one version of the accuracy conception, it means that the proposition *there is a pine tree present* is true in every possible world in which someone has an accurate phenomenal duplicate of t. But this is false. At a twin earth with no pine trees but only pine tree look-alikes, on any reasonable way of explaining accuracy, if S has an experience of a pine tree look-alike which is a phenomenal duplicate of t, then his experience might be perfectly accurate. On yet another version of accuracy conception, it is assumed that we can evaluate t – this very token-experience – for accuracy with respect to arbitrary hypothetical (centred) worlds. The claim is that the proposition *there is a pine tree present* is true in every world with respect to which t is accurate. Whether this is true depends on whether the claim presupposes the concept of accuracy$_e$ or the concept of accuracy$_d$. For the concept of accuracy$_e$ this claim is indeterminate (not merely epistemically opaque), because the examples used to introduce the concept of accuracy$_e$ are insufficient to determine a verdict on whether, say, t is accurate$_e$ with respect to a (centred) world containing an object which looks like the pine tree viewed in t, but is not a pine tree. (Likewise, it is indeterminate whether or not t is accurate$_e$ with respect to a centred world in which there is a pine tree other than the one viewed in t. Therefore on this conception of the content of an experience, it is indeterminate whether or not the content of t is a singular content about this very pine tree.) On the other hand, assuming the concept of accuracy$_d$, the issue of whether the content of S's experience t involves the property of being a pine tree becomes that of whether the viewed pine tree looks to S to have the property of being a pine tree. If S has the concept of a pine tree, then it will look to him to have the property of being a pine tree, and the claim will be true. If not, it will be false. If debates concerning the contents of experiences are to be more substantive, another conception of the contents of experience is required.

In my view, the only conception of the contents of experience which does not trivialize debates over what the contents of experiences are is theory-laden rather than theory-neutral. I call it the *identity conception*.[14] It may be introduced by analogy. What does it mean to say that a particular belief has a particular propositional content? Some theories, for instance, multiple relation theories and sententialist theories, deny that the property of having a certain belief is identical with the property of standing in a relation to a true or false proposition.[15] In contrast, the propositional theory upholds this identification. One reasonable conception of what it means to say that a particular belief has a particular content presupposes this theory. To claim that a particular belief has a particular proposition as its content is to claim that it is identical with standing in a relation, the *belief-relation*, to the proposition. Likewise, on the identity conception, to claim that a particular experience has a particular proposition as its content is to claim that having the experience is identical with standing in some relation (distinct from and more basic than belief) to this content, so that the claim that experiences have contents goes hand in hand with the intentionalist view that experience is explained in terms of content.

To develop this idea, I must first introduce the notion of an experiential property. Suppose S experiences a red and round tomato in normal

[14] This conception is employed in A. Pautz, 'Intentionalism and Perceptual Presence', *Philosophical Perspectives*, 21 (2007), pp. 495–541, at p. 497. It elaborates the formulation of intentionalism in M. Johnston, 'The Obscure Object of Hallucination', *Philosophical Studies*, 120 (2004), pp. 113–83, at p. 176.

[15] For a sententialist theory, see D. Davidson, 'On Saying That', in his *Inquiries into Truth and Interpretation* (Oxford UP, 1984), pp. 93–108. For the multiple relation theory, see B. Russell, *The Problems of Philosophy* (Oxford: Home University Library, 1912), pp. 124–30.

circumstances, so that it looks red and round to him. Next, suppose S experiences a green and oval tomato in abnormal circumstances, so that it looks red and round to him; and he also has a hallucination of a red and round tomato. Suppose, finally, that in all three cases his experience is phenomenally exactly the same. Despite the differences between the cases, there is a salient property which S possesses in the three cases and in any phenomenally identical case, and which S would not possess in any phenomenally different case. I shall call such properties of people *experiential properties*. Even disjunctivists should recognize experiential properties common to successful and unsuccessful cases; they will analyse them disjunctively.

Different theories of phenomenal character can be viewed as different accounts of the structure or real definition of experiential properties. (I assume that properties can be complex and hence can have structure; to give the real definition of a property is to reveal this structure.) On the *qualia* theory, the sense-datum theory and certain forms of disjunctivism, experiential properties are not analysed in terms of content. In contrast, intentionalism explains experiential properties in terms of content. Often it is formulated as the claim that what experiential properties a person has *supervene on* what the contents of his experiences are. But this formulation is problematic. As I have shown, the question then becomes 'What does it mean to say that a particular experience has a particular content?', and the standard answers make the supervenience claim trivially false. The solution has two parts. First, intentionalism should be formulated as a theory of the *identity* of experiential properties. Secondly, 'x has an experience with content y' should be treated as a theoretical term and removed from the formulation of intentionalism in favour of an existentially quantified bound variable, in accordance with the Ramsey–Lewis method for eliminating theoretical terms.[16] Then, in the case of visual experience, intentionalism may be formulated as follows:

Intentionalism about visual experience. There is a relation R such that for every visual experiential property E, there is a unique general content c such that having E is identical with bearing R to c (or there is a unique *type* of content t such that having E is identical with bearing R to some content or other of type t).

The parenthetical qualification is needed to make room for the possibility of *singular intentionalism*. On this view, when you have a red-round experience on viewing different tomatoes, you bear some relation R to different singular contents about the different tomatoes; and having a red-round experience is

---

[16] D.K. Lewis, 'How to Define Theoretical Terms', *Journal of Philosophy*, 67 (1970), pp. 427–46.

identified with standing in R to some proposition or other of a certain type, namely, one whose predicative constituent is the property of being red and round. This is in contrast with *general intentionalism*, which says that in every case the relevant content is the same general content, roughly *there is a red and round object present*.

I can now introduce two theoretical terms according to the Ramsey–Lewis method, which refer only if intentionalism is true. Let 'sensory entertaining' denote the unique relation R which satisfies the account provided by intentionalism of the structure of experiential properties. This is a mere referential tag which does not presuppose any analogy between sensorily entertaining contents in experience and entertaining contents in thought. Let 'the phenomenal content of token-experience *e*' denote the proposition which one sensorily entertains in having *e*. (By a *token-experience*, I mean a particular instantiation of some experiential property. Since it should be uncontroversial that there are experiential properties, it should be uncontroversial that there are token-experiences in this stipulated sense.) On singular intentionalism, phenomenally identical token-experiences have different singular phenomenal contents. On general intentionalism, they have the same general phenomenal content. If general intentionalism is true, we may speak of the phenomenal content of an experiential property E as well as of the phenomenal content of a particular experience-token: it is the unique general content *c* such that E is identical with sensorily entertaining *c*.

On typical supervenience formulations of intentionalism, the claim that experiences have contents is a presupposition of intentionalism which needs to be independently clarified and supported. As I have shown, existing clarifications make the supervenience claim trivially false. In contrast, on the identity conception, intentionalism and the claim that experiences have contents come together in a package.

One might think that this is less than ideal. Intentionalism holds that all experiential properties involve the same relation R. Therefore, as currently formulated, it entails that when they differ, they must differ in the contents which are the relata of this relation. In other words, intentionalism entails the supervenience of phenomenal character on content. Therefore on the identity conception as currently formulated, the claim that experiences have contents is wedded to this controversial supervenience claim. For this reason, one might introduce the *weak identity conception*. On this conception, the claim that experiences have contents is equated with *weak intentionalism*, which differs from *strong intentionalism* as formulated above. On weak intentionalism, every experiential property consists *in part* in bearing a relation to a content, which I shall call 'sensorily entertaining'. But this leaves it open that some experiential properties also involve non-intentional

properties, which might account for differences among experiential properties in which the same content is sensorily entertained.

In either version, the identity conception makes the three main debates
over the contents of experiences non-trivial. First, as I have shown, the
appears-looks conception and the accuracy conception trivialize the debate
over whether experiences have contents. The reason is that they equate the
claim that experiences have contents with the claim that experiences can be
non-arbitrarily *associated with* propositions, something everyone can accept.
In contrast, on the identity conception, the claim that experiences have
contents is equivalent to the non-trivial claim that experiential properties are
identical with relations to contents, so that contents enter into their real
definition.

It should be noted that on the identity conception the claim that experiences have contents is stronger than the claim that having experiences
involves standing in a propositional-attitude relation to contents.[17] The
problem with equating the claim that experiences have contents with this
involvement claim is that it seems that everyone can agree that having experiences involves standing in a relation to propositions, especially if we allow
'defined up' or unnatural relations. For instance, as I pointed out in connection with the appears-looks conception, everyone should admit that
having experiences involves standing in the relation *it appears to x that y is true*
to various propositions. Disjunctivism entails that having experiences involves standing in a relation R to general propositions, where one bears R to
the general proposition *there is an F* iff one cannot know by reflection that
one is not seeing the instantiation of F by something. Other theories, such as
the theory of appearing[18] and the sense-datum theory, entail that in having
experiences we stand in other such derivative relations to propositions,
definable in terms of the properties of sense-data or the properties objects
present to us. In response to the threat of triviality, the proponent of the
involvement claim might say that although these are relations to true or false
propositions defined in mentalist terms, they are not propositional-attitude
relations. But then it is unclear what more is needed for a relation to be a
propositional-attitude relation. In contrast, the identity conception which I
favour avoids the threat of triviality. While the sense-datum theory, the
theory of appearing and other theories entail that experiential properties
determine and thus involve relations to contents, they deny that experiences
are *identical with* relations to contents. Further, the identity conception avoids

[17] Alex Byrne formulated the claim that experiences have contents along these lines at the
Glasgow conference on the Admissible Contents of Experience.

[18] W.P. Alston, 'Back to the Theory of Appearing', *Philosophical Perspectives*, 13 (1999),
pp. 181–204.

the unclear notion of a propositional-attitude relation because it simply quantifies over relations in general without invoking this notion.

Secondly, the identity conception, in contrast with the appears-looks conception and the accuracy conception, does not trivialize the issue of whether phenomenal character supervenes on content, because it amounts to the issue of whether strong intentionalism provides the correct account of the structure of experiential properties.

Thirdly, the identity conception, unlike the appears-looks conception and the accuracy conception, does not trivialize the debate over what the contents of experiences are. On the identity conception of the content of experience, the issue of whether experiences have singular contents or only general contents becomes the non-trivial issue of whether singular intentionalism or general intentionalism provides the correct account of the structure of experiential properties. The debate over whether experiences have contents involving kind properties becomes the issue of whether kind properties must enter into the phenomenal contents of our experiences in order to explain phenomenal differences among experiences. Defenders of other theories of the structure of experiential properties, such as the sense-datum theory and the theory of appearing, face analogous issues. What are the properties of sense-data? What properties do objects phenomenally appear to have? But they should not formulate these issues in terms of some weak theory-neutral conception of the contents of experiences, because, as I have shown, such theory-neutral conceptions inevitably trivialize the debates. It is only those who accept the intentionalist view of the structure of experiential properties who should frame the issue in terms of the contents of experiences. I now turn to the case for this view.

II. WHY BELIEVE THAT EXPERIENCES HAVE CONTENTS?

Some philosophers (Travis, Brewer) have recently argued that the intentionalist account of illusion is not obligatory. I agree: disjunctivist theories and *qualia*-based theories also account for illusion. But elsewhere I have argued for intentionalism about visual experience, as opposed to rival theories, on the ground that it provides the *best explanation* of other features of visual experience. For instance, visual experience, even when illusory or hallucinatory, grounds the capacity for external thought.[19] Let R be the experiential property which S has on viewing a red and round tomato on a certain occasion. Necessarily, if a concept-user has R, then he will thereby

---

[19] Pautz, 'Intentionalism and Perceptual Presence'. Cf. also Johnston, 'The Obscure Object of Hallucination', p. 130.

have the capacity to have certain general beliefs with *being red* and *being round* as predicative constituents, even if he was previously unacquainted with these properties. This is no less true in a hallucinatory case in which these properties are not instantiated by physical objects before the subject. Some neglect hallucination. For instance, according to negative disjunctivists, in unsuccessful cases, one has R simply by virtue of not being able to know by reflection that one is not seeing the redness and roundness of something.[20] In addition to facing counter-examples (a rock is also unable to have this knowledge but does not have R), this theory is inconsistent with the explanatory role of hallucination. How might inability to have a certain piece of knowledge ground the ability to have certain thoughts? Against negative disjunctivism, a positive theory of hallucination is needed, according to which in hallucination S is *en rapport* with properties which are not instantiated by physical objects before him, such as *being red* and *being round*. Some such theories, for instance the sense-datum theory and the theory of appearing, postulate non-standard objects which instantiate or present the relevant properties. But they are problematic. Intentionalism avoids non-standard objects. In the hallucinatory case, having R simply consists in sensorily entertaining a content involving *being red* and *being round*. Since sensorily entertaining is more basic than believing, this state may ground the capacity to have general beliefs having these same properties as predicative constituents. If intentionalism works in unsuccessful cases, there are reasons to generalize it to successful cases as well.

Philosophers who argue that intentionalism is not obligatory also argue that it is not satisfactory. Travis argues against intentionalism on the ground that the contents of experiences are not *look-indexed*: they cannot be determined from looks-reports. I agree (see §III below). He also rejects functional theories according to which the content of a sensory state is determined by the state's typical causes and effects. I agree: there is no fail-safe algorithm for determining what contents a person sensorily entertains (just as there may be no algorithm for determining what a person knows or what is right or wrong). But I do not see the problem. People may nevertheless be sensitive to what contents they sensorily entertain, and thereby know what experiences they have.

A second objection to intentionalism is as follows. In the Müller–Lyer diagram, lines that are in fact the same length appear different in length. Brewer argues that this is not adequately explained in terms of a false intentional content to the effect that the lines differ in length. For instance, this view falsely predicts that if the distorting angles were to shrink in size, then there would be a phenomenal change in one's experience of the

---

[20] M. Martin, 'The Limits of Self-Awareness', *Philosophical Studies*, 120 (2004), pp. 37–89.

relative lengths of the lines. According to Brewer, the best view is that experiences are mere confrontations with the world which cannot be inaccurate or in error. It is only the beliefs which the subject is disposed to form which are in error. But this is only an objection to a version of intentionalism which explains the case in terms of a false content to the effect that the lines differ in length. To avoid the objection, the intentionalist might instead say that the phenomenal content of the original experience of the diagram is the true content *the top line has length l and the bottom line has length l*, and that they look different in length to *S* only in the sense that he is disposed to believe falsely that they are different in length.

Another point is that intentionalists could in a sense agree that experiences cannot themselves be inaccurate or in error. As I have said, everyone must admit that experiences can be inaccurate$_e$ and inaccurate$_d$. So when philosophers deny that experiences themselves can be accurate or inaccurate, they must have a thicker conception in mind. Perhaps they have in mind a conception that requires that experiences, like beliefs, are mental states with a mind to world direction of fit. I shall use accuracy$_t$ to mark this conception. As I have formulated intentionalism, it would be a mistake to say that intentionalism entails that experiences themselves can be accurate$_t$ or inaccurate$_t$, because it says nothing about 'direction of fit'. Intentionalism says only that experiences are relations to contents. But some relations to contents, for instance *desiring* and *entertaining in thought*, do not have a mind to world direction of fit. So even when they have a false content, one cannot say that the states themselves are inaccurate$_t$ or in error. Maybe it is the same with experiences. They tend to induce beliefs because they have a rich phenomenology. But maybe, unlike beliefs, they themselves do not have a mind to world direction of fit. Certainly, on standard explications of mind to world direction of fit in terms of sensitivity to evidence, they lack a mind to world direction of fit. In that case, even when they have false contents, experiences themselves cannot be said to be literally false or in error. Error only enters the picture when the subject takes the experience at face value and forms a false belief.

III. WHAT ARE THE CONTENTS OF EXPERIENCES?

I shall now address two issues concerning what the contents of experiences are. One issue is whether the contents of experiences include singular contents into which particular objects enter, or whether they are purely general. The second issue concerns what general properties enter into the contents of our experiences.

For the identity conception of the contents of experiences, the first issue is the issue of whether singular intentionalism or general intentionalism provides the best account of the structure of experiential properties. I favour general intentionalism on the grounds that it is simple and there is no good argument against it. A common argument against general intentionalism concerns examples in which the general phenomenal content of an experience is true, but the experience is inaccurate$_e$. An example would be a hallucination of a scene which is not present before S but which is by chance exactly duplicated at some other place or time, so that the purely general content of the hallucination is true. Or suppose S has an experience of an object which is in fact white and to his left. However, because of a mirror and abnormal light, it looks to him red and straight ahead.[21] If by chance there is a red object straight ahead of S behind the mirror, then the purely general content of the experience is true. But such cases are a problem only if the general intentionalist is committed to the *simple analysis* of accuracy$_e$ according to which an experience inherits its accuracy$_e$-conditions from its content. However, the general intentionalist is not committed to the simple analysis of accuracy$_e$.[22] Granted, the accuracy-conditions of a *belief* must match the accuracy-conditions of its content, because it is part of the definition of the content of a belief that it determines the accuracy-conditions of the belief. In contrast, the phenomenal content of an experience is not defined as what determines its accuracy-conditions (the accuracy conception), but as what constitutes its phenomenal character (the identity conception). So it is open to the general intentionalist to provide a more nuanced analysis of accuracy according to which an experience might be inaccurate$_e$ even though its purely general content is true. For instance, he might say that an experience is *accurate$_e$* iff it is a non-hallucinatory experience in which the viewed objects have the properties they look to have or a hallucinatory experience whose general content has among its witnesses objects directly before the subject. Then he might analyse *o looks F to S* as *o appropriately causes S to entertain sensorily the content that there is something that is F*. Alternatively, he might deny that there is any simple analysis of looks-reports in terms of content and causation.

I now turn to the second issue, that of what general properties enter into the contents of our experiences. As a bonus, the argument sketched in §II for believing that experiential properties are relations to contents naturally

---

[21] M. Soteriou, 'The Particularity of Visual Perception', *European Journal of Philosophy*, 8 (2000), pp. 173–89, at p. 187, fn. 3.

[22] For a similar point regarding the more ordinary concept of success, see Pautz, 'Intentionalism and Perceptual Presence', p. 513, fn. 1. For instance, the intentionalist could agree with some anti-intentionalists that success must be analysed in terms of a primitive form of awareness of states of the world.

also suggests a method for arriving at conclusions concerning what properties enter into the contents of particular experiential properties: intuitions
about the potential cognitive roles of particular experiential properties can
be used in order to arrive at hypotheses about what their contents must be if
they are to play this role. In fact, one can state a general principle. I shall say
that a single experiential property E *necessarily grounds* the capacity to have a
belief involving a property P iff it is metaphysically necessary that suitable
concept-users who have E will have the capacity to have beliefs involving P
because they have E, where a *suitable* concept-user is one who is not cogni-
tively impaired in comparison with a normal human. Then the following
principle is plausible:

The grounding principle. If experiential property E necessarily grounds the
capacity to have beliefs involving P *without imaginative extrapolation*, then P
enters into the phenomenal content of E.

Two comments. First, the 'without imaginative extrapolation' qualification is needed because of cases like the following: having an experiential
property E whose phenomenal content only involves the shades of blue B_1
and B_2 might necessarily ground the capacity to have thoughts involving an
intermediate shade of blue B'. But B' does not enter into the phenomenal
content of E. This is not a counter-example, because imaginative extrapolation is required to form beliefs involving B'. I have no definition of
imaginative extrapolation. But this does not make the grounding principle
useless, because we may nevertheless have justified beliefs about when it
takes place.

Secondly, the grounding principle can only help to determine which
properties figure in the contents of experiences. It cannot help to determine
which properties are bound together in the content (appear to be possessed
by the same object) and which properties are not bound together.

It may be said that the grounding principle is implausible. Let R be the
experiential property which one possesses when one experiences a particular
red and round tomato. It may be thought that having R in fact grounds the
capacity to have beliefs involving *being a tomato*, so that by the grounding
principle this kind property enters into the phenomenal content of the
experience. But, it may be said, obtaining this result should not be so easy.
This rests on a misunderstanding. It is not the case that having R *necessarily*
grounds the capacity to have beliefs involving *being a tomato*, as witness the
possibility of a community of perceivers on a tomato-free twin earth who
have R but not the capacity to have beliefs involving *being a tomato* because
they have no causal connection to this property. So the grounding principle
does not entail that *being a tomato* enters into the phenomenal content (which

is not to say that the principle entails that it does not). In contrast, as noted in §II, R does necessarily ground the capacity to have beliefs involving *being round*, for instance, the belief that something is round. So by the grounding principle this property enters into its phenomenal content.

What is the argument for the grounding principle? For a schematic case in which the antecedent holds, suppose that in every possible scenario having E grounds the capacity to have beliefs involving P without imaginative extrapolation – in hallucinatory cases in which P is not instantiated before the percipient, on twin earth, and so on. Then P itself must somehow be present in every case in which someone has E. Otherwise, how might this be the case? But on intentionalism, P is present in every case in which someone has E only if P enters into the phenomenal content of E.

To show how the grounding principle might be used to support more interesting results than the result that shape properties such as *being square* enter into phenomenal content, I can apply it to some debates. In each case, I shall try to make plausible a certain 'grounding intuition' to the effect that the antecedent of the grounding principle holds of an experiential property E and an external property P. Given the grounding principle, it follows that P enters into the phenomenal content of E.

To begin with a preliminary point, I believe that this *grounding method* should be used in conjunction with other methods. Siegel's *method of phenomenal contrast* begins by noting a difference in sensory phenomenology. For instance, in the cases of colour and shape constancy to be discussed presently, there are such differences. Given intentionalism, there is a difference in what properties enter into the phenomenal content. But the phenomenal difference alone fails to show what the different properties are. Siegel suggests that we should appeal to an argument from the best explanation to determine what the different properties are. My idea is that the best explanation will be the one which accommodates people's grounding intuitions.

First, in the debate between standard and non-standard intentionalists, *standard intentionalists* about colour experience hold that the properties which the phenomenal contents of our colour experiences attribute to external objects are simply the colours. *Non-standard intentionalists* hold that they are not the colours.[23] In fact, they hold that the relevant properties have no names in ordinary English. So they invent a name: for instance, they might call the relevant properties 'qualitative properties'. The dispute may be seen as a dispute about natural-language semantics, with standard intentionalists

[23] M. Thau, *Consciousness and Cognition* (Oxford UP, 2002); S. Shoemaker, 'On the Way Things Appear', in Gendler and Hawthorne (eds), *Perceptual Experience*, pp. 461–80; D. Chalmers, 'Perception and the Fall from Eden'.

claiming that the properties which enter into the phenomenal contents of colour experiences are the referents of colour terms in public language, and non-standard intentionalists claiming that colour terms denote properties lying outside phenomenal content.

Let E be the experiential property which S possesses on viewing a particular red object, a particular orange object and a particular green object together. Of course, both views agree that *in the actual world* having E grounds the capacity to have beliefs involving colours. Non-standard intentionalists might accommodate this by saying that thanks to a contingent correlation between the properties they call 'qualitative properties' and those they call 'colours', having an experience involving a certain 'qualitative property' grounds the capacity to have beliefs involving a certain 'colour'. But I believe that most people have a stronger grounding intuition, namely, that having E *necessarily* grounds the capacity to have beliefs involving colours. No matter what his environment is like, if S has E, then one naturally characterizes his beliefs using colour language: S might believe that *red* is more like *orange* than *green*, that *red* is a striking colour, and so on. Given the grounding principle, this 'grounding intuition' entails that the properties which enter into the phenomenal content of E are simply the colours, in favour of standard intentionalism and against non-standard intentionalism.

If you doubt that this 'grounding intuition' refutes non-standard intentionalism, suppose John, who has E but who does not track colours in the external environment, is a brain in a vat without an evolutionary history, or has evolved on a twin earth whose environment has never contained any coloured objects. On some versions of standard intentionalism, such a case is impossible. But on non-standard intentionalism, it is possible. In addition, on non-standard intentionalism, although John has E, he does not have the capacity to have any beliefs involving colours, since on this view to have beliefs involving colours one must bear certain naturalistic relations to the relevant properties instantiated in the external world. (Just as there might be someone who has a 'tomato-like' experience on a tomato-free twin earth, but, lacking connections to tomatoes, lacks the capacity for beliefs involving *being a tomato*.) So non-standard intentionalism conflicts with the grounding intuition. But since the grounding intuition is plausible for colour, it follows that the non-standard intentionalist's semantics for colour terms is mistaken, and colour terms refer to the properties given in phenomenal content in accordance with standard intentionalism (where it is left open whether these are reflectance properties, dispositional properties, primitive properties, or whatever).

Now for the debate over constancy phenomena. Let C be the experiential property which S has while viewing a particular white ball illuminated from above so that it looks white on top, white but shaded in the middle, and black at the bottom. The phenomenal contrast shows that different properties enter into the phenomenal contents of the experiences of the different regions, but it fails to show what they are. Presumably *white* at the top, *black* at the bottom, but what about the middle? There are two views. The *simple view* says that the phenomenal content of the experience of the shadowed region attributes *being grey*. The *complex view* is the negation of this. The phenomenal content only attributes *being white* and some property of the form *being subject to the occlusion of a light source to so-and-so degree*.[24]

I favour the simple view. I have already pointed out that colours enter into phenomenal contents, so the simple view is more conservative. Another point is that if the proponent of the complex view claims that the experience represents the bottom as black *simpliciter*, then at what point does the experience switch from representing *white* and (decreasing) *level of illumination* to not representing *white* or *level of illumination* at all, but merely *black*? It is hard to see how such a fact could be indeterminate. But the strongest case for the simple view is the grounding intuition that C necessarily endows people with the capacity to have beliefs involving the colour *grey* even if it is not instantiated before them, not only beliefs about *white* and *level of illumination*. For instance, if someone previously unacquainted with achromatic colours has C, one would naturally say that he now knows what *grey* is like, that he learns that *grey* is more like white than black, and so on. By the grounding principle, *grey* enters into the phenomenal content of his experience, not merely *white* and *under low illumination*.

The simple view does not have the consequence (which many would regard as implausible) that C is illusory. Since, on the identity conception, phenomenal content is defined as what constitutes phenomenology, not as what determines whether an experience is illusory or not, there is conceptual room for a view on which the phenomenal content of C is false but there is no sense in which C is *illusory*, as this notion is employed in ordinary thought. Further, in contrast with the appears-looks conception, the identity conception does not explain the content of experience in terms of looks-reports. So there is no reason to believe that phenomenal content is looks-indexed in any simple way. Hence the simple view also does not make the mistaken prediction that the middle region *looks grey* to observers. It is compatible with a more nuanced account of looks-reports which brings

---

[24] For the simple view, see W. Lycan, *Consciousness and Experience* (MIT Press, 1996); C. McGinn, 'The Objects of Intentionality', in his *Consciousness and its Objects* (Oxford UP, 2004), pp. 220–48. For the complex view, see M. Tye, 'In Defense of Representationalism', in M. Aydede (ed.), *Pain: New Essays on its Nature and the Methodology of its Study* (MIT Press, 2006), pp. 163–76, at p. 172; D. Hilbert, 'Color Constancy and the Complexity of Color', forthcoming in *Philosophical Topics*.

in factors outside phenomenal content. So it is compatible with the fact that in ordinary contexts the only correct description is 'the middle region looks white and under low illumination'. It follows that the intuition that C grounds beliefs about *grey* is not based on any intuition to the effect that the middle region looks grey.

A similar argument may be given in favour of a simple view of shape constancy, but I believe that there are problems here. Suppose D is the experiential property which someone has when he looks simultaneously at a tilted coin, a coin viewed straight on and a cube viewed straight on. The simple view says that the phenomenal content of D attributes *being elliptical* to the tilted coin (which, given the discussion of the last paragraph, is perfectly consistent with the report 'it looks round and tilted'). The complex view says that it does not attribute *being elliptical* to the coin; it attributes *being round* and *being tilted* (and maybe being such that it would be occluded by an elliptical object placed in front of it).[25] It might be said that having D necessarily grounds the capacity to have thoughts involving *being elliptical* without imaginative extrapolation: if John has never before encountered *being elliptical* in experience, then intuitively having D might give him the capacity to know what *being elliptical* is like and to believe that it is more like *being circular* than *being square*. In further support of this, the friend of the simple view might point out that John might think 'this [the shape-aspect of the tilted coin] is not exactly similar to that [the shape-aspect of the coin viewed straight on], but it is more like that [the shape-aspect of the coin viewed straight on] than this [the shape-aspect of the cube]'. Since this thought seems true, the referent of the first two demonstratives cannot be the *actual* shapes of the coins, for those resemble exactly. The only reasonable view is that the referent of the first demonstrative is *being elliptical* and that of the second is *being round*. The proponent of the simple view might now say that since having D necessarily grounds the capacity to have such thoughts without imaginative extrapolation, ellipticality must enter into its phenomenal content.

There are two problems with the argument. First, obtaining beliefs involving *being elliptical* from D seems to be more of a cognitive achievement than obtaining beliefs involving *being grey* from C. Hence the proponent of the complex view might say that the 'without imaginative extrapolation' clause of the grounding principle is not met here. Secondly, the defender of the complex view might accept the grounding intuition that D necessarily grounds the capacity to have thoughts involving *being elliptical* without

---

[25] For the simple view of shape constancy, see Lycan, *Consciousness and Experience*; McGinn, 'The Objects of Intentionality'. For the complex view, see Tye, *Consciousness, Color and Content*, p. 79.

imaginative extrapolation, and accept that the grounding principle entails that *being elliptical* somehow enters into its phenomenal content, but insist that this is compatible with the acceptance of the complex view and the rejection of the simple view. For he might grant that it enters into the content, while rejecting the key claim of the simple view that it is *attributed to* the coin itself. In particular, he might say that the phenomenal content attributes to the coin the relational property of exactly occluding an elliptical *region* behind it. Further, he might say that this is how the experience makes available thoughts involving ellipticality.

In addition, there is a problem for the simple view of shape constancy which does not arise for the simple view of colour constancy. If, as on the simple view, the phenomenal content attributes *being elliptical* to the coin, it is implausible that it also represents one side as being farther back than the other. So the simple view goes naturally with a two-dimensional view of visual phenomenal content. But if, as seems plausible, there is difference in depth phenomenology between viewing objects with two eyes and then with one eye, owing to the loss of stereoscopic depth-processing, then this view must be wrong: the only plausible view is that the difference is due to a decrease in the determinacy of the representation of object distances. In reply, the defender of the simple view might say that the experience of the coin has within the level of phenomenal content two contradictory contents: a two-dimensional content attributing *being elliptical* (accounting for the availability of thoughts about ellipticality), and a three-dimensional content attributing *being round and tilted* (accounting for the depth phenomenology). But this version of the simple view is unattractively complicated. For these reasons, while I endorse the simple view of colour constancy, I have doubts about the simple view of shape constancy.

To return finally to the debate over whether kind properties enter into the contents of our experiences, there is some reason to think that after Mabel learns how to recognize pine trees, the experiential property T she has on viewing a particular pine tree will differ from the visual experiential property which she had when she previously looked at the pine tree.[26] If so, then the phenomenal contrast shows that there is afterwards a different property in the phenomenal content, but fails to show what this property is. According to the *kind thesis*, it is simply the kind property *being a pine tree*. But there is reason to doubt this. Here is a plausible principle:

The reverse grounding principle. If the phenomenal content of an experiential property E involves P, then having E for a sufficient period necessarily grounds (in suitable concept-users) the capacity to have beliefs involving P.

[26] Siegel, 'Which Properties are Represented in Experience?'.

Contrapositively: if it is not the case that having E necessarily grounds the capacity to have a belief involving P, then the phenomenal content of E does not involve P.

Suppose Mabel's twin Tabel has always been on a twin earth where real pine trees are replaced by fake pine trees, so that *being a pine tree* is nowhere instantiated. Tabel gains the capacity to recognize fake pine trees. Suppose that, on viewing a particular fake pine tree, she now has experiential property T, the very same experiential property as Mabel has on viewing an exactly similar real pine tree after acquiring her recognitional capacity. It seems plausible that Tabel lacks the capacity to have beliefs involving the natural-kind property *being a pine tree*. So by the reverse grounding principle, *being a pine tree* does not enter into the phenomenal content of T, the shared content of Tabel's and Mabel's matching experiences. As I have shown, on the appears-looks conception and the accuracy conception, the kind thesis is trivially true or trivially false. On the identity conception, there is good reason to believe it is false.

The proponent of the kind thesis might reply by denying the key assumption that Mabel's and Tabel's matching experiences must share a phenomenal content involving the same properties. The singular intentionalist allows that the phenomenal contents of phenomenally identical experiences can differ in their subject constituents. Why not allow that they can differ in their predicative constituents? On this view, Tabel sensorily entertains a phenomenal content involving *being a pine tree*. Even though Tabel has the very same experiential property T, she sensorily entertains a phenomenal content involving *being a pine tree*$_1$, where this is the relevant kind property (distinct from *being a pine tree*) shared by fake pine trees on twin earth. The trouble with this reply is that it implies no plausible view concerning the identity of the experiential property T. The proponent of this reply must adopt the implausible view that T is identical with the infinitely disjunctive property of sensorily entertaining a content involving *being a pine tree* or sensorily entertaining a content involving *being a pine tree*$_1$ or sensorily entertaining a content involving *being a pine tree*$_2$ or ..., where these are properties of different classes of objects which are not pine trees but which look exactly like them.

To avoid this implausible view, one must retain the original assumption that when Mabel and Tabel share experiential properties, they sensorily entertain phenomenal contents involving the same properties. By the argument given, this rules out the kind thesis. But then how is the phenomenal change which Mabel and Tabel undergo, after they learn how to recognize pine trees (in the case of Tabel, fake pine trees), to be explained? One view is that they come to entertain sensorily a phenomenal content involving an 'overall pine tree *Gestalt*' which is shared by real pine trees and fake ones. Another view is that they come to entertain sensorily a phenomenal content attributing the property of being a familiar object in addition to colour and shape properties. A quite different type of view is that the phenomenal change which Mabel and Tabel undergo is not due to their sensorily entertaining a new phenomenal content at all, but rather is due to a difference at the level of thought in how they are disposed to classify pine trees (or in the case of Tabel, fake pine trees).[27]

[27] My thanks to an anonymous referee for helpful comments. Thanks also to David Barnett, David Chalmers, Benj Hellie, Susanna Siegel and all those who took part in the Glasgow conference on the Admissible Contents of Experience.

8

ASPECT-SWITCHING AND VISUAL PHENOMENAL CHARACTER

By RICHARD PRICE

John Searle and Susanna Siegel have argued that cases of aspect-switching show that visual experience represents a richer range of properties than colours, shapes, positions and sizes. I respond that cases of aspect-switching can be explained without holding that visual experience represents rich properties. I also argue that even if Searle and Siegel are right, and aspect-switching does require visual experience to represent rich properties, there is reason to think those properties do not include natural-kind properties, such as being a tomato.

I. INTRODUCTION

Philosophers have often asked what kind of information is available to vision. For instance, Berkeley argued that one cannot see depth, and Hume that one cannot see necessary connections.

Recently philosophers have asked what kinds of properties visual experience 'represents'. According to *sparse* views, visual experience represents a sparse range of properties, for instance, just colours, shapes, positions and sizes.[1] According to *rich* views, visual experience represents a rich range of properties, for instance, properties such as being a tomato and being sad.[2] Siegel and Searle have used cases of 'aspect-switching' to support the view that visual experience represents a rich range of properties. Roughly, their arguments are that when one aspect-switches on an object, the object comes to look different, but looks to have the same colour and shape properties. Therefore, so the arguments go, one's visual experiences represent these objects as having a richer set of properties than simply colour and shape properties.

[1] See C. McGinn, *The Character of Mind* (Oxford UP, 1982); T. Burge, 'Perceptual Entitlement', *Philosophy and Phenomenological Research*, 67 (2003), pp. 503–48; A. Millar, 'The Scope of Perceptual Knowledge', *Philosophy*, 75 (2000), pp. 75–88.

[2] See C. Peacocke, *The Realm of Reason* (Oxford: Clarendon Press, 2003); S. Siegel, 'Which Properties are Represented in Perception?', in T. Gendler and J. Hawthorne (eds), *Perceptual Experience* (Oxford UP, 2006), pp. 481–503; J. Searle, *Intentionality* (Cambridge UP, 1983); J. McDowell, *Meaning, Knowledge, and Reality* (Harvard UP, 1998).

In this chapter, I argue that one can explain well known cases of aspect-switching without having to assume that visual experience represents rich properties (i.e., properties other than colour, shape, position and size). Furthermore, I shall argue that even if my arguments are unsound, and cases of aspect-switching do require that visual experience represents rich properties, there is a reason to think that these rich properties do not include natural-kind properties such as the property of being a tomato.

In this chapter, instead of using the terminology of what properties visual experience represents, I define a kind of looking, *phenomenal looking*, which is individuated in terms of differences in visual phenomenal character. I identify phenomenal looking by arguing for a constraint on it, that is, a condition necessary for a kind of looking. My methodology is similar to that of someone who wishes to identify, say, a particular kind of justification, and does so by identifying a constraint on a particular kind of justification.

The following principle is a preliminary formulation of the constraint:

Restricted phenomenal character principle. Necessarily, for all objects x, y and z and all properties F and G, if x looks F to z, y does not look F to z, and y looks G to z, then there is a visual phenomenal difference between the ways x and y look to z.

I intend to apply the constraint diachronically and across worlds. Therefore the full constraint, the phenomenal character principle, quantifies over times and worlds, and is as follows:

Phenomenal character principle. Necessarily, for all objects x, y and z, all properties F and G, all times t_1 and t_2 and all worlds w_1 and w_2, if x looks F to z at t_1 at w_1, y does not look F to z at t_2 at w_2, and y looks G to z at t_2 at w_2, then there is a visual phenomenal difference between the way x looks to z at t_1 at w_1 and the way y looks to z at t_2 at w_2.

I assume that only one kind of looking satisfies the phenomenal character principle, and I call it *phenomenal looking*. What it means to say that there is a visual phenomenal difference between the ways two objects a and b look to S is that what it is visually like for S for a to look the way it does to S is different from what it is visually like for S for b to look the way it does to S.

The phenomenal character principle is phrased in terms of how things look to *a particular subject*. Sometimes I refer to the properties that objects phenomenally look to have, and leave it implicit that there is some particular subject to whom these objects phenomenally look to have the properties in question.

The phenomenal character principle uses the locution 'an object looks F', where 'F' is to be replaced by an adjective. In English, some properties can be expressed by predicates of the form 'is + adjective'. For instance, the property of being red can be expressed by the predicate 'is red'. However, some properties, for instance, the property of being a tomato, are not expressed by predicates of the form 'is + adjective'. There is no predicate 'is tomatoey' which expresses the property of being a tomato.

In order to express the question whether an object can stand in the phenomenal looking relation to the property of being a tomato, we could invent an adjective, 'tomatoey', stipulate that being tomatoey is identical with being a tomato, and then ask whether objects can phenomenally look tomatoey. Instead, however, I shall simply ask whether an object can phenomenally look *to be a tomato*, or whether an object can phenomenally look to have the property of being a tomato. Phenomenally looking to be an F and phenomenal looking to have the property of being an F obey the same constraint as phenomenally looking F: if an object x phenomenally looks to be F, and another object y does not phenomenally look to be F, but phenomenally looks to be G, then there is a visual phenomenal difference between the ways that x and y phenomenally look to be. The stronger principle which quantifies over times and worlds also applies to phenomenally looking to be F.

Some philosophers have argued that the expression 'looks to be' refers to a more epistemic kind of looking than the expression 'looks'. However, I do not use 'phenomenally looks to be' in a different sense from 'phenomenally looks': they both obey the same constraint. Using the locution of 'phenomenally looking to be an F' is merely a way of avoiding having to introduce new adjectives such as 'tomatoey'.

One way of understanding phenomenal looking is to compare it with kinds of looking which are not phenomenal. Consider *epistemic looking*. Some looks-statements refer to a state of a subject that is at least partly epistemic. For instance, if Joan is looking at a DVD cover, she may say 'This film looks intriguing', and this looks-statement refers to an epistemic kind of looking. Epistemic looking is not phenomenal looking. An object can change from epistemically looking F to epistemically looking G without any visual phenomenal difference in the way it looks. For instance, at one time Joan might look at the cover and say 'This film looks intriguing'. At a later time, when her interests have changed, she might look at the same DVD cover and say 'This film looks unappealing'. Intuitively, there may be no visual phenomenal difference between the ways the DVD cover looks at the two times.

Consider *externalist-looking*. Some philosophers have argued that there is a kind of looking which obtains between an object o, a perceiving subject S and a property F, when a certain internal state of S has been normally caused by a presence of Fness. For instance, consider a case of spectrum inversion in which what it is like to see tomatoes is different for two subjects Joe and Fay. Some philosophers would argue that the tomatoes *externalist-look* the same colour to Joe and Fay, namely, red; such philosophers would explain the difference between Joe and Fay by saying that what it is like for things to look red to them is different. It can be seen that externalist-looking is not phenomenal looking by considering that there is a world w_1 at which the actual internal states that Joe and Fay are in, when looking at tomatoes, are normally caused by objects having some property other than red, say, green. At w_1, given the definition of externalist-looking, tomatoes would externalist-look green to Joe and Fay, and given that Joe's and Fay's internal states are the same at w_1 as they are at the actual world, intuitively there would be no visual phenomenal difference between the way tomatoes actually look to Joe and Fay and the way tomatoes look at w_1 to Joe and Fay. It follows from the definition of phenomenal looking that externalist-looking is not phenomenal looking.

II. ASPECT SWITCHING

According to one view, objects phenomenally look to have a sparse range of properties, i.e., properties such as colour, shape, position and size. John Searle and Susanna Siegel use cases of aspect-switching to argue that this view is wrong, and that there are visual phenomenal differences which are not accounted for in terms of different colour and position properties that objects phenomenally look to have. Searle (pp. 54–5) gives two examples:

> [The shapes in Figure 1] can be seen as the word 'TOOT', as a table with two large balloons underneath, as the numeral 1001 with a line over the top, as a bridge with two pipelines crossing underneath, as the eyes of a man wearing a hat with string hanging down each side, and so on.... Consider, for example, the difference be-
>
>
> Figure 1
>
> tween looking at the front of a house where one takes it to be the front of a whole house, and looking at the front of a house where one takes it to be a mere façade, e.g., as part of a movie set. If one believes one is seeing a whole house, the front of the house actually looks different from the way it looks if one believes one is seeing a false façade of a house.... It is part of the content of my visual experience when I look at a whole house that I expect the rest of the house to be there if, for example, I enter the house or go round to the back.

Siegel (pp. 490–1) also gives two examples:

> The way [Cyrillic text] looks ... before and after [learning] to read Russian seems to bring about a phenomenological difference in how the text looks. (Christopher Peacocke makes a similar phenomenological claim in ch. 3 of *A Study of Concepts.*) When you

are first learning to read the script of a language that is new to you, you have to attend to each word, and perhaps to each letter, separately. In contrast, once you can easily read it, it takes a special effort to attend to the shapes of the script separately from its semantic properties. You become disposed to attend to the semantic properties of the words in the text, and less disposed to attend visually to the orthographic ones.

The second example involves a different recognitional disposition. Suppose you have never seen a pine tree before, and are hired to cut down all the pine trees in a grove containing trees of many different sorts. Someone points out to you which trees are pine trees. Some weeks pass, and your disposition to distinguish the pine trees from the others improves. Eventually, you can spot the pine trees immediately: they become visually salient to you. Like the recognitional disposition you gain, the salience of the trees emerges gradually. Gaining this recognitional disposition is reflected in a phenomenological difference between the visual experiences had before and after the recognitional disposition was fully developed.

The challenge posed by the above passages can be put as follows: there exist visual phenomenal differences which are best explained in terms of objects phenomenally looking to have properties other than colours, shapes, positions and sizes.

In §III and §IV I shall offer alternative explanations of the phenomena described by Searle and Siegel. In §V I shall argue that even if such phenomena do require that objects phenomenally look to have properties other than colours or positions, these properties do not include natural-kind properties, such as the property of being a tomato.

I shall consider two different kinds of case, first Searle's 'TOOT' aspect-switching case, and secondly Siegel's language and pine tree cases.

III. SEARLE'S CASE

Searle's 'TOOT' figure in Fig. 1 is one of a variety of ambiguous figures – figures which one can see under different aspects, or which one can see

as different types of object. Other familiar examples of ambiguous figures include the duck/rabbit picture (Figure 2) and also the young girl/old woman picture (Figure 3).[3]

I shall argue that the phenomenal shifts in these examples are explicable in terms of the following differences:

Figure 2

Figure 3

[3] The pictures in Figs 2 and 3 are from http://mathworld.wolfram.com.

- Differences in patterns of attention
- Differences in how one takes the objects to be
- Differences in how one visually imagines the objects to be.

Searle and Siegel argue that the best explanation of the visual phenomenal differences is that, in their terminology, visual experiences represent other properties in addition to colours, shapes, positions and sizes. I shall call this account of aspect-switching the *content view*. The account I shall defend, making use of the above three factors, I call the *non-content view*. I call it the non-content view because it does not hypothesize differences in the properties that the objects in question phenomenally look to have.

I shall use the expressions 'seeing as' and 'seeing under a certain aspect' in such a way that it is not controversial that one can see ambiguous figures as different kinds of objects, or under various aspects. I take the substantive question to be about what the best explanation of *seeing as* is.

III.1. *Patterns of attention*

Normally, aspect-switching on an ambiguous figure is accompanied by a shift in one's patterns of attention towards the figure, though these shifts need not be the same for different individuals. My own patterns of attention change in the following way when I see the above ambiguous figures under different aspects. When seeing the duck/rabbit as a rabbit, I tend to look at the picture from left to right, and when seeing it as a duck, I tend to look at it from right to left. Also, when seeing it as a rabbit, I attend to the rabbit's mouth and eye together; when I see it as a duck, I attend to the duck's eye and beak together. When seeing the 'TOOT' drawing as the word 'TOOT', I tend to attend to the whole word at once, whereas when I see it as a man wearing a hat with strings hanging down each side, I tend to attend to the eyes first and then the hat. When I see the young girl/old woman as an old woman, I tend to attend to the mouth and the eyes first, and when I see it as a young girl, I attend to her cheek and left shoulder first. Other people's patterns of attention may change in other ways.

Changing one's patterns of attention towards a figure can cause a phenomenal difference to occur, as with the picture in Figure 4. Initially, one's attention is evenly distributed over the shapes in the picture. After one sees the Dalmatian in the middle of the picture, one attends to the specific outline of the Dalmatian. There seems to be a phenomenal difference associated with this shift in one's pattern of attention.

Figure 4

Turning to Figure 5, one can see it as composed of a white triangle superimposed on black circles, and one can see it as composed of three black circles with wedges cut out of them. When one sees it as composed of a white triangle superimposed on black circles, it seems that one attends to the straight lines between the three black circles that would be the edges of the white triangle. When one sees it as composed of three black circles with wedges cut out of them, then one attends to these circles alone without attending to the straight lines that would be the edges of the white triangle.

Figure 5

III.2. *How one takes the object to be*

Cognitive states can have phenomenal character. There can be something it is like to understand a proposition. Switching between one's cognitive states can thus involve phenomenal shifts. For instance, one experiences a phenomenal shift when thinking of the two different meanings of the sentence 'Visiting royalty can be boring'. This phenomenal shift is not perceptual: one can be thinking about the different meanings of this sentence with one's eyes shut and without one's other sense modalities' being stimulated. It is natural to think that there is some shift in cognitive phenomenal character between thinking of the duck/rabbit figure as a duck and thinking of it as a rabbit. Bill Brewer relies exclusively on this factor in his account of aspect-switching:

> [When] I see it as a duck, say, this is again a phenomenological change, but one of conceptual classificatory engagement with the very diagram presented to me. Similarly, when I shift aspects, and see it as a rabbit, there is an alteration in this phenomenology of the categorization of what is presented.[4]

III.3. *Residual visual phenomenal differences and visual imagination*

One might argue that changes in one's patterns of attention towards the duck/rabbit figure, and changes in how one takes the figure to be, do not fully explain the phenomenal shift which one experiences. One might argue that one can prevent one's patterns of attention from changing, perhaps by looking only at the duck/rabbit's eye and beak/ears, and still experience a visual phenomenal shift when one aspect-switches on the figure.

If it is possible to aspect-switch on ambiguous figures without any change in one's patterns of attention, and if there is a residual, specifically *visual*, phenomenal difference between seeing the figure under the two aspects,

[4] B. Brewer, 'How To Account for Illusion', at http://www2.warwick.ac.uk/fac/soc/philosophy/staff/brewer.

then the above two factors which I have discussed are not sufficient to account for the phenomenon of aspect-switching.

The residual visual phenomenal differences can be explained by means of states of visual imagination. In particular, when one is looking at ambiguous figures, one may well be imagining unseen aspects of the figure. Unlike ordinary objects, ambiguous figures tend to be quite abstract, or lacking in detail. Thus it is not implausible to suppose that one's visual imagination may 'fill in' some detail when one looks at ambiguous figures.

For instance, when one sees the 'TOOT' picture as a man wearing a hat with two strings hanging down each side, one may visually imagine the boundary of a face below the eyes. This may be all that one visually imagines. One may not visually imagine features of the face such as a nose or a mouth. Merely visually imagining a small detail such as the boundary of the face would be sufficient to generate a visual phenomenal difference between seeing the picture as a man and seeing it as, say, a bridge. When one sees the figure as a bridge with two pipes passing underneath it, one may visually imagine the pipes as going off in such and such a direction. Again, this may be all that one visually imagines. Merely visually imagining brief lines going off in a certain direction would be sufficient to generate a visual phenomenal difference that would distinguish seeing the picture as a bridge from seeing it as a man.

The aim of using visual imagination to explain any residual visual phenomenal differences which occur when one aspect-switches on an ambiguous figure, having fixed one's patterns of attention is that the phenomenal character of visual imaginative states is similar to the phenomenal character of visual experiences. The kinds of phenomenal character in question do not seem identical, but they do seem similar. There seems to be a reason why visual imagination is called *visual* imagination. Thus shifts in one's visual imaginative states may be able to account for the residual visual phenomenal differences in question.

IV. SIEGEL'S CASES

Siegel argues that the acquisition of certain conceptual abilities, such as the ability to read Russian and the ability to recognize pine trees, can make certain kinds of objects, such as Russian sentences and pine trees, phenomenally look different.

Siegel argues that there is a phenomenal difference between looking at a page before and after one learns Russian. This claim seems plausible. Inevitably some phenomenal shift will result just because after one has learnt

Russian, one can read the text on the page, whereas beforehand one could not, and understanding the text on the page does have a certain kind of phenomenal character.

However, this account would not explain the *visual* phenomenal shift that occurs in this case. Siegel argues (p. 490) that after one has learnt Russian, one is 'disposed to attend to the semantic properties of the words in the text'. It is not clear that one needs the idea of attending to semantic properties of the words in order to explain the visual phenomenal shift in question. An alternative explanation is that one becomes disposed to attend to the linguistically significant aspects of certain letters, i.e., aspects that distinguish those letters from other letters. For instance, there are two letters in the Cyrillic alphabet that differ only by the presence of a hook at the foot of one of them. In Chinese the width, height and thickness of a stroke are relevant to determining which character it is part of. Learning Russian and Chinese will cause one to be disposed to attend to such features of the letters as these, and these altered patterns of attention towards texts in Russian and Chinese will produce a visual phenomenal shift.

If this explanation is correct, then the largest phenomenal shifts will occur when one learns a language which is written in an alphabet with which one is not familiar. A phenomenal shift may still occur when one learns a language which is written in an alphabet that one does know. The fact that one can read sentences written in the language will alter one's patterns of attention to sentences written in that language. For instance, depending on the language, one may come to look at newly intelligible sentences in a systematic way from left to right, whereas before one learnt the language one might not have looked at the sentences in a systematic way from left to right, because one might not have been attempting to read them.

A similar explanation may be offered for the phenomenal difference which occurs when one learns to recognize pine trees. After one learns to recognize pine trees, one starts to attend to those features of pine trees that distinguish them from other trees, for instance, the colour or thickness of the bark. Acquiring a recognitional disposition for pine trees will cause one's patterns of attention to shift when one looks at a grove containing pine trees and other sorts of trees.

V. NATURAL-KIND PROPERTIES

Suppose that acquiring a recognitional disposition for pine trees *does* cause pine trees phenomenally to look different. Suppose also that acquiring a recognitional disposition for tomatoes, a disposition which I shall henceforth

call 'the concept *tomato*', causes tomatoes to look phenomenally different. I
shall now discuss the question what new property tomatoes phenomenally
look to have after one acquires the concept *tomato*. I shall argue that even
supposing there is a property F such that acquiring the concept *tomato* causes
tomatoes to look F, being F is not the property of being a tomato.

On twin earth there are fruits, 'twin tomatoes', that look and taste just the
same as tomatoes do, but which are not tomatoes, since they are made
from different kinds of molecules from tomatoes. There is no visual phenomenal difference between the way twin tomatoes look to inhabitants of
twin earth and the way tomatoes look to inhabitants of earth. Here I am
assuming phenomenal internalism, which is as follows:

Phenomenal internalism. Necessarily, for all subjects S_1 and S_2, if S_1 is a
molecule-for-molecule duplicate of S_2 then S_1 does not differ from S_2 with
respect to the phenomenal character of the mental states of S_1 and S_2.

Suppose Oscar is an inhabitant of earth, and twin Oscar of twin earth.
Just as, by hypothesis, Oscar's acquisition of the concept *tomato* causes tomatoes phenomenally to look some new F to him, so twin Oscar's acquisition
of the concept *twin tomato* causes twin tomatoes phenomenally to look some
new F to *him*. It seems that the acquisition of the concept *tomato* will bring
about the same kind of visual phenomenal shift as the acquisition of the
concept *twin tomato*. The argument for this claim is that Oscar and twin
Oscar do not know the difference between tomatoes and twin tomatoes, and
they are thus in the same types of brain state, narrowly construed. Given
phenomenal internalism, the acquisition of the concepts *tomato* and *twin
tomato* by Oscar and twin Oscar will produce the same kind of visual phenomenal shift in Oscar and twin Oscar.

For the sake of argument, let us accept the claim that Oscar's acquiring
the concept *tomato* and twin-Oscar's acquiring the concept *twin tomato* bring
about the same kind of visual phenomenal shift for Oscar and twin Oscar. It
follows that there is some new F such that their acquisition of their respec-
tive concepts causes tomatoes and twin tomatoes phenomenally to look F to
Oscar and twin Oscar respectively. If being F is the property of being a
tomato, then twin tomatoes will not be the way they phenomenally look to
twin Oscar. This is counter-intuitive, since twin Oscar has as much right
to say that being F is the property of being a twin tomato, and that tomatoes
are not the way they phenomenally look to Oscar. To avoid an asymmetric
treatment of the cases, it seems that the only option is to hold that being
F is neither the property of being a tomato nor the property of being a
twin tomato. Even if aspect-switching cases do require that objects phenomenally look to have a rich range of properties, there is reason to think

that those properties will not include natural-kind properties such as being a tomato.

VI. CONCLUSION

I have argued that aspect-switching cases, such as the duck/rabbit, do not require that the properties which objects phenomenally look to have (or the properties which are represented by visual experience, to use Siegel's and Searle's terminology) must be richer than properties such as colour, shape, position and size. I have argued that aspect-switching cases can be explained by changes in patterns of attention, cognitive shifts and shifts in visual imagination. In the final section I argued that even if aspect-switching cases are taken to show that objects phenomenally look to have a richer range of properties than colour, shape, position and size, there is reason to think that those richer properties do not include natural-kind properties such as being a tomato.[5]

---

[5] Elsewhere I argue that objects phenomenally look to have just colour and position properties: see http://oxford.academia.edu/RichardPrice/attachment/21/full/Chapter-1---A-Sparse-View- About-The-Properties-That-Objects-Phenomenally- Look-To-Have.

9

THE VISUAL EXPERIENCE OF CAUSATION

By Susanna Siegel

The thesis that we can visually perceive causal relations is distinct from the thesis that visual experiences can represent causal relations. I defend the latter thesis about visual experience, and argue that although they are suggestive, the data provided by Albert Michotte's experiments on perceptual causality do not establish this thesis. Turning to the perception of causality, I defend the claim that we can perceive causation against the objection that its arcane features are unlikely to be represented in experience.

How is causation represented in the mind? We often *believe* that one event has caused another. But can we *visually experience* two things as causally related? If so, then experiences represent causation. A different question in the vicinity is whether we can ever see that something is causing (or has just caused) something else to happen. In the relevant sense of 'seeing' here, seeing is factive: you can see that *p* only if *p*. By contrast, experiential representation of properties or relations is not factive, so you can represent that *p* even if *p* is not true.

These questions are distinct. There are several ways in which visual experiences might represent causation, even if causation cannot be perceived. Most simply, there might be no such thing as causation – it might be a fabrication of the mind. In that case visual experiences could in principle still represent that causal relations obtain, though no such experiences would be veridical. (Some theories of intentionality for experience rule out this possibility, saying that an experience represents a property F only if experiences of that type are normally caused by instances of F.) Alternatively, experience could represent (even correctly represent) that causal relations obtain, but these experiences might fail to count as perception, if their relation to what they represent is never sufficiently direct.

In this chapter I shall argue that causation is represented in visual experience. The first part of the chapter makes a positive case for this claim. In §I, I introduce and clarify the central thesis. In §II, I discuss the bearing on this claim of the psychologist Albert Michotte's data, which are often said to show that adults 'perceive causality'. In §III, I introduce a strategy for defending the view that some experiences represent causal relations. In §IV, I present the central consideration which favours this view. The defence continues in §§V–VI. The last section of the chapter is devoted to defusing arguments that we cannot see or experientially represent causation. So while most of the chapter addresses the question about visual experience, the discussion at the end bears on the question about perception as well.

I. THE CAUSAL THESIS

The central thesis defended in this chapter is this:

Causal thesis.   Some visual experiences represent causal relations.

What is a causal relation? The relations of pushing, pulling, lifting, stopping, moving, supporting, hanging from, and preventing something from happening might naturally be considered modes of causation: they are specific ways of causing something else to happen. There also seems to be a more general relation which these relations exemplify – causation itself. There may be relations which are less specific than the modes I have listed, but more specific than causation itself, such as the varieties of 'launching' discussed by Michotte.[1] In plain launching, an object a approaches a stationary object b, which upon contact starts to move in the same direction as a was moving in. In launching-by-entraining, a pushes b along. In launching-by-expulsion, b moves as if thrown by a. The causal thesis should be interpreted as saying that visual experiences represent either the more general relation, or one of its specific modes.

What is it for a visual experience to represent a causal relation? The notion of representing a property in experience derives from the notion of representing that such and such is the case in experience. If experience represents that such and such is the case, then if such and such did not obtain, the experience would be inaccurate. For instance, if your visual experience represents that the square before you is red, then it will be inaccurate if there is a square before you that is not red. None of this is a definition of what it is for experience to represent that such and such is the case, but it is a start. To finish it, what is needed is an account specifying which accuracy-conditions are the ones at issue. Here the main constraint is that the accuracy-conditions are supposed to reflect the phenomenal character of the experience, so that a statement of the accuracy-conditions of the experience would characterize the subject S's experience, from S's point of view.

[1] A. Michotte, *The Perception of Causality* (London: Methuen, 1963).

One reason to think that visual experiences are assessable for accuracy is that we regularly classify some of them as 'veridical' or 'illusory'. A straightforward account of this is that they are *correct* when they are veridical, and *incorrect* when they are illusory. Some philosophers think this account is flawed, and they deny that such experiences are assessable for accuracy.[2] Here I am just going to assume, contrary to these claims, that visual experiences are assessable for accuracy.[3]

Once it is granted that visual experiences have accuracy-conditions, it is a short step to defining what it is for experiences to represent a property. In the visual experiences of the sort at issue, the properties that are experientially represented are the properties that the objects S sees appear to S to have. For instance, ordinary objects appear to have colour and shape properties, and the causal thesis says that they can appear to stand in causal relations as well. If the causal thesis is true, causal relations are represented in experience in the same way as colour and shape properties are.

To maximize the interest of the causal thesis, it will be useful to make two stipulations about the kind of mental state that can count as an experiential representation of a property. First, since no one doubts that we form beliefs about the causal relations between things, beliefs will not count as experiential representations (if they did, then the causal thesis would be true just in virtue of the fact that people believe that one thing caused something else to happen). Secondly, some philosophers think of experiences as a conjunction of judgements and sensations. In the case of the experiences to be discussed here, this view categorizes them as conjunctions of judgements that one thing has caused another thing to happen, where the judgement itself is not systematically or intrinsically related to any phenomenal character, with sensations which are intrinsically phenomenal, but not systematically or intrinsically related to any representation of causation, judgemental or otherwise. On such a view, experiential representations of causation are structured much as Thomas Reid supposed perceptions to be: the sensational and the representational aspects can vary independently. I shall interpret the notion of an experiential representation in such a way that the causal thesis would not be made true by such a conjunction of states.

---

[2] Further discussion of this point can be found in E.N. Zalta (ed.), *The Stanford Encyclopedia of Philosophy*, http://plato.stanford.edu/archives/spr2005/entries/perception-contents, §2.1.

[3] Even if experiences are not assessable for accuracy, something very much like the question of whether causation is represented in experience would still arise. For instance, if some experiences consist in a subject's perceiving an object as F, as some naïve realists about perception hold, then one can ask whether the values of F can include causation. Likewise, if experiences consist in adverbial modifications of the subject whereby one is 'appeared-to F-ly', one can ask in which ways one can be appeared-to, and specifically whether one may be appeared-to by two (or more) relata in a causal manner.

Whenever causal relations are represented in an experience, the experience has accuracy-conditions, and so represents that such and such is the case, where a causal relation R is part of such and such. This raises the question of what the relata of the causal relation are. The causal thesis leaves this open. The contents of an experience illustrating the causal thesis could be naturally (albeit approximately) expressed by a sentence of the form *x causes y to happen*, in which case *y* would be an event. Or the contents could be naturally expressed by a sentence of the form *x R y* which posits a relation between two things – sometimes objects ('Bob lifted Jack', 'The laundry hangs on the line'), sometimes events ('The scream caused the shudder'). Still another option would be contents roughly expressed by a sentence of the form *x causes y to φ* ('Bob caused Jack to fall', 'The scream caused me to shudder'), where *y* and φ are pairs of objects and properties that bear some close relation to events. If you applied a systematic semantic theory to each of these sentences, it would posit different truth-conditions for each of them, involving different ontological commitments.

The causal thesis is neutral on which of these truth-conditions (if any) experiences have when they represent causal relations. Experiences may not always be sensitive to these differences in truth-conditions, so that there is sometimes some indeterminateness in how exactly the world must be, if the experience is accurate. In other cases experiences may have more determinate truth-conditions. All that matters for the causal thesis, however, is that the truth-conditions include a causal relation.

II. MICHOTTE'S RESULTS

In the 1960s Michotte published the results of about 150 experiments which showed that adults are inclined to describe scenes of launching and entraining in causal terms. In launching, object *a* moves towards a stationary object *b*, makes contact with it, and *b* then without delay begins to move in the same direction as *a* while *a* stops. Entraining is the same except that *a* moves along with *b*. It will be useful to keep these vividly in mind for the subsequent discussion.[4]

Michotte's experiments were attempts to isolate the exact parameters of motion that elicited such descriptions from adults. In some of the experiments the 'objects' were lights or shadows projected on a screen, in others they were ordinary hefty objects such as wooden balls, and some experiments combined both. Subjects knew that no actual causal relations were

---

[4] Readers are encouraged to view these at http://research.yale.edu/ perception/causality/ capture-launchAlone.mov and http://research.yale.edu/perception/causality/entraining.mov.

operative in many of the situations they saw (such as where a shadow 'launches' a ball or *vice versa*), but that did not influence their descriptions. This led Michotte to posit a representation of causality which was something other than a belief about what was happening in the environment. He called it an 'impression of causation'.[5] Michotte's results establish that adults regularly describe launching and entraining in causal terms, saying things like 'The red square moved the blue one along', or 'The ball pushed the shadow'.

What, if anything, do Michotte's results establish about the contents of the visual experiences their subjects report? In general, how people report what they see is a poor guide to the contents of their visual experience. People may use different expressions to describe a scene that looks the same – for instance, two people might try to guess how large or how far away something is, and differ in how good they are at making such estimations. Taking their reports as a guide would force us to conclude that tables (say) look as if they are of different sizes and at different distances from each subject, when in fact there might be no such differences at all. So if Michotte's results tell us anything about the contents of his subjects' visual experiences, this will not be because we can simply read the contents off their reports. In general, one cannot do that.

Michotte's results do not by themselves entail the causal thesis. At best, they entail it when combined with further theoretical assumptions about the relation between experience, beliefs and reports. Suppose, in a case of launching, the 'launching' object (sometimes called the 'motor object') is a ball and the 'launched' object is a patch of light. Adults know that hefty objects cannot cause patches of light to move. Suppose also that we take the following substantive assumption as a rough guide to the contents of experience: these are the contents of what one would believe if one relied on what one knows about the relata. Then we should probably say that the contents of experience are roughly that there is a certain pattern of continuous motion between the ball and the 'moving' patch of light. If we changed the substantive assumption so that the guide to the contents of experience is instead what one would believe if one bracketed what one knows about the nature of the relata, then we might get a different result – that the ball causes the patch of light to move. Either way, we get a verdict that bears on the causal thesis only when Michotte's results are combined with substantive theoretical assumptions linking reports to background beliefs and contents of experience.

[5] Psychologists today use 'perceptual causation' to refer to the kind of mental representation that Michotte posited to explain this description, though sometimes this term is used to label the kinds of scenes that adults are prone to describe as causal – launching, entraining or expulsion.

Furthermore, Michotte's results are compatible with the claim that the visual experiences reported in his experiments (and others like them) merely represent the input-conditions that elicit the causal reports, as opposed to representing causation (or a kinetic mode of causation) itself. The input-conditions are the specific spatiotemporal pattern of continuous motion that elicits the reports. These conditions are features of the world that obtain (we may assume) independently of the subjects' having any experiences. When we ask what contents experiences have, we are asking how experiences present things to the subject. We are asking, roughly, how a specific pattern of motion looks. Michotte's results are compatible with the claim that the subjects' experiences have contents which exactly match this pattern of motion. It is this pattern that elicits the causal descriptions, even when people know that there is no actual causation. Moreover, there are also cases of actual causation, such as heat causing water to boil, or pressure on a button making a light go on, that do not elicit the causal descriptions, as well as cases without actual causation that do elicit it. So an opponent of the causal thesis might say that the natural conclusion to draw is that Michotte's subjects represent the spatiotemporal pattern of continuous motion, rather than causation.

The central question that Michotte's results pose for the causal thesis, then, is whether there is a defensible principle relating report-contents and experience-contents which can be added to Michotte's results to support the causal thesis. This would be one way to try to defend the causal thesis. But instead of trying to develop such a principle here, I am going to pursue a different strategy.

III. HOW TO DEFEND THE CAUSAL THESIS

If the causal thesis is true, then some visual experiences represent causal relations. One candidate for illustrating the causal thesis is experiences of certain static scenes. Suppose there is a cat sitting on a loose mesh hammock, forming a sitting-cat-shaped dip in the hammock's surface. The causal thesis allows that your experience of seeing the cat represents that the cat is pulling the hammock downwards. If the causal thesis is false, then your experience can represent that the part of the net directly under the cat is closer to the ground than the rest of it, but not that the cat is pressing on it. The opponent of the causal thesis holds that experience simply remains neutral on whether any force is being continuously exerted in such a case.

The descriptions of these static experiences championed by an opponent of the causal thesis do not strike me as phenomenally apt. But the phenomenal aptitude of a proposed content for visual experience can be hard to judge when we are given only a single case. Given only a single case, it can be difficult to discern what the phenomenal character of the visual experience is, and hence hard to discern which contents most adequately reflect it. How, then, might we proceed if we want to know whether the causal thesis is true?

One way to proceed is to focus on a pair of cases that fairly obviously differ phenomenally. At this stage, what is important is that people who may ultimately disagree about what, if anything, is represented in experience would agree that these are cases that differ phenomenally. All that introspection is relied upon to do is to recognize a phenomenal contrast, without taking any stand on whether it is also a difference in what is represented, let alone on what the representational difference, if there is one, may be. Once we have such a phenomenal contrast in hand, the following method is available for reaching a reasoned verdict about whether the contrasting experiences represent causal relations. The method is to reason about the best explanation of the phenomenal difference, ruling out some hypotheses and making the case for others. This method is general: it can in principle be used with respect to any property or relation that is putatively represented in experience. How successful it is may vary from case to case, depending on the properties or relations in question, and on the sort of considerations that are available for assessing alternatives.[6]

So far I have spoken of representational differences that 'accompany' the phenomenal ones. One might wonder what 'accompaniment' is, and more specifically whether representational features are explanatorily more fundamental than phenomenal features, or the converse, or neither. All these options can be respected by the causal thesis. If the fact that visual experience has certain contents – say, causal ones – explains why it has the phenomenal character it does, then it will be natural to say that the fact that experienced causal contents exist in one of the cases but not the other accounts for the phenomenal contrast. On this way of thinking about things, the opposing sides in a debate about whether experience has causal contents may agree about what phenomenal character the experience has, but disagree about its contents. In contrast, if the fact that experience has a certain phenomenal character explains why it has causal contents, then it will be more natural to say that the view that the experience has causal contents offers a further characterization of the phenomenal character. On this way of thinking about things, what the opposing sides disagree about is in part what the phenomenal character of the experiences in question is in

---

[6] I discuss and defend this method in 'How Can We Discover the Contents of Experience?', *Southern Journal of Philosophy*, 45 (2007), pp. 127–42.

the first place. I shall talk as if the causal thesis is one way to explain the phenomenal difference, but this is just a manner of speaking. My defence of the causal thesis is indifferent to which of these is the way in which it is developed.

IV. CAUSAL UNITY IN EXPERIENCE

In defending the causal thesis, I shall discuss pairs of experiences which differ phenomenally. These pairs will bring into focus a specific and familiar kind of unity in experience. Suppose you are playing catch indoors. A throw falls short and the ball lands in a potted plant, with its momentum absorbed all at once by the soil. You see it land, and just after that, the lights go out. The ball's landing in the plant does not cause the lights to go out, and by hypothesis you do not believe that it does. Nevertheless it may seem to you that the ball's landing somehow caused the lights to go out. This is the first case. In the second case, you likewise see the ball land and the lights go out. But this case is unlike the first: you do not have any feeling that the ball's landing *caused* the lights to go out. Your visual experience represents the ball's trajectory and landing, and it also represents the lights going out, but so far as your visual experience is concerned, these events merely occur in quick succession.

It seems plain that there can be a phenomenal difference between two such experiences. This provides a starting-point for the method described above. But in this case, a bit more can be said at the outset about the phenomenal contrast to be explained. This contrast seems to have something to do with the connection between events: the difference stems from how the lights' going off seems to you to be related to the landing of the ball.[7] The successive events seem to be unified in experience in a way that is not merely temporal.

There are also cases of a similar sort of experienced unity involving simultaneous events. Suppose you draw open the curtain from a window and let in some light. Here there is one event, the uncovering of the window, that occurs simultaneously with another event, the increased illumination of the room. These events occur simultaneously. They can also, let us assume, be experienced as occurring simultaneously. Contrast this with a case in

---

[7] I have focused on how the observed events seem to be related: the light's going off seems related to the trajectory of the ball. Arguably, the associated experiences (or parts of experience) also seem to be related: the experience of seeing the lights go off seems related to the experience of seeing the ball land in the plant. I am setting aside the question of how these two kinds of unity may be related.

which you draw open a curtain that does not block out any light in the first place (perhaps because it is translucent). Just as you uncover the window, the sun comes out from behind a dark cloud, causing the room to lighten progressively as the curtain is drawn open. Here we have a very similar event of uncovering the window, coupled with an event of the room gradually lightening, and (we can suppose) these events have and are experienced as having the same duration. But it seems that there could none the less be a phenomenal difference between the two experiences, with respect to how the window's uncovering and the room's illumination are experienced as related to one another. I am taking this to be an intuition. In this application of the method for investigating whether a certain content is a content of visual experience, I am taking the *explanandum* to be not merely a phenomenal contrast, but more specifically a contrast with respect to whether the events in question seem to be unified – leaving open, at the outset, just what kind of unity those events seem to have.

In what way might the events seem to be unified? A natural suggestion is that in the one case there is an experiential representation of causation, whereas in the other case there is not. If so, then in the ball case one of the experiences represents the ball-landing and the lights' going off as causally unified, and in the curtain case one of the experiences represents that the uncovering of the window lets in the light. The main merit of the causal thesis is that it provides a plausible account of the phenomenal difference between each pair.

To defend the causal thesis properly, what is needed is reason to think that this is the best account of the phenomenal contrast. There seem to be two main alternative types of hypotheses. Either the difference is due to a cognitive element, such as a disposition to form a causal belief, or else it is due to a difference in exclusively non-causal contents.[8] In the next section, I discuss the latter alternative – agreeing with the causal thesis that experiences have contents, but holding that in the pairs of cases in question these contents are exclusively non-causal.

V. NON-CAUSAL CONTENTS

One might think that the phenomenal difference between the two cases in each pair (the ball and the curtain) is a difference exclusively in non-causal contents. The central question about this proposal is whether the contents of

---

[8] The further alternative that the experiences in question are simply 'raw feels', with no content at all, is at odds with the starting assumption that the visual experiences in question have contents. Some responses to the two-component view in §VI address this view as well.

the experiences in question could be exhausted by non-causal contents.

I shall focus for a moment on motion, illumination and temporal contiguity in the curtain case. An opponent of the causal thesis might say that if the two events – the uncovering and the lightening – unfold in such a way that the increases in light are correlated with the movement of the curtain in just the right way, then there will be an impression of unity between these events. But this need not be an impression of causal unity, the opponent might say; it is merely an impression of a special correlation between the rates at which two things happen.

Could it be the rate at which the window is uncovered and at which light streams in that makes it seem as if uncovering the window has let in the light? If so, then while these rates could be the same in each of the curtain cases, they could not be visually represented as the same – since if they were, then (on this proposal) there would be an impression of causation in both cases, whereas by hypothesis there is such an impression only in one.

This opponent of the causal thesis thus has to hold that if there were a pair of curtain experiences with the phenomenal difference described, one of the experiences would have to be falsidical. *Mutatis mutandis* for the ball experiences.

This prediction seems implausible. Why must either experience involve any error in how fast the uncovering or the lightening is experienced as occurring? Taken separately, each case in the pair can perfectly well be imagined to be a completely veridical experience. So this alternative requires illusion where intuitively there does not seem to have to be any. If so, then both the actual rates of the events and the rates at which they are experienced as occurring can be the same, on both occasions. It seems that opponents of the causal thesis will have to look elsewhere to account for the phenomenal difference.

Where else might they look? The curtain cases were described in such a way that the colour and thickness of the curtain differs in the scenes, and there were corresponding differences in the contents of experience. The difference in perceived colour, however, seems irrelevant to experienced unity between the uncovering of the window and the lightening of the room. Changing the perceived colour of the curtain does not seem to affect whether or not the visual experience represents the light as being let in as a result of the curtain's moving, so long as the curtain is thick. (Moreover, if one could have such an experience at all, it seems that one could have it without even registering the colour of the curtain.) What about the curtain? Suppose, for the sake of argument, that the curtain's luminous properties are unlike its colour in that at least one of the experiences has to represent that the weave of the curtain is either opaque or transparent. (This leaves open whether or not the other experience is neutral on the curtain's luminous properties, either by failing to represent anything about them at all, or by representing a more general luminous property of which opacity and translucence are determinates.) One might claim that the phenomenal difference between the two curtain-openings is due to a difference in representation of luminous properties. In effect, this proposes to explain an impression of unity between the window-uncovering and the room's getting lighter by focusing exclusively on the illumination properties of the curtain.

If the impression of unity has any content at all, however, then it would concern the relation between the lightening and the uncovering of the window, since these are the events that seem to be unified. This proposal looks for the key representational element in a different relational property – the relation between the curtain and light in general. So it seems to be looking in the wrong place.

Another option is that visual experience represents the events in question as unified, without representing them as causally unified. What kind of unity might this be? Perhaps there is a kind of unity analogous to the kind discussed by Husserl in connection with the experience of the passage of time. Suppose you hear a series of five sounds: the clink of a cup against a saucer, the groan of an accelerating bus, a creak from a chair, a snippet of a loud voice, and the honk of a car's horn. Compare this auditory experience with hearing five notes of a melody. We experience the notes of the melody as unified in a way in which we need not experience the five sounds as unified, even if at each moment we remember the sounds from the previous moments. Husserl observed that such remembering does not suffice to make us experience any remembered series of motley sounds as integrated, as we hear the notes of a melody to be integrated. Rather, when we hear the sounds as a melody, the previous ones remain present to us in a distinctive way even after they have ceased. Husserl had a special term, 'retention', for this way of remaining present to us. In the case of the melody, the previous notes are 'retained', whereas in the motley series they are not, and that is what makes it the case that we hear the notes as a melody, but not the motley sounds.[9]

There seems to be a phenomenal difference between these two experiences, one which stems not just from the different qualities of the individual sounds, but from the way in which the sounds seem to be related to one another in each experience. One might think that analogously, the ball's

[9] Husserl discusses the notion of retention, in connection with hearing melodies, in lectures given between 1893 and 1917, in *On the Phenomenology of the Consciousness of Internal Time*, tr. J.B. Brough (Dordrecht: Kluwer, 1980). I have discussed the contrast between melody and motley sounds in Siegel, 'The Phenomenology of Efficacy', *Philosophical Topics*, 33 (2005), pp. 265–84.

landing in the plant seems in the first case to be unified with the lights' going out, while it does not seem like that in the second case. The general idea seems to be that the events somehow belong together as a unit – perhaps in something like the way in which the *Gestalt* psychologists thought that the geese in a flock appear to be a unit.

As stated, this proposal is not a very specific one. Moreover, it does not make clear what accuracy-conditions it is positing. Likewise, in the case of retention, it is difficult to say how the world has to be in order for experiences of retention to be accurate. It is clearly not enough that the notes of the melody occur in succession. The opponent of the causal thesis I have been considering draws an analogy between retention, on the one hand, and a kind of unity that can be visually represented in the case of the ball or the curtain, on the other, where the unity experiences have exclusively non-causal contents. This raises the question of which contents these are. A proposal which we can assess needs to say, at a minimum, how things in the world have to be in order for the experience to be accurate.

To return to the case of the ball landing in the plant and appearing to turn off the lights, suppose the ball's landing does not really turn off the light. So the proponent of the causal thesis (if in agreement that this experience illustrates the thesis) predicts that the experience is falsidical, because it represents two events as causally related when they are not. What does the opponent predict about the experience? Is it veridical because the events really are unified in the way in which experience presents them as being (and there is no other illusion), or is it falsidical because the events only appear to be 'unified'? Similar questions apply to the experience of seeing the light coming on at 6 a.m. and then hearing the neighbour's whirring coffee grinder. There does not seem to be any obvious relation that events in the world can have when such experiences are veridical but lack when they are falsidical. This suggests to me that we should not conclude from the analogy with Husserlian retention that the curtain and ball cases have non-causal unity content. Rather, the lesson of the analogy should just be that there is a special kind of temporal relation which one can experience events as having, and that sometimes such events also seem to be causally related, but at other times they do not.

How else might one try to account for the feeling of unity in the ball and curtain cases (and others like them), without accepting the causal thesis? A more specific proposal is that in the ball case, experience represents that if the ball had not landed in the plant, then the lights would not have gone out. According to this proposal, what is represented is a relation of counter-factual dependence: specifically, the lights' going out counterfactually depends on the ball's landing in the plant.

Some philosophers think that causation is a kind of counterfactual dependence, and they may hear this proposal as a proposal in favour of the causal thesis, rather than a proposed alternative to it. But even those who favour counterfactual analyses of causation do not identify this relation with causation itself. For example, according to Lewis, if c and e are two events such that e would not have occurred without c, then c is a cause of e – so counterfactual dependence is sufficient for causation. But he denies that it is necessary. Others who have developed counterfactual theories of causation take counterfactual dependence as a starting-point rather than a stopping-point of analysis. Because it has struck many philosophers as such a reasonable starting-point for analyses of causation, one might think that it is the perfect candidate for being a non-causal relation which is represented in experience: it is (relatively) simple, but close enough (by their lights) to causation itself to account for unity phenomenology in the cases at issue.

More generally, the proposal says that for two events x, y that occur, if an experience represents that y would not have occurred had x not occurred, then it will seem to the subject as if x and y are unified in the way in which the ball's landing and the lights' going off seem to be unified. This proposal predicts that if visual experience represents that an event y counterfactually depends on an event x then those events will be experienced as unified in the way exemplified by the ball and the curtain cases.

Some philosophers think that counterfactuals cannot be represented in visual experience. Colin McGinn seems to voice this claim:

> You do not see what *would* obtain in certain counterfactual situations; you see only what actually obtains. When you see something as red you do not see the counterfactual possibilities that constitute its having a disposition to appear red. Your eyes do not respond to *woulds* and *might have beens*.[10]

There are several different things McGinn might have in mind. One is that we do not see events other than the actual ones that occur at the time of the experience. This is true. Another claim is that if you see that an object has a property F, then F has to be instantiated by the object you see. This claim is also true. But it does not follow from either of these claims that it is impossible to see that an object has a dispositional property. If a thing has a disposition, then it is part of 'what actually obtains' that the thing has the disposition. If a counterfactual is true of an object you see, then the counterfactual is part of what actually obtains too.

A different thing McGinn might have in mind is simply that counterfactuals cannot be represented in visual experience – not because they are

---

[10] C. McGinn, 'Another Look at Color', *Journal of Philosophy*, 93 (1996), pp. 537–53, at p. 540.

not part of what actually obtains, but because their antecedents and consequents describe occurrences that are not occurring in the very situation being seen (or if it is a case of hallucination, in the situation which is experientially represented). If this claim is true, then it is incorrect to propose that instead of representing causal relations between the ball's landing and the lights' going off, the subject's experience represents that the lights' going off counterfactually depends on the ball's landing.

I think this proposal is false, but not because counterfactuals in general cannot be represented in visual experience. Gibson suggested that we sometimes perceive 'affordances' of things, where these are possibilities for interaction with them – such as the rollability of a ball, or that a flat solid surface would support us, or that we shall not find support beyond a 'cliff' where the floor suddenly drops off.[11] If we can perceive affordances, then there will be cases where we can perceive possible – and sometimes merely possible – continuations of what we actually see. Perhaps one of the simplest cases of such an affordance would be a ball's continuing along the path on which it is thrown. If someone catches it, the catcher interrupts its path, and arguably there are cases (curve balls aside) in which we can perceive and experientially represent the direction in which it would have continued had it not been caught. More exactly, we can experientially represent that the ball would have continued in the direction it was moving, had its path not been interrupted. Some other examples: you see Joe trying to grab hold of a cup sitting on a high shelf. He stands on his toes, stretching one arm up high, straining to reach a bit higher. But the cup is just out of reach. In the counterfactual *If he reached just a bit farther, he could grab the cup* the antecedent describes a continuation of a motion that one can see – the motion of reaching for the cup. Similarly, suppose you are watching a powerful windstorm, with wind blowing so hard that a cloth stuck to a branch of the tree is waving furiously, and remains attached to the branch only by a small corner. The antecedent of the counterfactual *If the wind blew harder, the cloth would fly away* describes a strengthening of the wind. One can imagine a rock balancing precariously on the pointed tip of another rock. Could your visual experience represent that the rock would tip over if pushed, Joe could grab the cup if he reached farther, or that the cloth would fly away if the wind blew harder? As proposals about the contents of the visual experience, these are not obviously incorrect. If these counterfactuals can be represented in visual experience, then McGinn goes too far if he suggests that no counterfactuals can be so represented.

None the less there is something correct in McGinn's general doubt. He

[11] E.J. Gibson and R.D. Walk, 'The "Visual Cliff"', *Scientific American*, 202 (1960), pp. 67–71.

seems correct about cases in which the antecedent of the counterfactual does not specify any natural continuation of an event that you see. In the ball case, it is the event of the ball's landing and the event of the lights' going off that seem to be unified. So if the proposal challenging the causal thesis by appealing to counterfactual dependence were correct, then we should expect that the visual experience in this case represents that if the ball had not landed in the plant, then the lights would not have gone off. In the curtain case, it is the event of moving the curtain and the lightening of the room which seem to be unified. So if the proposal were correct, we should expect that the subject's visual experience represents that if the curtain had not moved, the room would not have lightened.

In both these counterfactuals, the antecedents do not describe natural continuations or movements of scenes that the subject sees. Instead, the antecedents merely negate a description of something that happens, without any indication of what would have happened instead. The reason to think that this could not be represented in visual experience derives from the intuition McGinn voices when he says that our eyes do not respond to woulds and might have beens. The antecedent of the counterfactuals in the ball and curtain cases are not closely enough connected to what the subject actually sees to be represented in visual experience. The possibilities they describe are visually unconnected with the actual events we see. The hypothesis that we represent counterfactual dependence in the ball case (and others like them) demands much more powerful insight into modal space than is demanded by the proposal that we represent counterfactuals about the direction in which the ball will continue once it is thrown. Perception is not that powerful.

VI. TWO-COMPONENT VIEWS

So far, I have criticized one alternative to the account of the phenomenal differences provided by the causal thesis, the alternative that the phenomenal differences discussed can be accounted for by a difference between the non-causal contents of the experiences in each pair. I now turn to another alternative to the causal thesis, which chalks up the unity phenomenology to a cognitive element, such as a disposition to form a causal belief.

According to the simplest version of this view, experience proper consists of a state without causal content – perhaps a state with exclusively non-causal contents, or perhaps a raw feel with no contents at all. But, this position says, when two events seem to be unified in a visual experience, in addition S is disposed to form a causal belief (as it might be, a belief that uncovering the window let in the light). According to a different version of the view, experiences are identified with a sensory–cognitive complex, rather than with the sensory component alone. Either way, there are two components in the vicinity of the experiences in the ball and the curtain cases: the sensory component, and a disposition to form a causal belief.

What, according to these views, explains how it is that one has a disposition to form a causal belief? I shall first consider the version which identifies experiences with the sensory–cognitive complex. It is not open to proponents of this view to say that S has the disposition because S has an experience, since by their lights the disposition is part of the experience. The reasonable alternative is that it is the sensory component alone that gives the subject this disposition. The simple version of the view, which identifies experience with this sensory component alone, can agree that the sensory component makes S disposed to form this belief – and proponents of this view can thereby simultaneously embrace the natural idea that the experience is responsible for S's being so disposed.

Whichever state or pair of states is identified with experiences, the crucial question is what exactly makes S disposed to form a causal belief. Here is a crucial difference between the Michotte cases and the case of the ball and the light. In Michotte's cases, an impression of causation is inevitable. It is easy to imagine a version of the ball case, however, where one did not feel that the ball landing in the plant and light going off were unified. One might just experience this as a succession of events that are not unified as they are in the initial example. Indeed, the two-component view is committed to allowing such cases, since each component could in principle be had without the other. But if the sensory component can be had without S's being disposed to form a causal belief, then it is doubtful that the sensory component is what gives S that disposition. The two-component view, then, seems to lack a good account of why in the ball case S is disposed to form a causal belief.

Another challenge to two-component views concerns the relation between the putatively separate components of experience. Since it is possible to have the sensory component without the cognitive component, the relation must fall short of lawlike regularity. One option is that the sensory component causes the causal representation, without there being any lawlike connection between the property of being that kind of sensory state and the property of being a belief or disposition to believe with the specific causal content posited. (This is compatible with there being some other sort of nomic connection between the two events, connecting some other properties they each have.) But such a causal link does not seem to be able to account for how closely the cognitive component would be *felt* to be associated with the sensory component. A pang of sadness could cause you to remember that you need to buy light bulbs, but this would not be enough to make it seem to you that the sad feeling and the memory content have anything to do with each other. In contrast, even by the lights of the two-component views, the putative sensory component and causal contents seem to S to be associated, since the sensory component presents the relata that seem to be causally related. So the relation between these components would have to be something other (or more) than mere causation.

The proponent of the two-component view might posit a higher-order state which represents that the sensory component and the component representing causation are appropriately connected. This would be one way to ensure that the two components seem to S to go together. But it is pretty clearly not necessary to have such a higher-order state in order to have the kind of experience of unity of the sort illustrated by the ball and curtain cases. Such higher-order states about relations between other mental states are comparatively rare, since they require elaborate self-reflection.

One might wonder where in the scheme to fit Hume's claim that the idea of causation arises when the mind makes a transition between ideas. There are two ways in which this might be done. First, the transition between ideas could be part of the content of the experience, in which case the result would be a higher-order content of the sort just discussed. Secondly, the claim that there is such a transition could just be a description of some psychological structure underlying experience. If so, it is neutral on the causal thesis.[12]

A different two-component view, perhaps loosely related to Hume's claim, is that one component is non-causal contents (with whatever phenomenal character goes along with having those), while the second component is a sensation, or raw feel, which is associated with causation. According to this view, when these two components are put together, we get the distinctive feeling of causal unity.

In order for these components really to be separate, it must be coherent to suppose that the alleged raw feel of causation could occur without the non-causal contents – since if these could not occur separately, then there would not be two components after all. To focus on the supposed raw feel, the proponent of this view is committed to the possibility that someone could have an experience with this very raw feel, but without the overall feeling of causation. This possibility is not obviously coherent. Our initial grip on what phenomenal character this is comes from the sorts of examples

---

[12] I am focusing just on Hume's claim about a transition between mental items, ignoring other commitments about the nature of ideas Hume may have had which might rule out the causal thesis.

I have discussed, in all of which there is uncontroversially some feeling of causation (just *which* kind of feeling is what is in question). Do we really have any grip on what the phenomenal character is, apart from those experiences of causation? Proponents of this two-component view are committed to saying that we have, since for them the relation between phenomenal character and the feeling of causation is contingent. They are committed to there being something recognizable as the same feeling as is had in my examples, but without it being a feeling of causation.

I have argued that the causal thesis is a good explanation of the unity experienced in the ball and the curtain cases. There are of course alternative explanations, and I have not addressed every possibility. One alternative I have set aside is that there might be no contents involved in the experiences in question at all. But if there are, then the options seem to fall exhaustively into two broad categories: there are non-causal contents, and there are combinations of cognitive causal contents with sensory components lacking causal contents. I have tried to address the main considerations surrounding each of these alternatives.

In the rest of the chapter, I consider an argument against the causal thesis which also opposes the thesis that causation can be perceived. My attempts to defuse it thus bear on both of the questions with which the chapter began – the question about perception, and the question about visual experience.

VII. ARE ARCANE FEATURES OF CAUSAL RELATIONS REPRESENTED IN EXPERIENCE?

Someone might doubt the causal thesis on the ground that causal relations are the wrong *kind* of thing to be represented in visual experience, given the nature of our perceptual apparatus. Causation, the thought goes, is a kind of counterfactual dependence, or a kind of energy transfer, or a kind of lawful necessitation; none of these things can be represented in visual experience. I shall criticize two specific instances of this doubt, and then respond to the doubt in its general form.

This doubt about the causal thesis has a two-part structure. The first part identifies a factor X such that to represent experientially that a is causing b would be to represent factor X. Factor X could be a relation which (some true theory in metaphysics tells us) is the causal relation, or it could be a related property such that any instance of causation is also an instance of X. The second part provides what is supposed to be a principled reason to deny that factor X can be so represented.

One instance of the doubt focuses on counterfactual dependence.

According to this version of the doubt, to represent experientially that *a* and *b* are causally related would be to represent that certain counterfactuals hold. For instance, if your visual experience represents that the knife is cutting the bread, then it would have to represent that if the knife stopped moving and no other force were applied to the bread, then the bread would not continue to be sliced; if your visual experience represented that uncovering the window lets in the light, then it would have to represent that if the window were covered again, then the light would be blocked, and so on.

The second part of this instance of the general doubt is the claim that counterfactuals are not represented in visual experience. This claim contradicts the central idea in Gibson's work on perception, that we perceive 'affordances' of things, such as the rollability of a ball. To oppose the claim, however, one need not think that we perceive nothing but affordances. It is enough to refute McGinn (on this interpretation of the remark I have quoted) if there are some cases in which we see that *p*, where *p* would be naturally expressed by using a counterfactual. I have examined earlier some cases in which it is not obviously incorrect to say that experiences represent counterfactuals.

Another instance of the doubt focuses on what is useful to call *nomic generalism* about causation, where this is the view that two (or more) relata are causally related only if the relation they stand in instantiates an (exceptionless) law. In contrast, *singularism* about causation holds that causal relations need not instantiate such laws.[13] It has been suggested that nomic generalism about causation is incompatible with the thesis that causation can be perceived. I shall call this 'the incompatibility claim'. In a summary of Anscombe's chapter 'Causality and Determination', Sosa and Tooley endorse this incompatibility claim, and suggest it as an interpretation of Anscombe's main point.

> ... there would seem to be a close relation between a singularist conception of causation and the thesis that causation can be directly perceived – a thesis which [Anscombe] certainly is defending. For if two events could be causally related only if that relation were an instance of some law, to observe that two events were causally related would be to observe that there was some relevant law, and it not easy to see how a single observation could serve to establish such a conclusion. So it is hard to see how causation could be directly observable if a singularist conception of causation were not true.[14]

Suppose nomic generalism about causation is true. Taking '*S* observes that *p*' to be non-factive, and substituting '*S*'s visual experience represents'

---

[13] Sometimes 'singular causation' is used differently, to pick out causal relations holding between particulars as opposed to properties.

[14] E. Sosa and M. Tooley (eds), *Causation* (Oxford UP, 1993), introduction, p. 13.

for 'S sees that' (plus minor adjustments), yields the following argument:

1. If S's visual experience represents that a causes b, then that visual experience represents that (a, b) instantiates a law
2. For any events (a, b), one's visual experience cannot represent that (a, b) instantiates a law
3. Therefore one cannot represent in visual experience that a caused b.[15]

There are many ways to elaborate what it would be for two causal relata to instantiate a law, and how this is elaborated will determine exactly what (1) and (2) come to. For now, I set this complication aside. On virtually any account of what nomic subsumption is, (1) seems open to question. One may grant that if a causes b, then (a, b) instantiates a law. It does not follow from this that if one's experience represents that p, and p entails q, then one's experience represents that q. That there is an ice cube on the table entails that there is a chemical compound on the table. But one can see that there is an ice cube on the table without seeing that there is a chemical compound on the table. An analogous point holds for representations in visual experience. So the argument seems to start off badly.

In its general form, the doubt considers a feature X closely tied to causation itself – either by being a feature had by any relata of causal relations, or by being the *analysans* of an analysis of causation. I shall call X a 'distinctive feature of causation'. The doubt then claims that the distinctive feature X cannot be represented in visual experience, and concludes that causal relations cannot be either. So far, I have considered two possible values for X – relations of counterfactual dependence, and lawfulness. But something more general can be said. From the fact that X is a feature distinctive of causal relations, it does not follow that an experience representing a causal relation would have to represent X. An experience could correctly represent that a succession (or a pair of simultaneous relata) is a case of causation, without representing any of the features that (putatively) make it a case of causation. Even if feature X is the property that some theory of causation tells us *is* causation itself, and even if that theory is correct, one could still represent in experience that one thing causes something else to happen without representing X in experience. Visual experience might just be neutral on whether anything, or any relation between things, has feature X.

Holes provide an analogy. It is hard to say what makes something a hole. But it is clearly possible to see holes, and to represent them experientially as

---

[15] Sosa and Tooley's remarks could also be developed into an argument about seeing, taking 'S observes that p' to be factive, and substituting 'see' for 'observe': if S sees that a causes b, then S sees that (a, b) instantiate a law; we cannot see that a law obtains; so we cannot see that a causes b. The criticism raised against the argument presented in the text applies to this argument as well.

holes. Here we seem to have a case in which there is a property – the property of being a hole – that is represented in experience, even though we do not represent in experience any more specific feature that distinguishes holes from non-holes.

Suppose you see some cheese with a hole in it, and your visual experience is veridical. According to one theory of the metaphysics of holes, they are immaterial particulars. According to an opposing theory, they are material but negative parts of material particulars.[16] When the cheese appears to have a hole in it, does it appear to host an immaterial particular, or does it appear to have a material part – or neither, or both? If the cheese appeared to have both of these more specific properties, then the experience could not be veridical after all, since the hole cannot be both material and immaterial. The best answer seems to be 'neither': visual experience just seems neutral on whether the hole in the cheese is a material but negative part or an immaterial part hosted by a material particular. Visual phenomenology does not seem to count for or against either of these theories, even if there are faults to be found with the theories on other grounds. If so, it seems likely that visual experiences do not take a stand on the metaphysics of holes.

Suppose some metaphysical theory of holes turns out to be correct (one of the two I have mentioned, or some other). If experience is neutral in the way I have described, then we have a case in which an object has a distinctive feature H if it has a hole, and experience represents the property of having a hole, but does not represent distinctive feature H. So – returning to the general doubt – it will not in general be true that if X is a distinctive feature of causal relations, an experience represents that a causal relation holds between two things only if it represents X. To support the doubt, then, some argument is needed that the case of causation is not like the case of holes.

An opponent of the causal thesis might say that the case of causation is indeed disanalogous to the case of holes or ice cubes: whereas it is not analytic that ice is H_2O or that holes are, say, immaterial particulars, it is supposed to be analytic that causation is a kind of counterfactual dependence. Or one might try to make a similar point using the notion of concepts instead of analyticity: it is supposedly a conceptual truth, if it is true at all, that causation is a kind of counterfactual dependence, but supposedly not a conceptual truth that ice is H_2O, or that holes are immaterial particulars – assuming that they are. But while this point shows a disanalogy between the ice case and the case of causation, there does not seem to be any disanalogy

---

[16] The first theory is defended by R. Casati and A.C. Varzi, *Holes and Other Superficialities* (Cambridge: Bradford Books, 1994), the second by D.D. Hoffman and W.A. Richards, 'Parts of Recognition', *Cognition*, 18 (1985), pp. 65–96; see also D.K. and S.R. Lewis, 'Holes', *Australasian Journal of Philosophy*, 48 (1970), pp. 206–12, repr. in D.K. Lewis, *Philosophical Papers*, Vol. 1 (Oxford UP, 1983), pp. 3–9.

between the case of causation and the case of holes. Whatever relation
theorizing about causation has to the concept of causation or the meaning of
'causation' seems to be in place in the case of theorizing about holes and the
meaning of 'hole' as well.

I have argued that causation may be like holes, in that we can represent
causation in visual experience without representing its distinctive features.
This rebuttal emphasizes what you do *not* have to represent in visual experience in order for your experience to represent causation. One might then
wonder whether there is any way causation *must* look, if it is represented in
visual experience. At one extreme is the position I have just discussed, which
says that causation could be represented only if its distinctive nature were
revealed in experience as well. At the other extreme is the position that
things could look in *any* way to S compatible with S's visual experience representing causation (e.g., an experience could count as representing causation, even if all that S seemed to see was an undifferentiated expanse of
yellow). This extreme seems implausible as well. If both positions are false,
then there are only some ways in which events (or other relata) can appear
when they appear to stand in a causal relation. But which ways are these?
To put it differently, what are the phenomenal constraints on the representation of causation in visual experience? Are there any?

One proposal for a minimal constraint is that things look as if they stand
in a causal relation only if they look contiguous spatially or temporally. (The
events in the ball case are not and do not appear to be spatially contiguous,
but they do appear to occur in quick succession.) Michotte's results seem to
provide some support for this minimal constraint. If you show adults (and, as
it happens, chimpanzees) a scene of launching with a temporal gap (the
second ball does not start moving until after the first one has collided with it
and stopped), they do not report what they see as a case of causation.

Although this constraint cannot differentiate representation of causation
from the representation of mere contiguity, it may be a necessary phenomenal condition for experiential representation of causation. The deeper
question in the vicinity, however, is why there should be any phenomenal
constraints at all on how causation may look.[17]

[17] Versions of this chapter were presented at the Arizona Ontology Conference, Bates
College, the On-Line Philosophy Conference and the University of Warwick. Thanks to audi-
ences for their responses. For further discussion, thanks to Stephen Butterfill, Elizabeth Camp,
Imogen Dickie, Andy Egan, John Hawthorne, M.G.F. Martin, Casey O'Callaghan, Laurie
Paul, Brian Scholl, Jessica Wilson, and especially David Chalmers.

IO

THE ADMISSIBLE CONTENTS OF VISUAL EXPERIENCE

By Michael Tye

My purpose is to take a close look at the nature of visual content. I discuss the view that visual experiences have only existential contents, the view that visual experiences have either singular or gappy contents, and the view that visual experiences have multiple contents. I also consider a proposal about visual content inspired by Kaplan's well known theory of indexicals. I draw out some consequences of my discussion for the thesis of intentionalism with respect to the phenomenal character of visual experience.

One thought inspiring disjunctivist theories of experience has been that in cases of veridical perception, the subject is directly in contact with the perceived object.[1] When I perceive a tomato, for example, there is no tomato-like sense-impression that stands as an intermediary between the tomato and me. Nor am I related to the tomato as I am to a deer when I see its footprint in the snow. I do not experience the tomato by experiencing something *else* over and above the tomato and its facing surface. I see the facing surface of the tomato *directly*.

This, of course, is the view of naïve realism. It seems as good a starting-point as any for further theorizing about the nature of perception. Some disjunctivists have suggested that to do proper justice to the above thought, we need to suppose that the objects we perceive are *components* of the contents of our perceptual experiences in veridical cases. This supposition is supported further by the simple observation that if I see an object, it must look some way to me. But if an object looks some way to me, then intuitively it must be experienced *as* being some way. How can the object be experienced as being some way unless the object itself figures in the content of the experience, assuming that experience is representational at all?

A third related consideration is that in cases of illusion the perceived object appears other than it is. In such cases, intuitively, the perceptual

---

[1] See, e.g., J.M. Hinton, *Experiences* (Oxford: Clarendon Press, 1973); P. Snowdon, 'The Objects of Direct Experience', *Proceedings of the Aristotelian Society*, Supp. Vol. 64 (1990), pp. 121–50; M. Martin, 'The Transparency of Experience', *Mind & Language*, 17 (2002), pp. 376–425, and 'On Being Alienated', in T.S. Gendler and J. Hawthorne (eds), *Perceptual Experience* (Oxford UP, 2006), pp. 354–410.

experience is inaccurate.[2] It is so precisely because the object is not as it appears to be. This strongly suggests that at least in those cases where there is a perceived object, a perceptual experience has a content into which the perceived object enters along with its apparent properties.[3] The experience, then, is accurate if and only if the object *has* those apparent properties.

Once it is acknowledged that the content of visual experience is singular in veridical cases, it must also be acknowledged that in cases of hallucination, the content (if there is one) is not singular.[4] For in these cases there is no object with which the subject is in perceptual contact. This has led disjunctivists to conclude that there is no shared mental state common to veridical and hallucinatory visual experiences.[5] The class of such experiences is not like the class of beliefs, say. Instead, the former class is more like the class of tigers or tables.

This is not to say that to their subjects veridical and hallucinatory experiences never *seem* the same. Upon occasion, the former may be introspectively indistinguishable from the latter. But when this happens, the veridical experience and the hallucinatory experience are no more closely related than a lemon and a bar of soap that looks just like a lemon.[6] The one experience is indistinguishable from the other via introspection, just as the lemon and the soap are indistinguishable from one another visually. Even so, the two are very different kinds of thing.

The purpose of this chapter is to take a close look at the nature of perceptual content. The chapter is divided into nine sections. In §I, I discuss further the view, at odds with this introduction, that experiences have only existential contents, and I raise a further serious objection to it. In §II, I lay out the thesis that experiences have only singular contents in normal veridical cases and gappy contents otherwise. I bring out some difficulties for this thesis. In §III, I consider a proposal about visual content inspired by

---

[2] Not everyone accepts this claim. One notable exception is C. Travis, 'The Silence of the Senses', *Mind*, 113 (2004), pp. 57–94.

[3] Not all disjunctivists grant that in cases of illusion, perceptual experiences have contents of the same sort as veridical perceptual experiences: see, e.g., Martin, 'On Being Alienated'. Obviously those disjunctivists who take this view cannot use the present consideration to support their theory.

[4] Assuming that the term 'singular content' is used in the usual way. For an opposing usage, see M. Sainsbury, *Reference without Referents* (Oxford UP, 2006).

[5] This is an over-simplification. Martin, for example, sometimes seems to hold that there is 'no distinctive mental event or state common to these various disjoint situations': Martin, 'The Reality of Appearances', in M. Sainsbury (ed.), *Thought and Ontology* (Milan: Franco Angeli, 1997), p. 37. But he also says (p. 86) that 'the disjunctive view itself should be viewed as strictly neutral between views which assume that experience is a common element and those that deny it'. In the text, I assume that disjunctivism is a definite metaphysical thesis. For more on varieties of disjunctivism, see A. Byrne and H. Logue (eds), *Disjunctivism: Contemporary Readings* (forthcoming).

[6] Cf. J.L. Austin, *Sense and Sensibilia* (Oxford: Clarendon Press, 1962), p. 50.

Kaplan's well known theory of indexicals. In §IV, I elaborate the thesis that experiences have multiple contents. In §V, I consider an attempt to reinstate the existential thesis. §VI returns to the proposal that visual experiences have only either singular or gappy contents. In §VII, I draw out some consequences of my discussion for the thesis of strong intentionalism with respect to the phenomenal character of visual experience. §VIII discusses a new intentionalist proposal. The final section summarizes my conclusions.

I. THE EXISTENTIAL THESIS

The thesis that experiences do not have singular contents into which their experienced objects enter is endorsed by Colin McGinn in the following passage:

> ... the content of experience is not to be specified by using any terms that refer to the object of experience, on pain of denying that distinct objects can seem precisely the same.... we are to say that a given experience is as of *a* book that is brown, thick, and has the words 'The Bible' inscribed upon it; we are not to say, when giving the content of the experience, *which* book it is that is seen.[7]

In a later passage (p. 42), McGinn qualifies the above remarks by saying that the concepts used to characterize the content of visual experience should be restricted to concepts of 'colour, superficial texture, shape, etc.'. Concepts such as the concept *book*, in his view, really only enter into associated beliefs.

It is clear that McGinn supposes that experiences can have the same content but different objects. What is not so clear is why he supposes this. He says above that to hold that particular objects enter into the content of experience is to be compelled to deny that distinct objects can seem precisely the same.[8] This seems too hasty. Singular contents that include different experienced objects are certainly different contents, but why should this be taken to show that how one object seems to a given perceiver cannot be precisely the same as how another object seems? Perhaps McGinn's thought

---

[7] C. McGinn, *The Character of Mind* (Oxford UP, 1982), p. 39. Other philosophers who take a similar view include D.K. Lewis, 'Veridical Hallucination and Prosthetic Vision', *Australasian Journal of Philosophy*, 58 (1980), pp. 239–49, and A. Millar, *Reasons and Experiences* (Oxford: Clarendon Press, 1991).

[8] McGinn also says in an earlier passage (p. 38) that we cannot deduce the identity of the object of an experience from knowledge of its content. His thought here may be that we can know the content of an experience via introspection without thereby knowing which object, if any, is present. However, this claim is open to dispute. If experiences have multiple contents (see here §VI below), it is not at all obvious that we can know each content via introspection. Further, even if experiences have only a single content, it could be held that what we can know via introspection is not the content but the phenomenal character.

is that when the singular contents are different, the *total* 'seemings' cannot be the same. However, if one total 'seeming' is the same as another if and only if the two experiences have the same phenomenal character, the fact that the two experiences have different singular contents clearly does not show that the total 'seemings' must be different. Given the thesis of strong intentionalism, together with the further claim that each perceptual experience has only a single representational content, the negative thesis that McGinn advocates in the quoted passage follows. But why make these assumptions? McGinn does not say.

The positive thesis that experiences have only existential contents is embraced by Martin Davies. He comments

.... we can take perceptual content to be existentially quantified content. A visual experience may present the world as containing an object of a certain size and shape, in a certain direction, at a certain distance from the subject.[9]

Davies' reason for adopting this view is essentially the same as the one McGinn offers for his own position. One immediate objection, then, to the existential thesis is that, as yet, it lacks a clear reason for adopting it. For present purposes, I shall put this to one side. The objection to the existential thesis I shall develop in this section is that it yields an unequivocal result of veridicality in certain cases in which such a result is not warranted. Thus the existential thesis should be rejected.

Suppose I am looking directly ahead, and without my knowledge there is a mirror in front of me placed at a 45° angle, behind which there is a yellow cube.[10] Off to the right of the mirror and reflected in it is a cube that is white in colour. Through special lighting conditions, this cube appears yellow to me. According to the existential thesis, in these circumstances, my experience is accurate or veridical. It 'says' that there is a yellow cube located in front of me, and there is such a cube. But I do not see that cube. I see something else, something that does *not* have the properties in question. *That* cube looks to me other than it really is. My experience misrepresents its colour. So my visual experience cannot be counted as accurate *simpliciter*, as the existential thesis requires. It follows that the existential thesis should be rejected.

One way to try to defend the existential thesis against this objection is to make the existential content more elaborate. Thus it might be held that my experience represents that there is a yellow cube that stands in such and such a causal/contextual relation to this very experience, where the relevant

---

[9] M. Davies, 'Perceptual Content and Local Supervenience', *Proceedings of the Aristotelian Society*, 92 (1992), pp. 21–46, at p. 26.

[10] This case is similar to one Grice discusses in H.P. Grice, 'The Causal Theory of Perception', *Proceedings of the Aristotelian Society*, Supp. Vol. 35 (1961), pp. 121–52.

causal/contextual relation is the one needed for seeing the relevant cube.[11] Now my experience is inaccurate, since the object causing it is *not* yellow.

This proposal does not do full justice to the thought that the cube I see looks to me other than it is. Intuitively, I misperceive *that cube*. My experience misrepresents *it*. This is possible only if the cube I see is itself a component of the content of my experience. Furthermore, the proposal that experiences, in part, refer to themselves is not easy to swallow. Intuitively, when I see a tomato, for example, my visual experience is directed upon the tomato. It is not about *itself* in addition to the tomato.

A third difficulty is that if deviant causal chain counter-examples are to be avoided, it will have to be stipulated that the relevant causal chain is not deviant. But the conditions needed to spell out non-deviance are surely not ones that are *perceptually* available.

A fourth problem can be brought out by considering the case of memory. For me to remember that *p*, there must be a causal connection between the historical event that makes '*p*' true and my current memory state, or so it is usually supposed. But patently that causal connection is not part of the content of the memory. To think otherwise is to confuse the satisfaction-conditions for '*A* remembers that *p*' with those for '*p*'. It is also standardly held that truly believing that *p* is not enough for knowing that *p*. In addition, the belief must be appropriately caused. This fits with the causal requirement on memory, given that memory is a species of knowledge. But again it would clearly be silly to hold that the relevant causal connection must be in the known content. This is not what is known, although its existence is a necessary condition of subjects' knowing what they know. Correspondingly, in the case of perception and perceptual experience.[12]

Finally, the proposal is *ad hoc*. This can be seen from the case of a police radar gun *R*. Trained on Claude's Ferrari, it represents that the car is going at 90 mph. But the gun does not represent that it is Claude's car upon which it is trained. *R*'s reading represents the speed of his Ferrari via a certain causal contextual relation which connects the two. It is the existence of this relation which determines that *R* is then representing Claude's Ferrari and not Paul's Porsche. The relation which *R*'s reading bears to the Ferrari and the speed which *R* registers are why Claude gets the speeding ticket and not Paul. But the relation itself is surely not part of the content of *R*'s

---

[11] John Searle has a proposal along these lines in his *Intentionality* (Oxford: Clarendon Press, 1983). In Searle's formulation, the content of my experience is that *there is a yellow cube (ahead) and the fact that there is such a cube is causing this experience*. This obviously will not do as it stands. Without some restrictions on the causal connection, it is easy to construct more complex mirror-case counter-examples.

[12] I am indebted to Mark Sainsbury here.

reading. The reading does not 'say' that there is a car owned by Claude which bears the appropriate relation to that very reading.

There is no clear reason to treat the case of visual experiences any differently. What makes it the case that my veridical experience of a tomato is about one particular tomato is not *how* that tomato is represented by my experience but rather a certain causal/contextual relation the experience bears to that tomato. This causal/contextual relation is not itself part of the content of my experience, any more than the causal/contextual relation which the radar gun reading bears to the speed of Claude's car is part of the content of that reading.[13]

The upshot is that the existential thesis is in trouble.

II. THE SINGULAR (WHEN FILLED) THESIS

A china frog sits by one of my house-plants. As I view it, I think to myself that *that* is a china frog. A little later, I look up from the book I am reading and again I think to myself that *that* is a china frog. Without my knowledge, a mischievous demon has made the frog disappear in the intervening time period while still making it appear to me that the frog is present. In the second case, then, there is no frog for my thought to be about. Even so, in the second case I did think something, just as I did in the first. According to one standard use of the term 'content', what I thought was the content of my thought. So in the second case my thought has a content, just as in the first.

My first thought, as I looked at the china frog, had a singular content, into which the china frog entered. The second thought did not have a singular content, at least on the usual use of the term 'singular content'. How, then, are we to conceive of the content of the second thought?

The natural proposal, I suggest, is that the second content is just like the first except that where the first has a concrete object in it, the second has a gap. The two contents thus have a common structure. This structure may be conceived of as having a slot in it for an object. In the case of the first content, the slot is filled by the china frog. In the case of the second content, the slot is empty. I shall call such structures 'content schemas'.

Some may be disinclined to count the second content as a content at all. But, as noted above, I am certainly thinking something in the above case. (Of course, the term 'content' is a term of art, and there is no one correct

---

[13] Cf. F. Dretske, *Naturalizing the Mind* (MIT Press, 1995). The problems do not end here. Veridical hallucinations cannot be handled on the causal version of the existential thesis. On this, see fn. 16 below and the surrounding discussion in the text.

way to use it. As I use the term, the content of a thought is what is thought. It is expressed in the 'that'-clause and it is either true or false, or, on three-valued views, neither true nor false.) Furthermore, there are other independently plausible examples of thoughts with gappy contents, for example, the thought that Vulcan does not exist; this thought is true. But with the demise of descriptivist theories of proper names, arguably the best account of the content of this thought is that it is gappy.

Returning now to the first thought that that is a china frog, this thought is true: the object in the content has the property in it. What of the second thought? Well, the second thought that that is a china frog is true if and only if that is a china frog. Since there is no object picked out by the demonstrative 'that' on the right-hand side of this biconditional, there is no demonstrated object to have the property of being a china frog. So the sentence on the right-hand side of the biconditional is naturally classified as false. Correspondingly, then, given the truth of the biconditional, the thought is naturally classified as false too.[14]

Hereafter, I shall call content schemas of the above sort 'SWF content schemas' (schemas yielding singular contents when their slots are filled). With the failure of the existential thesis, it might now be suggested that the general line sketched above for singular (or putatively singular) thoughts can be applied to perceptual experiences.[15] I shall develop this suggestion further.

Whether one is undergoing a veridical perceptual experience, an illusory experience or a hallucinatory one, one experiences *something*. One's experience has a content, or so it seems very reasonable to suppose. The singular (when filled) thesis, as I shall call it, holds that in the case where a visual experience is veridical it has a content that is an instance of an SWF content schema, the slot in which is filled by the seen object, where the properties attributed in the content are properties the seen object has. (It need not always be a common or garden manifest object such as a tomato. If I am surrounded by a white mist, for example, the seen object is the part of the mist in my field of view.) In the case where an illusion is present, the experience again has a content that is an instance of an SWF content schema, the slot in which is filled by the seen object, but now the seen object lacks one or more of the properties attributed in the content. In the case of a

---

[14] Another possible view is that the thought is neither true nor false, since there is no object the thought is about either to have or to lack the attributed property. One difficulty for this view is that *prima facie* it requires us to give up the claim that the thought that this is a china frog is true if and only if this is a china frog in the second case.

[15] Philosophers who emphasize the singularity or particularity of visual experience include M. Soteriou, 'The Particularity of Visual Perception', *European Journal of Philosophy*, 8 (2000), pp. 173–89; Sainsbury, *Reference without Referents*.

hallucination, the experience has a content that is an instance of an SWF content schema, the slot in which is empty. (This is not quite true. There are cases of *de re* hallucination, as, for example, when I dream with respect to my mother that she is being strangled by a snake. Here there is a particular – my mother – and so obviously the content of my visual experience, assuming it is agreed that dreams involve visual experiences, cannot be gappy. Such an experience is singular though the object involved is not seen. For present taxonomical purposes, I am ignoring cases of this sort, but obviously they present no special difficulty for the singular (when filled) thesis.)

One way to conceive of the relevant SWF schemas in the above cases is on the model of Russellian singular propositions having a slot in place of an object. When the slot is filled by a seen object, a Russellian singular proposition results. In other cases, when the slot is empty, there is a gappy proposition. This, of course, is not the only way to view the SWF schemas.

What if the experience is one of multiple objects? Now the relevant SWF schemas have multiple filled slots. In the case of hallucinations of multiple things, there are multiple empty slots. Exactly how the metaphysics of empty slots (and correspondingly gappy propositions) is to be elaborated is a topic that deserves further discussion but upon which I take no position here.

It may be replied that what I am calling 'gappy propositions' or 'gappy contents' for cases of hallucination are not really contents at all, on the ground that they are not truth- or accuracy-evaluable. But this would be too hasty. As noted earlier, the thought that this is a china frog is plausibly classified as false where there is no china frog, even though it has a gappy content. Why not take the same view for hallucinatory experiences (and for essentially the same reasons)? This also fits with the intuitive idea that hallucinatory experiences are inaccurate: the world is not as it seems to the person who is having a hallucination.

Here is a serious worry for the singular (when filled) thesis. In the mirror case from the last section, the present thesis yields the *unequivocal* result that my visual experience is inaccurate, since the cube I am seeing enters into the content of my experience as does the colour property it appears to have, and the latter is a property it actually lacks. But this does not seem the right thing to say. After all, it certainly *appears* to me that there is a yellow cube in front of me; and there is such a cube. The world is as it appears in this respect.

A further problem case for the singular (when filled) thesis is this. In front of me, there is a blue bouncing ball. Without my knowledge, the information in the light reflected from the ball and reaching my retina is not being processed any further. An evil neuroscientist has blocked the signals from my retina to my optic nerve while simultaneously and serendipitously activating my visual cortex by means of electrical probes in just the way it would have been activated had the signals got through. In these circumstances, I do not see the bouncing ball. There is no item out there in the world in front of me that causes my visual experience. Nor do I misperceive the bouncing ball for the same reason. I am not subject to an illusory experience. The experience I undergo is hallucinatory. I have a hallucination of a blue round bouncing object before me. Even so, my experience is accurate. The world is just as it appears to me. I am undergoing a veridical hallucination.

It seems, then, that the singular (when filled) thesis cannot accommodate cases of veridical hallucination.[16] According to that thesis, where there is no seen object, the visual experience has a gappy content; and the gappy content is false, or at least neither true nor false.

Next I shall consider a thesis, according to which not all perceptual experiences have content.

III. KAPLANIANISM

Indexicals are terms that change their reference from utterance to utterance. Examples are 'I', 'here', 'she', 'that', 'today' and 'here'.

Intuitively, the two utterances

TIM: 'I am hot'
TOM: 'I am hot'

have the same linguistic meaning, but what Tim says is different from what Tom says. Tim, who is cold, says something false; but Tom, who is hot, says something true. So the content of Tim's remark is different from the content of Tom's.

On Kaplan's theory, indexicals have contents with respect to contexts.[17] For example, the content of 'I' with respect to a given context c is the subject or agent of c; the content of 'that' with respect to c is the object demonstrated in c; the content of 'here' with respect to c is the location of c. The content of a sentence containing an indexical is a structured proposition having as its constituents the content of the indexical (the agent, place, object demonstrated, etc.) and the contents of the other terms, where these contents

---

[16] Nor can the causal version of the existential thesis discussed in §I. According to that thesis, there can be no such thing as a veridical hallucination, since when a hallucination is present, there is no object of the relevant sort in the scene before the subject's causing his experience. So every hallucination must be counted as falsidical. This obviously will not do.

[17] D. Kaplan, 'Demonstratives' and 'Afterthoughts', both in J. Almog, J. Perry and H. Wettstein (eds), *Themes from Kaplan* (Oxford UP, 1989), pp. 481–614.

are taken to be worldly entities: particulars, properties and relations. Thus in the case of Tim's utterance of the sentence 'I am hot', the content of Tim's remark is a structured proposition containing Tim himself (the subject in this context) and the property of being hot (the content of the predicate 'is hot'). The sentence is false in the context, given that Tim is cold.

On Kaplan's theory, the linguistic meaning of an indexical term is a function that maps contexts onto contents, where the latter are those contents the term has at each context. Kaplan calls this function the term's *character*. Thus the character of the term 'here' is a function from contexts whose value at each context is the location of that context. Similarly, the character of the term 'that' is a function from contexts to the objects demonstrated in those contexts. In the case of sentences containing indexicals, their characters are functions from contexts to the structured propositions which are the contents of the sentences in those contexts.

One case not explicitly discussed by Kaplan which is relevant to the theory below is that of demonstratives used in failed demonstrations. Suppose, for example, I mistakenly think that I have demonstrated something and that I have used the term 'that' to refer to it. In reality, there is nothing to be demonstrated, no referent for my utterance of 'that'. The content of the term 'that' in any given context, on Kaplan's theory, is the object demonstrated in that context. But what counts as a context here? Each context has associated with it at least an agent or subject, a time, and a location. In the case of 'that', it seems plausible to hold that each context is a context of demonstration and thus that it also has associated with it a demonstrated object. So where there is no demonstrated object, there is no context.

It follows that in the case of a failed demonstration, the term 'that' has no content. But it does have a linguistic meaning. This is a function that maps contexts (of demonstration) onto the objects demonstrated in those contexts.

As for the case of the content of visual experience, I shall begin my development of a Kaplanian approach here by saying a little more about the case of illusion. Here there is a seen object. That object appears other than it is. The natural further account of this is that the subject's experience represents the object as having some property that it lacks. The case is one of misrepresentation. Thus when I see a straight stick in water, and it appears bent to me, my experience represents it, the seen object, as bent. The difference between this case and the veridical one is not that in the latter I am in direct contact with an object whereas in the former I am not, but rather that the singular content into which the seen object enters is accurate in the latter case but not in the former.

If it is indeed true that veridical and illusory perceptual experiences have singular contents, then one possible view to take of cases of hallucination is that their phenomenology is misleading. It is for the subject of a hallucination as if the experience has a singular content, but in reality there is no content there at all. Thus hallucinations are like cases of failed demonstration. Just as a token of 'this', uttered in a failed demonstration, has a linguistic meaning but no content, so a token experience, occurring in a hallucination, has a phenomenal character but no content.

For tokens of 'that', a context, I suggested above, is a context of demonstration. Thus where there is no object demonstrated, there is no context in the relevant sense. In the case of perceptual experience, what experiences *fundamentally* aim to do is to put us in contact with objects around us. Where there is no object, as in the case of hallucination, there is no contact and so, as one might say, no context of experiential contact. The experience is a failed experience.

On this view, each token experience has a phenomenal character, but not every token experience has a representational content. However, each token experience is a token of an experiential type for which there is a function having as its arguments contexts of experiential contact in which tokens of that type occur and having as its values the appropriate singular contents of those tokens. Again the model is that of demonstratives. Each token of 'that' is a token of a linguistic type for which there is a function having as its arguments contexts of demonstration in which tokens of that type occur and having as its values the objects demonstrated via the use of those tokens.

I am disinclined to accept this view, though it does have some appeal. My reasons are two. First, in my discussion of the singular (when filled) thesis in §II, I held that when one has a demonstrative thought for which there is no object, none the less one's thought has content. For one certainly does think something in such a case. However, on Kaplan's account, there is no *content* in the case of a failed linguistic demonstration. Of course, the Kaplanian could reply that even though there is no linguistic content in this case, the subject is expressing a thought which does have content. But if one does says this, it is very hard to see why one would not then be prepared to grant that the sentence one utters has content too. If that is the case, then there no longer seems any reason to deny that visual experiences have content in hallucinatory cases.

Secondly, the view requires a denial of a basic presupposition of any sort of intentionalism or representationalism with respect to visual phenomenal character, namely, that all visual experiences have representational content. However, as I have argued elsewhere at length, this presupposition is extremely plausible.[18]

---

[18] M. Tye, *Ten Problems of Consciousness* (MIT Press, 1995), and *Consciousness, Color, and Content* (MIT Press, 2000).

IV. THE MULTIPLE CONTENTS THESIS

So far it has been assumed that each visual experience has (at most) a single content. It is this assumption which the multiple contents thesis (MCT) challenges.

What drives (MCT) is really two thoughts. First, it seems natural to suppose that vision involves direct contact with external things in standard veridical cases. In those cases, the objects seen are just as they appear. One straightforward explanation of this fact, perhaps the most straightforward explanation, is to hold that visual experiences in such cases have accurate singular contents into which the seen objects enter. Secondly, it also seems natural to suppose that when something o appears F (even though there is really no something other than o – an appearance o presents – which is F, as the sense-datum theorists would have us believe), still it surely does *appear* to us that something is F. This, in turn, seems best further understood in terms of the experience representing that something is F. So experiences have a layer of content that is existential, according to (MCT). This layer is to be found in all perceptual experiences, accurate or not, whereas singular contents are missing in some perceptual experiences (namely, the hallucinatory ones). Singular contents, thus, are not *essential* to perceptual experiences, whereas existential contents are.

Obviously there is room for disagreement among those who advocate (MCT) about how rich this layer of existential content is and whether it requires the subject of the experience to possess the concepts needed to state the conditions under which it is accurate. This issue is one that I shall pass over in this chapter.

This position has no difficulty either with the mirror case of §I or with the case of veridical hallucination. In the mirror case, my visual experience is accurate with respect to its existential content and inaccurate with respect to its singular content. It appears to me that there is before me an object of a certain shape and size and colour at a certain distance away and in a certain direction and, as it happens, there is an object with the relevant apparent features, namely, the yellow cube hidden behind the mirror. So my experience has an accurate existential content. However, the cube I am actually seeing is *not* as it appears to be. It is white rather than yellow, as I am led to suppose on the basis of my experience. So my experience has an inaccurate singular content.

In the case of a veridical hallucination, the subject undergoes an experience with an accurate existential content. The world appears to contain a blue round bouncing object before the subject, for example, and there is such an object. But the subject does not see the object, being the subject of a hallucination. So there is no singular content.

One interesting question is whether the multiple contents theorist needs to acknowledge a gappy SWF content in addition to an existential content in the case of hallucinatory experiences. One argument for this view is that we need to suppose that there is a gappy SWF content for such experiences in order to explain the deceptive nature of hallucinations and further to explain the actions hallucinations generate. Suppose for, example, that Sebastian has a hallucination of a large furry spider crawling up his leg. He forms the belief that *that* spider is dangerous. In great fear, he reaches for a nearby book to hit it with. That is why he reaches for the book.[19]

The general point that hallucinations are deceptive seems to me unpersuasive; for if hallucinatory experiences have existential contents then they have false contents (leaving aside those experiences occurring in veridical hallucinations). Unsurprisingly, then, they give rise to false beliefs and thus they deceive their subjects. They are also failed experiences in that they do not succeed in putting their subjects in contact with things in the world even though their subjects typically suppose otherwise.

However, it is true that the supposition that some experiences have gappy SWF contents provides a straightforward explanation of the action performed by the victim of the hallucination. It is the spider in Sebastian's hallucination which he intends to squash with a book. He reaches for a book with the aim of killing *that* spider, and not the much smaller innocuous-looking spider on the ground to his left. Sebastian did not want to kill *a* spider. He wanted to kill one particular spider – the spider which, according to his hallucination, was on his leg.

Still, this consideration seems to me indecisive. Suppose I say to you that Winston believes that there is a burglar in the house. I may then continue by remarking that Winston wants to find him and shoot him. That is why Winston is going upstairs, gun in hand. Clearly the use of the pronoun 'him' here does not show that the content of Winston's belief is singular. What Winston believes has an existential content. Why not suppose something of the same sort is going in Sebastian's case? On this view, it is perfectly acceptable to say both that Sebastian has a visual experience of *a* spider on his leg and that he wants to kill it.

Perhaps it will be replied that even if the example does not tell definitely in favour of the admission of gappy contents, it is none the less the case that the supposition that there is gappy content in hallucinatory cases preserves

[19] Sainsbury (p. 254) offers an example of this sort.

as much similarity as can be preserved between those cases and the veridical ones. So given the overall introspective similarity between the two sets of cases, this is a point in favour of the view that some visual experiences have gappy contents.

I shall return in the next section to the question of whether gappy contents are needed in an account of the admissible contents of visual experience.

V. THE EXISTENTIAL THESIS REVISITED

In my introduction, I noted that adherence to naïve realism requires us to accept that we see the facing surfaces of common or garden material objects directly. The first point I intend to make in this section is that granting this point about what is directly seen does not necessitate that we also accept that ordinary objects enter into the contents of our experiences. Indeed, consistently with this point, we could even deny (as, for example, adverbial theorists do) that perceptual experiences *have* contents. The strongest support for the view that perceptual experiences have singular contents into which the seen objects enter is the thought that when we see those objects they look some way to us, together with the further thought that an object can only look some way if it is experienced *as* being that way. This in turn, seems to require that the object be represented as being that way. In the case of an illusion, then, there is misrepresentation since the seen object is not as it is represented as being. Here the seen object looks other than it is.

One possible response to this line of reasoning, consistent with the general view that experiences have representational contents, is to grant that one sees an object if and only if it looks some way to one, but to deny that the object's looking some way requires one to undergo an experience which represents it as being that way. Thus one might hold that what it is for an object to look F is for it to cause (in the distinctive way appropriate to seeing) an experience of an F, where the experience so caused has an existential content. If this response is cogent (I return to it later), then existential theorists have a way of handling the mirror case discussed earlier: they can say that while it is true that the subject misperceives the white cube on the right, this is because the cube the subject sees *looks* yellow and straight ahead, and its so looking requires only that it causes (in the right way) an experience which represents that there is a yellow cube ahead. So the content is accurate, even though the case is one of misperception. So this, existential content theorists may say, is a case of *veridical illusion*. The case is thus a counterpart to the earlier case of veridical hallucination. The latter case did not demand an inaccurate or falsidical content, so why suppose the former does?

Here is an answer. Having a hallucination, Sebastian tries to grab what he takes to be a spider crawling up his leg. Suppose the hallucination is veridical: there really is a spider crawling up his leg, so that what Sebastian succeeds in grabbing is the real spider. Did Sebastian manage to grab the spider in the hallucination? It seems not, for that spider is unreal. Nevertheless, *that* is the spider he tried to grab – the one which, *according to his hallucination*, was on his leg. To explain what Sebastian was trying to do in this case and, further, his failure to do it, it seems that we really must suppose that his experience has a gappy content, one with a *quasi*-singular character. That content is inaccurate or falsidical. At any rate, it is not accurate. So the claim that cases of veridical hallucination do not demand inaccurate or falsidical contents is mistaken.

Again, however, the existential theorist has a reply. Winston believes that there is a burglar upstairs, whom he is trying to catch. That seems a perfectly good explanation of why he is running up the stairs, gun in hand, even if there is no burglar. But his belief certainly does not have a gappy content.

Admittedly, in the case of veridical illusions, some of the beliefs formed directly on the basis of experience are singular. For example, in the mirror case, I believe falsely that *that* cube is yellow, where that cube is the one I am seeing located off to the right. The most straightforward account of the formation of beliefs with singular contents in such cases, it might be insisted, is that the experiences have singular contents too.

Once again this point does not refute the existential theory. Winston believes that there is a burglar upstairs. Given the direction of the noise, Winston forms the belief that *he* is in the red room. Even so, Winston's initial belief has an existential content.

It seems, then, that the above considerations do *not* refute the view that visual experiences have existential contents. The point I seek to establish next is that even if there are such experiential contents, they are not pure (that is, without any constituent particulars).

Suppose I am seeing a tomato at 2:00, and then I close my eyes for ten seconds, after which I view it again. How is this to be captured in terms of existential content? The obvious answer is that in both cases my experience represents that there is something red, round and bulgy. But this will not do. For suppose at 2:00 there was something red, round and bulgy before me whereas at 2:10 there is nothing red, round and bulgy in the world at all, notwithstanding how things then seem to me. In this case, intuitively, my later experience is inaccurate. However, its existential content is correct (on the assumption that 'there is' is tenseless).

The obvious response to this difficulty is to say that my experience at 2:00 represents that there is something red, round and bulgy at 2:00, whereas my experience at 2:10 represents that there is something red, round and bulgy at the later time. The difficulty now is that the existential content of my experience at 2:00 is no longer pure: it includes a particular time.

One way around this problem is to say that the relevant existential content is that there is *currently* something red, round and bulgy. The question now becomes how to understand 'currently'. If 'currently' means *at the present time*, that is, at the time of occurrence of the relevant token experience, then the above difficulty recurs. For in the case of the experience at 2:00, the content involves a token experience different from the content of the experience at 2:10. Perhaps 'currently' picks out a way or mode of being. If clear sense can be made of this, then the immediate difficulty dissolves.

Another difficulty is not far behind, however. Suppose there is currently something red, round and bulgy in front of a perceiver in Lithuania even though there is nothing red, round and bulgy anywhere else. Intuitively, my visual experience of a tomato, occurring in Texas, is inaccurate. Unfortunately, its existential content is accurate, if we suppose that its content is just that there is something red, round and bulgy. It is also accurate if we suppose that the content is that there is currently something red, round and bulgy in front of some perceiver.

There may be some who would be inclined to bite the bullet here and allow that experiences need not have the same accuracy- or correctness-conditions as their contents. But those who value their teeth should pause. After all, if what you believe is true, then your belief is true. Why should the situation be any different for experiences? Furthermore, on a causal co-variational account of experiential representation, if the content of my experience, as I view the tomato, is (simply) that there is currently something red, round and bulgy then my experience is of the type that, under normal conditions, is tokened if and only if, and because, there is currently something red, round and bulgy. But patently no visual experience is of this type; to suppose otherwise is like supposing that the height of a mercury column in a thermometer normally tracks the temperature of air *somewhere or other* rather than the temperature of the *surrounding* air.

One simple way to handle the above difficulty is to introduce the subject into the content. What my experience at 2:00 represents is that there is currently something red, round and bulgy in front of *me*. But again the existential content is not pure: the subject of the experience now enters into it.

It does not help, of course, to remove the subject from the content and replace him with an objective place; for again the existential content is not pure. Likewise, if we say that the relevant existential content is one which brings in a causal relationship with the appropriate token experience, even setting to one side the earlier objections to this proposal.

The conclusion I draw is that if it is supposed that visual experiences have existential contents, these contents must be *partly* singular.[20] The seen object does not itself enter into the content, but other objects do – such objects as particular times or particular places or subjects of experiences or particular experiences themselves. This does not refute the existential view, of course, but it does naturally lead us to ask why once *some* singularity is admitted, it is necessary to insist, as the existential theorist insists, that the seen object in particular does *not* enter into the relevant content.

I shall respond to this question by arguing for the stronger conclusion that even with the introduction of impure existential contents, there is no good reason to suppose that any such contents attach to visual experiences. This counts against both the existential theory and the multiple contents thesis.

VI. STILL MORE ON EXISTENTIAL CONTENTS

Earlier it was urged against the singular (when filled) thesis that it must at least be admitted that there is a layer of existential content in order to account for cases of veridical hallucination. The thought was that without such a layer of content, we cannot understand how it can be true that it appears to me that there is something blue, round and bouncing ahead (or before me) in the case where there is such an object even though I am not seeing it.

I suggest that there is another explanation available: my visual experience has a gappy content – a content with a gap in it where a seen object should go along with such properties as blueness, roundness and bounciness. But this gappy content disposes me to believe that there is something blue, round and bouncing. This is what makes it the case that it appears to me that there is something blue, round and bouncing. Cases of veridical hallucination are veridical, then, only to the following extent: the visual experiences they involve dispose their subjects to form true beliefs. The experiences themselves, however, are falsidical or at least neither true nor false.

This proposal does not entail that when it appears to me that *p*, I do actually believe that *p*. Evidently that would be too strong. In the Müller–Lyer illusion, for example, it appears to me that the lines are of different lengths, but I do not believe this. Still, I am disposed to believe it if I go by the content of my experience alone. Moreover, the proposal does not assume any specific account of how the relevant disposition is to be cashed. Consistently with this proposal, it could be denied that there is any

[20] For further discussion here leading to the same conclusion, see T. Schroeder and B. Caplan, 'On the Content of Experience', *Philosophy and Phenomenological Research*, forthcoming.

straightforward further analysis of the relevant disposition. Certainly there is reason to resist any account of the disposition in simple if–then terms, as is shown by counter-examples of the sort proposed by C.B. Martin to straightforward if–then analyses of dispositions.[21]

Another virtue of the above proposal is that it allows it to be true that, say, it visually appears to me that there are more than three red objects before me, that there are fewer than one hundred such objects, that there are more than seven red objects before me, fewer than three hundred, that there are at least twice as many red objects as green ones, and so on indefinitely, even though I am not subject to any occurrent thought with any of these contents. Nor in this case need any of the given contents attach to my visual experience. I need not see the scene before me as having more than three red objects, etc., in order for it to appear visually to me that it has. It suffices that my visual experience has a content which disposes me to believe that there are more than three red objects before me, fewer than one hundred, and so on, if I go by the content of the experience alone. The relevant contents, thus, are *potential* cognitive contents and not actual visual contents of my experience. Further, what goes for these contents is plausibly held to go for *all* contents expressible via sentence of the form 'It visually appears to me that *p*'.

So where does this leave us? Even though no knockdown argument has emerged yet against the view that visual experiences have existential contents, there is no clear reason left to accept the view. Neither veridical hallucinations nor veridical illusions provide any strong support. Admittedly, McGinn, in the passage quoted at the beginning, did offer an additional reason, namely, that we must suppose that the seen object does not enter into the content of experience 'on pain of denying that seen objects can seem precisely the same'. This reason has not yet been discussed; but patently it is not compelling. Different objects seem the same, it is natural to suppose, if they are visually represented as having the same properties. Their being so represented does not preclude them from entering into the contents of the relevant experiences. Indeed, it seems that they must so enter in order for *them* to be represented at all.

This brings me back to the suggestion made earlier on behalf of the existential theorist that what is it for an object *o* to look F is for *o* to cause (in the way involved in seeing *o*) an experience of an F. To accept this proposal is to be committed to denying that if *o* looks F then *o* is visually experienced as being F. For *o* cannot be experienced as being F unless the relevant experience represents *o* as F, assuming that experience is representational at all. But there seems to me a very strong intuitive pull to the thought that if

---

[21] C.B. Martin, 'Dispositions and Conditionals', *The Philosophical Quarterly*, 44 (1994), pp. 1–8.

o looks F, *o* is represented as F; and this is lost, on the existential proposal. Furthermore, there is a difficulty lurking for the existential theorist's account above of what it is for *o* to look F, a difficulty I have so far ignored. Suppose I am seeing two objects *a* and *b* such that *a* looks red to me and *b* looks green. The object *a* causes my experience of something green, and it does so in the way involved in seeing *a*. But equally, so does *b*. In seeing both *a* and *b*, I undergo an experience that represents something green, on the existential proposal. This experience, however, also represents something red. So *b* not only causes my experience of something red but it also causes my experience of something green, and it does so in the way involved in seeing *b*. So *b* looks red, but it also looks green. Clearly something has gone wrong. The obvious diagnosis of the trouble is that the account of what it is for an object to look some way proposed by the existential theorist makes the mistake of removing the seen object from the content of the experience involved in seeing it.[22]

A related thought counting against the existential view is that intuitively visual experiences have a singular content, or at least a putatively singular content. They simply do not present the world to us in the way the existential thesis requires. There is a particularity in our experience which the existential thesis fails to capture fully.

The upshot, I suggest, is that the layer of existential content should be discarded. The best view to take, on balance, of the content of visual experience is the one offered by the singular (when filled) thesis.

What about the contents of experiences in the other sensory modalities? Again, I am inclined to favour the singular (when filled) thesis. In the case of auditory experience, for example, the relevant particular (if there is one) is a particular sound. Things are heard by hearing the sounds they emit and sounds are particulars. Similarly, in the case of olfactory experience, the particular are smells. We smell things by smelling the odours they produce, and odours are particulars. Odours begin and end. They have spatio-temporal locations, even if these locations are not at all precise.

VII. CONSEQUENCES FOR STRONG INTENTIONALISM

Strong intentionalism or representationalism is the view that phenomenal character is one and the same as a certain sort of representational content.

---

[22] I do not deny that further conditions could be imposed that would handle this objection. But these conditions would require there to be a sensitivity in the relevant part of the content of the token experience to the relevant object. Given such a sensitivity, it is no longer clear that the object has not been smuggled into the content after all.

Weak intentionalism, unlike strong intentionalism, is not an identity thesis. It does not purport to identify phenomenal character with representational content. It is, rather, a supervenience thesis. It asserts that, necessarily, experiences with the same representational content have the same phenomenal character.

On the assumption that veridical and hallucinatory experiences sometimes share the same phenomenal character, strong intentionalism is falsified by the arguments given so far; for there is no common representational content. But should this assumption be made? The lemon and the bar of soap, though very different objects, may none the less be visually indistinguishable. The best explanation of this fact, it could be urged, is not that the two items are intrinsically the same but rather that they produce experiences that cannot be told apart introspectively.[23] On this view, the visual indistinguishability of the soap and the lemon is grounded upon a relational fact about them, the fact that they cause introspectively indistinguishable experiences.

Likewise, then, perhaps what the strong intentionalist should reject is the assumption that some veridical experiences and some hallucinatory ones have the same phenomenal character. What is really true, the strong intentionalist might say, is merely that these experiences sometimes have indistinguishable phenomenal characters, where this is to be understood in terms of their possession of a common relational property. Now there is no immediate difficulty in identifying phenomenal character with representational content.

The trouble with this retort is that there is no plausible candidate for the relevant relational property. The best alternative seems to be that both the phenomenal character of the veridical experience and the corresponding phenomenal character of the hallucinatory experience cause their subjects to believe, when they introspect, that the two experiences are exactly alike. But alike in which respect? Presumably, phenomenal character. The subjects of the relevant experiences are simply not conscious of any phenomenal difference via introspection.

The question now becomes *why* they are not conscious of any such difference. Surely the most straightforward and natural answer is that in some cases there is no difference: the phenomenal character is the same. But if this is the case, then strong intentionalism should be rejected.

---

[23] Actually, it is a mistake to suppose that the soap and the lemon are not intrinsically the same. They are, in that they have the same colour and the same three-dimensional shape.

VIII. A NEW INTENTIONALIST PROPOSAL

Weak intentionalism is not threatened by the arguments presented in this chapter. However, weak intentionalism is a thesis which cries out for further development. Surely it is not simply a brute fact that necessarily experiences which share the same content have the same phenomenal character. Some explanation is needed.

When I view a tomato my experience has a singular content; when you have a hallucination of one your experience has a corresponding gappy content. The contents are different, but none the less they are of the same type. Each experience has a content that falls under the same SWF content schema. What the two experiences have in common, thus, is the possession of a content of a certain sort.

One way to capture this is to say that the two contents fall under an SWF content schema having a slot in it that is filled by an object in the one case but which is left empty in the other. Another way to put the point is to say that each experience has an SWF content into which all the same (non-object-involving) properties enter. The obvious, way, then, to begin to develop the weak intentionalist position further without its collapsing into strong intentionalism is to hold that the phenomenal character P of a given token experience e is a matter of e's having within its content a certain cluster of properties.[24]

In my view, for reasons I have elaborated elsewhere (see fn. 18), the relevant properties, in addition to being within e's content, should be non-conceptually represented, and the content should be suitably poised to bring about cognitive responses. What emerges from these reflections, thus, is a form of intentionalism that bears the same sort of relationship to strong intentionalism as functionalism bears to the type-identity theory. Just as functional properties are multiply physically realizable, so phenomenal properties, on this proposal, are multiply realizable via strong intentional properties of the sort which strong intentionalism took to be identical with them. There is no one poised content which an experience must have in order to possess a given phenomenal character. Instead, its phenomenal character resides in its having a poised content within which such and such a

[24] It might seem that this view cannot distinguish having a hallucination of a red square and a green triangle from having a hallucination of a green square and a red triangle, since each experience represents the same colour and shape properties, *viz* greenness, triangularity, redness and squareness. But there are other properties represented by each experience too. In the former case, the property of being a red square is represented; not so in the latter. In the latter case, the property of being a green square is represented; not so in the former.

cluster of properties is non-conceptually represented. One might call this view 'second-order intentionalism'.

One objection to this proposal is that it seems somewhat contrived. Can it really be that the phenomenal character of an experience is a *second-order* intentional property? However, in my view, the biggest difficulty this proposal faces is that does not do justice to the phenomenon of transparency. So the attempt to identify phenomenal character with representational content or to find any intentional property, first or second-order, with which phenomenal character is identical seems to be in serious trouble.

The solution, in my view, is to take phenomenal character to be the cluster of properties within the content (singular or gappy). The property cluster becomes the phenomenal character of a given visual experience, of course, only if it is represented by that experience (just as Benjamin Franklin becomes the inventor of bifocals only if he invents bifocals). This view is developed in detail elsewhere.[25]

IX. CONCLUSION

So the multiple contents thesis is to be rejected, as is the existential thesis. What remains is the singular (when filled) thesis, and this is the thesis I embrace. The thesis is a form of disjunctivism, in that it concedes that the content of visual experience in hallucinatory cases is different from the content of visual experience in veridical cases. At the level of content itself, there is indeed no common factor. For each experience, there is only a single admissible content, but this content is different in veridical and in hallucinatory cases. There is, however, in some such cases a common phenomenal character. This necessitates the rejection of strong intentionalism. But it leaves open another intentionalist view of phenomenal character – that of second-order intentionalism. Unfortunately, second-order intentionalism faces difficulties of its own. The solution is to look to the properties represented to find phenomenal character, and not to the representing of those properties.[26]

[25] On this, see my *Consciousness Revisited: Materialism without Phenomenal Concepts* (MIT Press, 2008).

[26] I would like to thank Alex Byrne, Tim Crane and Susanna Siegel for helpful discussion. An earlier version formed the basis for a talk at U.N.A.M. in Mexico City. I thank members of that audience for their comments.

INDEX

aboutness 85–6, 109, 111
abstract objects 98–9, 115
abstraction 19, 36–7, 49–50, 58
accuracy conception of content 115, 118–23, 126–7, 137
accuracy, not the same as truth 85, 88–9, 93
   special notion 119
accuracy-conditions 2–6, 13–14, 87–9, 92–3, 99, 116, 118–22, 151–3, 161, 173, 179, 187
actionism 107–13
affordance 163, 168
after-images 77–8
agency, experience of 38
agnosia, apperceptive 21–2
   associative 14, 21–2, 24–8, 34
alexia 23
Alston, W.P. 78–9
ambiguous figures 21, 106, 143–6
amodal perception 1, 54, 104
Anscombe, G.E.M. 39, 168
appearing, theory of 78–9, 126–8
appears as F 78–9
appears/looks conception of content 115–17, 120, 126–7, 134, 137
Armstrong, D.M. 37, 81, 88
as of 5–6, 8, 83
aspect-switching 139–40, 142–6, 148–9
aspects 86–7, 98, 144
assertion 90, 93
attention 12, 65, 96, 103–4, 106, 143–7, 149
Austin, J.L. 76–7, 80
awareness, of shape 55, 58–9
   phonological 56–7

ba-da-ga 45

backs of things 9, 15, 101–2, 105–6, 110, 142
Baillargeon, R. 53
ball in pot 40–1, 157–8, 160–5, 167
bananas 24
Bayne, T. 14
behaviour, explanation of 4, 7, 165, 184
belief 2–4, 9, 12, 14, 85–6, 97
belief in 91–2
belief, caused by experience 8, 11, 26–7, 165, 192
   content of 2, 61, 84, 88, 97, 123, 130, 177, 182, 184
   content of, singular 186
   contrasted with experience 8–9, 11–12, 14–15, 26–7, 43, 76, 88, 97
   phenomenology of 12, 34
beliefs, conflict between 81–2, 188
Berkeley, G. 139
black 134
Brentano, F. 86
Brewer, B. 61, 67, 78, 100, 116–17, 121–2, 127–9, 145
Butterfill, S. 14
Byrne, A. 14, 84, 94–5, 100, 116, 118

Campbell, J. 100, 109
canonical characterization 97–9
category perception 14, 19, 22, 24, 42, 45–52, 54, 56–8
causal belief, origin of 164–5
causal connection not part of content 176–7
causal relations, represented in experience 9, 15, 25, 36–7, 41, 150–6, 158–9, 165–7, 169, 171
causation, and laws 168–9
   concept of 153, 162, 167, 169, 171

distinctive features of 169–71
how represented? 169–71
in static scene 155
modes of 151, 153
perception of 14–15, 30, 36–40, 42–4,
48, 50–5, 57–9, 150–71
raw feel of 166–7
centaurs 74–5
change blindness 117
cheese 79, 96, 170
chicken-sexing 18, 29–30
Chisholm, R. 70–4
classifying *perceptibilia* 11–12, 22, 24, 26–7,
52–4, 63, 74, 143, 145
co-variation 3–4, 9, 13, 51, 187
cognitive penetration 14
coins 20, 135–6
collisions 36, 41–3, 49–50, 171
colour 8–10, 16, 18, 23–4, 29–33, 47, 67,
73, 80, 103–4, 115, 132–4, 136,
139–40, 142–4, 149, 152, 174
colour constancy 30, 103
colour-blindness 9
colours, in phenomenal content 133–4
concept-acquisition 148
conditions of satisfaction 61
conservative/liberal, see *phenomenal
character, high/low level*
constancy 103–4, 132–6
constancy, in speech recognition 45–6
content view 61–2, 66–9, 79–80
content view, attacked 70, 72, 75
not about experiences 66
content, as a matter of looks 116
conceptual 84
'content', definition of 1, 14–15, 85–8,
96–7, 114–27, 129–31, 177–9
content, existential component 11, 183–4
merely described 99
non-conceptual, content/state view of
97–9
non-propositional 88
of judgement 84
singular or general? 10–11, 129–30
contents, potential 189
context-sensitive 3

contrast cases 10–12, 14–15, 21, 23–4, 34,
40–1, 80, 132, 140, 156–61, 164–5
contrast cases, not applicable 41
counterfactual dependence, experience of
161–4, 167–8, 170
counterfactual-supporting 108
cow-shaped 71–2, 74
Crane, T. 14
cross-modal experience 1, 26–7
curtains 157–61, 164–5, 167

Dalmatian 144
Davies, M. 175
defending, visible 39–40
demonstratives 91, 94, 178
demonstratives, failed use of 180–2
depth phenomenology 51–2, 136, 139
desire 2, 4, 85–6
deviant causal chain 108, 175–6, 179–80
disjunctivism 5–7, 10, 95, 109–10, 116,
120–1, 124, 126, 128, 172–3, 193
dispositions 189
dispositions, experience of 162–3
dogs 24
dreams 179
Dretske, F. 47, 58
Ducasse, C.J. 39
duck/rabbit 106–7, 143–5, 149

elliptical 135–6
epistemology 14, 58
Escher, M.C. 4
events, unified series of 157–62, 164–7
evidence 71, 75–6, 117, 129
exing 68, 70, 73–4, 76, 78–82
experience causes disposition to believe
96, 188–9
experience not given by representational
content 121–2
experience, accidentally veridical 175–6
after training 11–12
assessable for accuracy 152
awareness of 56, 58
content of 87–9, 93, 95–6, 98, 114
content/state view of 97–9
contrasted with propositions 93–4

'experience', definition of 61–6, 87–8, 115, 117–19, 123, 126
experience, describing 55, 85, 94, 99
   direction of fit 121, 129
   existential component of 15, 79, 183–90, 193
   explains capacity to believe 127–8
   has representational content 182
   not true/false 129
   of duplicates 5, 7, 10–12, 24, 27–30, 124–5, 137, 174–5, 189, 191
   of singulars 174–5, 186–9
   reports of 38, 42, 45, 48–9, 65, 153–8
   reports of, unreliable 9, 39–40, 55, 154
   rich/sparse 14, 16–20, 23, 129, 139–40, 149
   singular component of 185, 192
'experience', special sense of 14, 62, 64–6, 68, 117, 119, 121, 129
experience, supervenes on content? 123–5
   with event as content 95–6
experiences are events 62–4, 68, 88
experiences, are particulars 62, 64
   have only existential content 175–7
   have representational content 60–82, 96
   types of 1–2, 6–7
   without content 180–2
experiential contents, potential 189
experiential properties 10, 123–7, 130–7
experiential properties, ground capacity for belief 55, 127, 131–2, 137
expert 11–12, 31–2, 55
explanation, need for 40–4, 46–7, 50–1, 54, 57–8, 132, 156, 158
explanatory gap 33–4

feels 1, 17, 96
focus 103–4
Fodor, J. 18–19, 47
Frege, G. 87
Fregean conception of phenomenal content 183, 193
functional-role theory 13

gappy content 15, 173, 177–80, 182–6, 188, 192–3

Gestalt 74, 81, 138, 161
Gibson, J.J. 163, 168
green 77–8
grey 24, 77–8, 134–5
Grice, H.P. 108
grounding method 131–7

hallucination 5, 7, 15, 67, 79, 116–17, 119, 124, 128, 130, 163, 173, 178–84, 186, 193
hallucination, not of singulars 173
hallucinations, cause beliefs 184, 188
hearing 16–18
Heck, R. 96–7
Heider, F. 39
high/low level properties, see *phenomenal character, high/low level*
Hinton, J.M. 62, 64, 66
holes 169–71
how things look 116
Hume, D. 32, 36, 40, 53, 59, 139, 166
Husserl, E. 160–1

identity claims about theoretical terms 1, 10, 27, 29, 31, 35, 61–2, 78, 88, 115, 119–21, 123–7, 134, 137, 165, 167, 191–3
identity conception of content 115, 119–20, 123–7, 130, 134, 137
illumination, level of 134–5
illusions 67–70, 75–8, 80, 82, 88, 110, 112, 119, 127, 134, 172–3, 178–82, 185
illusory crescents 41–3, 51
impossible objects 4
indexicals 179–82
indistinguishability 11–13, 28–30, 34, 191
indubitability 30–1, 34
information-carrying 58
intentional content 61
intentional objects 61, 85–7, 92, 109–10, 112, 117, 183–4
intentional states, have content 87, 93–4
   not necessarily propositional 93–4
intentionalism 115, 118–20, 123–5, 127–30, 132–3, 182
intentionalism, second-order 193
   standard/non-standard 132–3

strong, rejected 191
strong/weak 125, 127, 174–5, 190–2
  varieties of 133–7, 150, 175, 190–3
intentionalism. singular/general 115, 150
intentionality 2, 85–7, 109, 111–12, 115, 150
introspection 5, 9, 13, 21, 55, 58, 63, 65–8,
  156, 158, 173, 185, 191

Jackson, F. 31–3, 71–4
Johnston, M. 69
judgement 88, 94–6

Kaplan, D. 174, 179–82
Kelly, S.D. 106
kinds, content of perception? 8–9, 11–13,
  18–19, 114
  recognition of 14–15, 17–20, 22, 24–8,
  31–2, 81
knowledge argument 31–3
Krushke, J.K. 52

Langsam, H. 78–9
launching 36, 38, 41–4, 48–53, 151, 153–4,
  171
lemons 67–8, 70, 75, 79–81, 173
Lewis, D. 108, 162
liberal/conservative, see *phenomenal
  character, high/low level*
Liberman, A.M. 44–7
Lissauer, H. 21
looking 11, 25–6, 28–31, 67, 69–70, 73,
  75–7, 106, 108, 116–17, 120, 140–1,
  145
looking, epistemic 141
  externalist 141–2
  phenomenal 140–2, 149, 151
looks as if 71–2, 74–80, 102, 116–17, 120–1,
  123, 126, 139, 141, 172, 183, 185,
  188–9
looks F 25, 30, 69–70, 72, 75–6, 78, 116,
  134–5, 140–1, 148, 183, 185, 189–90
looks like 76
looks red 73
looks to be of a kind 141, 143–4
looks, as signs 70–1
  comparative/epistemic 25, 70–7, 80
  non-comparative 25, 74–8

not connected to content 70–1
objective 76–8
phenomenal 72–4
reports of 134
'looks', sense of 25, 70
looks-indexing 70–1, 74–5, 128, 134
love 94
Lycan, W.G. 63, 79
Lyons, J. 18

McDowell, J. 84, 88, 94–6, 109
McGinn, C. 10–11, 162–4, 168, 174–5, 189
Marr, D. 37, 54
Martin, C.B. 189
Martin, M. 109
Mary (thought-experiment) 31–3, 134–5
Matthen, M. 47
melody 160–1
mental states, types of 5–7, 12–14, 43, 63,
  86–7, 97, 112, 129, 152
Michotte, A. 14–15, 36–8, 40–1, 43–4,
  48–52, 55, 59, 150–1, 153–5, 165, 171
Millikan, R. 69
mirrors 72, 130, 175–6, 179, 183, 185–6
misrepresentation 3–6, 13–14, 28–9, 67–9,
  78, 175–6, 179–83, 185–6
missing shade of blue 32, 131
modality 19
modality, perceptual 16
mode of presentation 29, 81, 86, 92, 98–9,
  187
mole rats 74–5
Moore, G.E. 65
motion 16, 36, 38, 42, 48, 50–1, 53, 80,
  153–5
multiple contents thesis 183, 188, 192–3
multiple realizability 192
Müller–Lyer diagram 67, 69–70, 76–8,
  80–2, 119, 128–9, 188

Nakayama, K. 102–3
Napoleon 90–1, 94–5
natural indicators 2–4, 39, 70–1, 172
natural kinds 9, 11–12, 15, 140, 147–9
naïve realism 172, 185
necessary truths 3, 6, 118

neurophysiology 1, 33, 102
nomic generalism 168–9
non-conceptual content 96–9
non-human perception 19–20, 109, 117, 171
Noë, A. 15

object identity 51–3
object, presence of 109–12
objects of mental states 2, 85–6
objects of perception, accessible by moving 105–8, 110
objects, components of experience? 172–5, 187
 in perspective 103, 106–7, 119, 135–6
 not part of experiential content 185
 perception of 51–4, 58–9
occlusions 9, 15, 101–4, 136
old 73–5
old woman picture 21, 143–4
optical illusions 41, 67

paintings 2, 4, 93, 106
Pautz, A. 15
Peacocke, C. 61–3, 99–100, 142
'perceive', grammatical contexts of 83
percept stripped of meaning 22, 27
perceptible relations 79
perceptible, as accessible 15, 104–13
perception - conceptual? 35
perception, accidentally veridical 179
 after training 18, 21, 23–4, 56–7, 81, 137
 amodal 104
 and belief 26–7, 61, 67–70, 81–2, 84, 88, 96–7, 114, 117, 128–9, 138, 152, 154, 157, 164–6, 174, 188
 and thought 110, 112
 as access to world 58, 100, 105–6
 as propositional attitude 14, 68–70, 76, 78–81, 83–5, 88–9, 95–100, 116–18, 122, 126–7
 causal chain of 65–6
 causal theory of 108
 common sense talk about 39–40, 75
 contact with world 67, 129, 172–3, 178–9, 181–5, 190

 excludes error 60, 67, 101, 118, 121, 129, 150
 hypotheses about 37, 45–54, 68
 in children 56–7, 117
 involving inference 37, 53
 non-conceptual 96–9
 not a matter of looks 46–7
 not like a picture 104, 106
 object of 83, 110, 113–14
 object of, existing 116–17
 of kinds 17, 127, 136–7, 181–3, 190
 of singulars 114, 117, 124–5, 127, 137, 173–4, 180–4, 190
 related to representation 60
 talk about, unreliable 47
 veridical 183
perceptual error 14, 78, 82
perceptual experience, cannot be inaccurate? 5–7
 object of 87
perceptual modalities 68
perceptual modules 18–19, 46, 68
perceptual objects 85
perceptual presence, as availability 103–5
phenomenal character and experience 20
phenomenal character has cluster of properties as content 192
phenomenal character identical with representational content? 190, 193
phenomenal character of experience 151
phenomenal character shared by veridical and hallucinatory experience? 191
phenomenal character, and belief 41, 43
 and representational content 11–13, 17
 change of 13, 139–40
 high/low level 7–25, 27–8, 30–1, 33–5, 114–15, 127, 130, 136, 139–40, 142–3, 148–9, 174
 high/low level, a real distinction? 20
 non-conceptual 23, 68
 propositional? 69, 75
 relation to experience 21–2
 relation to representation 10, 24–5, 28–30
 supervenient on content? 25, 122, 125
 supervenient on representation 10, 17–18

the cluster of properties in the content
193
thin 81
types of 192
phenomenal consciousness 17–18, 26,
30–1, 34–5
phenomenal content 17–35, 120, 125, 127,
129–38
phenomenal distance 32–3, 164
phenomenal looks, changes of 141, 143–9,
156–61
phenomenal state 17
phenomenology, mandatory 41
phonic gestures 44–7, 51–2, 54, 56–7, 59
photographs 2, 4, 23
Piaget, H. 40
pictures 74, 85, 89–91, 95
pictures, content expressed/described by
sentence 91–5
content of 89–91, 93
contrasted with propositions 89–93
pigs 4, 65
pine trees 11–12, 18, 80, 115, 117, 119,
122–3, 136–8, 143, 146–7
pipes 22, 26–7
possible-worlds arguments 6, 19, 29, 118,
121–3, 142
present as absent 15, 102–4, 111
presentation 6–7, 67, 116, 190
presentation, simple 67–8
Price, H.H. 30–1
Price, R. 15
primary qualities 32–3
Prinz, J. 18
proper names 132, 178–9
properties, non-visual 8–9, 25, 36, 162
types of 8–10, 16–18, 28–9
propositional attitudes 2
propositional content 85–6, 98
propositions 85, 88–90, 94, 97
prosopagnosia 23
pulling 38, 49–50, 151, 153
Putnam, H. 107, 109

qualia 104, 115–16, 121, 124

radar 176–7
Ramsey–Lewis definition 124–5
reading 142–3, 146–7
recognition 24
recognition, after training 80, 136, 142–3,
146–8
red 16, 18, 30–2, 67, 72–3, 75, 77, 123–5,
127–8, 133, 141–2
red, knowledge of, see Mary
red-haired 75
reference (see also Russellian) 112
Reid, T. 152
'represent', definition of 2
representation 1, 3–8, 13, 61, 66, 71, 77,
86–8, 90–2, 96, 98, 100, 118, 139,
150, 189, 193
'representation', minimal sense of 6
representation, not necessarily conscious
30
of particulars 10–11
representational content 17, 87
representational content, propositional?
61, 68
supervenient on phenomenal
character 191
representational state 2–4, 6–7
representationalism 10, 13
retention 124, 135, 160–1
round 123–5, 127–8, 132, 135
Rubens, A.B. 27
Russellian propositions 29, 89, 92, 99, 179

salience 12, 71–2, 122, 124, 143
Sartre, J.-P. 111
scenario content 99
Scholl, B.J. 37, 41–3, 49, 51, 59
scripts, foreign 142–3, 146–7
Searle, J.R. 40, 61–3, 65, 73, 87, 139,
142–4, 149
secondary qualities 28
seeing as 144–6, 189
seeing that 8–9, 26, 36, 67, 71, 83–4, 162,
168, 189
seen object, component of experience?
178, 188–90
semantic properties, attention to 146–7
sensation 58, 152, 166

sense-data 30–1, 60, 71, 73, 102, 106, 121,
    124, 126–8, 183
sensorimotor knowledge 15, 101, 105,
    107–12
sensory entertaining 69, 125–8, 130, 132,
    137–8
sensory modality 1
sentences 2–3, 89–91
shadows 28–9, 153–4
shape 8, 11–12, 16, 18, 21–2, 32–3, 36–7,
    39, 42, 54–5, 57–9, 67, 73, 80, 107,
    115, 132, 135–6, 139–40, 142–4, 147,
    149, 152, 174–5
sharks 4–7
Siegel, S. 6, 11–12, 15, 18, 20, 40–1, 80–1,
    100, 118, 120, 132, 139, 142–4, 146–7,
    149
smells 79, 95–6, 190
soap, lemon-like 80, 173, 191
Sosa, E. 168
sounds 1–2, 8–9, 16–18, 21, 44–5, 68, 96,
    160, 190
sounds, recognition of 23
space 54
spectrum inversion 141–2
speech perception, motor theory of 44,
    46–7, 55
speech recognition 23–4, 37, 44–59
speech, understanding 21
Spelke, E. 53
squares 32–3, 72
Strawson, P.F. 37, 39, 59, 108
supervenience 10, 13, 17–18, 25, 30, 115–17,
    122, 124–5, 127, 191
SWF content schemas 177–9, 183–4, 192
Szabó, Z. 91–2

tastes 16–17, 28, 79, 96
Teuber, H.-L. 22, 27
Thau, M. 73, 75, 100
thought, about particulars 177
    being struck by 41
    content of 177–8
    object of 109–12
    phenomenology of 26, 34–5, 145
    relation to perception 111–12
three-dimensional, see *depth*

tigers 28–30
toads 11–13
tomatoes 16–17, 21, 30–3, 67, 101–6,
    109–10, 123–4, 127, 131, 133, 139–42,
    147–9, 172, 176–8, 186–7, 192
Tooley, M. 168
toot picture 142, 144–6
transparency 65–6, 176, 193
Travis, C. 64, 69–72, 75–8, 100, 121, 127–8
tree-rings 2–4
triangle picture 145
twin earth arguments 28, 80–1, 131, 133,
    137, 148
two-component views 165–7
Tye, M. 15, 18, 20, 23, 26–9, 65–6

understanding 101, 105, 107–12

van Gulick, R. 18, 20, 184–5
Vendler, Z. 64
veridical hallucination 5, 108, 119, 179–80,
    183–6, 188–9
veridical illusion 185, 189
visual experience, not like a picture 93, 101
visual imagination 131, 135–6, 144, 146,
    149, 163–4
visual system, hypotheses about 37, 42–4,
    52, 103, 155
    using inference? 103

walls 103–4
Wang, S. 53
what it is like 10, 16–17, 20–1, 23, 31
white 134
White, P. 38, 40, 43, 50
windows 103–7
writing 56, 142–3, 146–7

yellow 28–9, 67–8, 70, 79

zeeing 68